THE MAN
in the
IRON MASK

ALSO BY JOSEPHINE WILKINSON

Louis XIV: The Power and the Glory

Richard III: The Young King to Be

Mary Boleyn: The True Story of Henry VIII's Favourite Mistress

Anne Boleyn: The Young Queen to Be

*The Princes in the Tower: Did Richard III Murder His Nephews,
Edward V and Richard of York?*

Katherine Howard: The Tragic Story of Henry VIII's Fifth Queen

EDITED BY JOSEPHINE WILKINSON

Anne Boleyn by Paul Friedmann

THE MAN
in the
IRON MASK

The True Story of Europe's
Most Famous Prisoner

Josephine Wilkinson

PEGASUS BOOKS
NEW YORK LONDON

THE MAN IN THE IRON MASK

Pegasus Books, Ltd.
148 West 37th Street, 13th Floor
New York, NY 10018

First Pegasus Books cloth edition July 2021

Interior design by Maria Fernandez

Library of Congress Cataloging-in-Publication Data is available.

ISBN: 978-1-64313-742-1

10 9 8 7 6 5 4 3 2 1

Printed in the United States of America
Distributed by Simon & Schuster
www.pegasusbooks.com

CONTENTS

THE MAN
in the
IRON MASK

ONE

"Only a Valet"

I t began with a letter written to an obscure jailer in the distant fortress of Pignerol at the end of July 1669. Saint-Mars, the governor of the donjon of Pignerol, was alerted to the imminent arrival of a new prisoner. It was of the utmost importance to the king's service, he was told, that the man whose name was given as "Eustache d'Auger" should be kept under conditions of the strictest security. Particularly, it was imperative that this man should be unable to communicate with anyone by any means whatsoever.

Saint-Mars was being warned in advance of the arrival of his prisoner so that he could prepare a secure cell. He was ordered to take care that the windows of this cell were "so placed that they could not be approached by anyone," and that it was equipped with "enough doors closing one upon the other," that Saint-Mars's sentries would not be able to hear anything. Saint-Mars himself was once a day to take to this "wretch," whatever he might need for the day, and he was not under any pretext to listen to what the prisoner might say to him, but instead to threaten to kill him if he tried to speak of anything except his basic needs. The sieur Poupart, commissioner for war at Pignerol, was on standby waiting to begin work on the secure cell, while Saint-Mars was authorized to obtain some furniture for the prisoner, bearing in mind that "since he is only a valet," this should not cost very much.[1]

The letter to Saint-Mars, which was dated July 19, 1669, was written on the orders of Louis XIV by François-Michel Le Tellier, marquis de Louvois. Still only twenty-eight years old, Louvois was destined to play a vital role in the story of the Man in the Iron Mask. Serving as Louis XIV's minister of state for war, Louvois had been educated at the Jesuit Collège de Clermont in the rue Saint-Jacques in Paris. Upon leaving the school in 1657, he was instructed in French law by his father, the formidable secretary of state for war, Michel Le Tellier. Louvois then served at the Parlement of Metz as counselor before obtaining the survivance of his father's office.[2] He worked in the ministry for war for a time, learning the job under his father's guidance, but Le Tellier would hand over increasing amounts of ministry work to his son and, upon being made chancellor in 1677, he would leave Louvois in sole charge. As the minister for war, the garrison and prison of Pignerol came under Louvois's jurisdiction, as did any prisoner who might be held there.

Seven days after Louvois's letter to Saint-Mars had been dispatched, Louis issued a lettre de cachet, or royal warrant under the king's seal and signed by his own hand. Dated July 26, this document, which was countersigned by Michel Le Tellier, was addressed to Captain Alexandre de Vauroy, sergeant-major of the town and citadel of Dunkirk. "Captain Vauroy," it began, "being dissatisfied with the behavior of the man named Eustache Dauger, and wanting to make sure of his person, I am writing this letter to tell you that, as soon as you see him, you are to seize and arrest him and conduct him yourself in all security to the citadel of Pignerol." On the same day, Louis wrote to Saint-Mars at

Pignerol to advise him that Vauroy was bringing the prisoner he had been told to expect:

Captain de Saint-Mars,

Sending to my citadel of Pignerol under the escort of Captain de Vauroy, major of my city and citadel of Dunkerque, the man named Eustache Dauger, there to be kept securely, I write you this letter to tell you that when the said Captain de Vauroy has arrived in my citadel of Pignerol with the said prisoner you have to receive him from his hands and keep him in good and safe custody until further orders from Me, preventing him from communicating with anyone either verbally or by writing. And so that you do not encounter any difficulty in the execution of what is my will, I order the sieur marquis de Pienne,[3] and in his absence he who commands in the said citadel, to give you for this purpose all the help and assistance you need, and may require. And the present [letter] being for no other purpose, I pray to God that he will have you, captain de Saint-Mars, in his holy keeping.

Written at Saint-Germain-en-Laye, le 26 July 1669.

Louis did not elaborate upon what Eustache had done to displease him, nor did he have any reason to: he had only to express his dissatisfaction and Eustache would be held in prison without trial for as long as Louis thought appropriate.

The lapse of nine days between Saint-Mars being alerted about his new prisoner and the lettre de cachet being issued for Eustache's arrest was vital. Secrecy in such matters was paramount lest Eustache should somehow learn that he was about to be captured and make good his escape.

It was assumed that Vauroy knew Eustache, or that he knew who he was, for he was ordered to arrest him on sight and no mention is made of further verbal information being sent with the courier. Eustache's face, therefore, was well known or had become so, at least in certain circles. Vauroy was ordered to take the prisoner directly to Pignerol, a long and difficult journey that would take some three weeks. In order to explain his absence, a cover story was invented, with Godefroy d'Estrades, the governor of Dunkirk, being told that Vauroy had been ordered to capture Spanish officers who were chasing deserters believed to have had fled into French territory.[4]

The risk that Eustache might escape was very real, for he was known to be in Calais, a major port and one of the gateways between France and England. It would be a relatively simple matter for him to board any ship leaving for England, where he could disappear into obscurity. It was with a sense of urgency, then, that Vauroy traveled to Calais as soon as he received his orders, taking with him three soldiers from the Dunkirk citadel. They appear to have had no problems in tracking down the fugitive and taking him into custody. This part of his orders having been carried out successfully, Vauroy and his men escorted their prisoner without delay to Pignerol. There was never any mention of hiding the man's face or disguising who he was. Instead, the small group traveled on horseback by regular roads and stopped at convenient post-houses along the way.[5]

Nestling among the pine forests in a valley made lush by the crystal waters of the Chisone and Lemina torrents, Pignerol could hardly be more idyllic.[6] Sheltered by the soaring Cottian Alps to the west, the town lies on the road connecting Briançon with Turin. Standing guard over one of the main routes to the Italian states, Pignerol was of major strategic importance in the 17th century. It had long been coveted by the kings of France and, in 1532, had been captured by François I only to be restored to the dukes of Savoy forty-two years later. Then, in 1630, Cardinal Richelieu, at the head of 20,000 men, seized the town for Louis XIII, his victory secured by the Treaty of Cherasco that was signed the following year.

Although now in French hands, the charming medieval town continued to be inhabited by the native and hostile Piedmontese population, whose loyalties remained with the duc de Savoy. It was heavily fortified, surrounded by bastions, moats, demi-lunes and counter-gardes,[7] which protected it from enemy attack. Two main gates pierced these outer defenses: the Porte de France to the west and the Porte de Turin on the eastern side.

The town was guarded by the citadel, which had been built on its northeastern outskirts, and which was separated from the town itself by a strong wall, complete with ditches and drawbridges. The citadel housed a garrison, and this was manned by troops from several regiments, their colorful uniforms breaking the monotony of the drab gray walls of the surrounding buildings. Sitting on the edge of the citadel and looming over the town was the dark and sinister donjon. The citadel could be accessed from the town through the heavily guarded Porte de la Citadelle, but there was another gate, the secret Porte de Saint-Jacques, which led directly into the donjon from the outside. It was here, on August 21, 1669, that Eustache's long journey came to an end and he passed into the care of his jailer, Saint-Mars.

The early life of Bénigne Dauvergne de Saint-Mars is sketchy, but some facts are known. He was born circa 1626 in Les Mésnuls to a family of minor gentry.[8] Having lost both parents as a child, he was brought up by his uncle, Gilles de Byot de Blainvilliers, who sent him off to the army at the age of twelve. In 1650, the young man joined the musketeers, and it was at this point that he adopted Saint-Mars as his nom de guerre. Although his career progressed relatively slowly, he was promoted twice, first to the rank of brigadier, and then, at the age of thirty-four, to that of sergeant.

Saint-Mars served under the command of Charles Ogier de Batz-Castelmore, comte d'Artagnan, captain-lieutenant of the first company of the king's musketeers. D'Artagnan was the historical figure upon whom Alexandre Dumas would later base his celebrated hero. When Louis XIV was looking for a man to take on the governorship of the donjon of Pignerol, d'Artagnan suggested his sergeant. He had recognized in Saint-Mars those qualities essential for a jailer, especially one who would be guarding state prisoners, where discipline and security were important considerations. As a military man, Saint-Mars knew well how to take orders and act upon them without question. He was generally pleasant, at least at this stage in his career, and discreet, and he could be relied upon to take his responsibilities seriously.

Pignerol was no ordinary prison. It was reserved for those who were considered to be dangerous to the state. It had first been used as a state prison in 1645, when Jean-Jacques de Barillon was incarcerated there on the orders of Anne of Austria. President of the Chambre des Enquêtes at the Parlement de Paris, Barillon was a political adversary of both Cardinal Richelieu and his successor, Cardinal Mazarin. He was arrested when he opposed the Edict de Toisé, which regulated the size of buildings constructed in the suburbs of Paris. He died shortly after his arrival at Pignerol.

Because of Pignerol's importance as a state prison, as well as its position in territory hostile to the French, Louis authorized Saint-Mars to form a *compagnie-franche d'infanterie*, a free infantry company, which he was confident would be "very fine and very good."[9] At the same time, he promoted the former sergeant of the musketeers to the rank of captain. In addition to Saint-Mars, the compagnie-franche initially comprised four officers, three of whom were musketeers on detachment from their regular regiment, as well as two sergeants and fifty men. Within a few months, the company would be augmented with one more sergeant, three corporals, and five *anspessades*, or police officers, who ranked just below the corporals.[10]

Saint-Mars's life had changed radically. The former musketeer was now captain of his own army and stationed on a strategically important frontier post. He was a jailer to a mysterious prisoner who had to be kept securely. In his private life, things had changed, too. On July 4, 1669, shortly before he received Eustache, Saint-Mars married Marie-Antoinette Collot, the daughter of a postmaster, at the church of Saint-Maurice in Pignerol. The couple would go on to have two sons. The eldest, Antoine Bénigne, born on June 17, 1672, would follow his father into the army, achieving the rank of lieutenant-colonel of the king's dragoons. The couple's second-born son, André Antoine, was born on

6

November 29, 1679. He would marry Marguerite Ancel des Granges, a daughter of Louvois's clerk. He would follow his father and elder brother into the military, becoming a guard in the gendarmes of Berry.

Madame de Saint-Mars had two sisters. The eldest, Françoise, was married to Louis Demorezan, commissioner for war at Pignerol. Marie, the younger sister, married Elie du Fresnoy, first clerk to Louvois in the ministry for war. Famed for her beauty, Marie would famously become Louvois's mistress. She was appointed lady of the queen's bed in 1673, a post that she no doubt owed to her lover, and which excited the imagination and amusement of the court. In a further connection, Louvois, acted as godfather to Saint-Mars's eldest son, Antoine Bénigne, in November 1674.

The family connection did not end there, however. When he took up his post at Pignerol, Saint-Mars took with him two of his cousins, both of whom had also served in the musketeers. One cousin was Zachée de Byot, Seigneur de Blainvilliers, who was the son of Saint-Mars's guardian, and who was appointed lieutenant of Saint-Mars's *compagne-franche*. In time, two of Saint-Mars's nephews would enter his service.[11]

The running of the donjon of Pignerol was indeed a family affair, but there were limits. While Saint-Mars had been placed in command of the donjon and given full control of every aspect of his prisoner's life, he was not to act autonomously. Instead, he relied upon the guidance and orders of Louis as transmitted through a constant stream of correspondence with the marquis de Louvois. As time went by and more prisoners were committed to his care, Saint-Mars would send several letters each month containing minute details about those in his charge, how they lived, how he watched over them, and even what they said to him or to his staff.[12] Upon receiving these communications, Louvois would read them out to Louis at one of their regular meetings. The king would dictate his response, which Louvois would dictate to a secretary before sending it back to Saint-Mars. A lone courier riding post could make the journey from Saint-Germain, or wherever the court happened to be, and Pignerol in about a week.

Now that he had taken charge of his prisoner, Saint-Mars had only to lodge him securely, but the special cell he had been ordered to prepare was not yet ready. A temporary cell, therefore, would have to do for the present; but Saint-Mars had some stern words of warning for his prisoner. As he wrote to Louvois: "As soon as I put him in a very safe place, while waiting for the cell that I was making ready for him, I told him in the presence of M. de Vauroy that if he spoke to me, to me [*sic*] or anyone else of anything other than of his needs, I would run him through with my sword."[13] Under no illusion about the dire consequences of disobeying the restrictions placed upon him, Eustache entered his cell. In this forbidding place, Eustache faced a life of loneliness and despair, his days long and without hope; but, whether or not he was aware of it, he was not the only prisoner at Pignerol.

TWO
Nicolas Foucquet

S everal years before Eustache's ordeal began, Nicolas Foucquet had been arrested and put on trial for his life. One of the most powerful men in France at the time, Foucquet had enjoyed a successful career as *procureur-général*, where he put his extensive legal skills to good use on behalf of the crown in the Parlement of Paris. He had also held the post of superintendent of finances, in which capacity he was responsible for raising the funds needed by the state. The superintendence, however, had been in disarray for several decades, and although Foucquet had developed some sound ideas about the best way to reform it, he was prevented from implementing them because, for most of his tenure, France was at war with Spain. Money was always needed, usually urgently, to pay for men, horses, munitions, and other supplies. Much of this revenue had to be raised by extraordinary measures, which included borrowing at illegal rates and creating offices that were then sold to the highest bidder. While these practices were effective in raising the much-needed funds in the short term, they did nothing to alleviate the disorder in the finances.

During the life of Cardinal Mazarin, who had served as first minister during his minority, the young Louis XIV was content to leave the affairs of state to him. Mazarin was not only Louis's godfather, he was also his mentor, instructing the inexperienced king in the art of statecraft. Upon the cardinal's death, Louis announced that he intended to take the reins of power into his own hands. He would have no first minister and his ministers and secretaries of state were required to consult him on all matters. While most accepted this, Foucquet thought that the king, who was still only twenty-two and showed a great fondness for dancing, hunting, and women, would soon tire of endless council meetings and the complex affairs of state, and he looked forward to the day when the king would turn to him to direct the kingdom's affairs as Mazarin had done. It was no secret that this had been Foucquet's ambition, indeed, his expectation, but the superintendent had not reckoned on Louis's determination and capacity for work, no matter how dull. Fallen from favor, Foucquet had been arrested on charges of malversation and lèse-majesté.

At his trial, Foucquet had protested that he was being made a scapegoat, taking punishment that should have been meted out to another, by which he meant the late Cardinal Mazarin. The truth of this argument was secretly recognized and accepted by a majority of Foucquet's judges and, after more than three years of investigations and interrogations, followed by a show trial based upon unsound evidence, the packed panel of judges could not find sufficient cause to condemn Nicolas Foucquet to death, as Louis had wanted. Instead, by a majority of thirteen to nine, Foucquet was convicted of negligence and malfeasance in the exercise of his office as superintendent of finances. The recommended sentence was banishment beyond the borders of France for life and the confiscation of his possessions in favor of the crown, with the exception of a small amount of money to be donated to charity.[1]

The sentence was much less than had been expected, and desired, by the king; but, although Louis had pressed for Foucquet's execution throughout the process, he was not prepared to break the law in order to achieve it. On the other hand, he knew that Foucquet had gained extensive knowledge of foreign affairs during his time in office. The former superintendent's intelligence and affable nature made him particularly suited to diplomacy, and Louis had entrusted him with several sensitive missions. In Sweden, Foucquet had assisted the secretary of state for foreign affairs, Hugues de Lionne, strengthen ties with France, but he had acted independently in Holland, where he opened trade negotiations. He had also sent men and money to assist the French-born Queen Marie-Louise de Gonzague as she endeavored to secure the nomination of her nephew, the duc d'Enghien, as heir to the Polish throne.

Foucquet greatest success, however, had been in diplomatic relations with England. The people of France had embraced the Treaty of the Pyrenees, which brought peace between France and Spain, and which was sealed by the marriage of Louis XIV to the Spanish Infanta, Maria-Teresa. Amid the rejoicing, there were those who were not entirely satisfied with the treaty and thought that France should have benefited more from it. Specifically, the terms of the treaty prevented France from assisting its ally, Portugal, which was struggling to gain independence from Spain.

Even at this early stage in his personal reign, Louis was harboring ambitions in the Spanish Netherlands, and he had recognized that hostilities between Spain and Portugal could prove useful to him. Since Foucquet had been one of those who expressed reservations about the Treaty of the Pyrenees, Louis entrusted him to negotiate with the English in a bid to bring Charles II, recently restored to the throne, into an alliance with the Portuguese. Such a pact would bring England into France's network of European allies. It would be sealed by Charles's marriage to the Portuguese Infanta, Catherine of Braganza, and further sweetened with large subsidies from France.[2] The mission was so secret that Louis did not wish to use his own diplomats. Instead, he ordered

Foucquet to use his own intermediary to induce Edward Hyde, the Earl of Clarendon, to accept the plan and press Charles into marrying the Infanta Catherine.[3]

The sensitive nature of these diplomatic missions and the secrecy that had surrounded them persuaded Louis of the danger of allowing Foucquet to live freely beyond the borders of France. There was, however, another reason why Louis was reluctant to allow the sentence of banishment to be conferred on Foucquet: the ex-superintendent was well aware of the inner workings of French finances, a system that kept power and wealth in the hands of a few at the expense of the poor and powerless. Louis was keen not to let this "secret" be known.

The king was a fair and just man, but on this occasion, and for the first time in the history of the French monarchy, he used his powers not to moderate a sentence against an offender, but to augment it. On December 22, 1664, the same day that Foucquet learned of the verdict and his punishment, Louis issued a decree to be read out in council:

> *The king judged that there might be great danger in letting the sieur Foucquet leave the kingdom, given the peculiar knowledge he had of the most important affairs of the state; that is why he commuted the punishment of perpetual banishment, carried by this judgment, to that of perpetual imprisonment.*[4]

The prison Louis had selected for the incarceration of the man who had served him so faithfully as superintendent of finances, procureur-général, and diplomat was the donjon of faraway Pignerol.

Foucquet, who left behind a wife, five children, four of whom were very young,[5] and his elderly mother, began his journey at eleven o'clock in the morning of December 22, 1664, just three hours after the verdict of the trial and his amended sentence had been read out to him. His carriage, which was adapted for security rather than comfort during the long journey ahead, was heavily fortified with bars on the windows and across the doors. Louis had turned Foucquet's carriage into a cage on wheels.

His greatest fear was that the former superintendent would attempt to escape, or that his loyal friends and allies would try to mount a rescue. As an added precaution, the carriage was escorted by a company of one hundred musketeers under d'Artagnan's command.[6] Four of the musketeers sat inside the carriage, one on either side of the prisoner, while the other two occupied the seats facing him.

D'Artagnan had been the one to arrest Foucquet on the king's orders and, apart from a break of a few weeks, had remained with him throughout the entire legal process. Although he obeyed his orders meticulously, he was a benevolent jailer and treated Foucquet with kindness and humanity. As the carriage pulled out of the courtyard of the Bastille, Foucquet's loyal servant,[7] La Forêt, rushed forward, prompting d'Artagnan to order the coach to slow down sufficiently to allow the two men to exchange a few last words: "I am delighted to see you," Foucquet called out through the heavy grating. "I know your fidelity and your affection. Tell our wives that they should not be downhearted, that I have courage to spare, and that I am well."[8] It was an emotional farewell, and Foucquet's words were immediately circulated among his friends.

Foucquet reached the Porte Saint-Antoine to find a large crowd had assembled. They cheered and wished him well on his way as the carriage thundered through the gates of Paris and out into the wintery countryside beyond. At seven that evening, with the night already closed in, d'Artagnan gave orders for the company to stop at Villeneuve-Saint-Georges.

The following morning saw the unhappy prisoner passing through the town of Melun, a poignant moment because he had formerly been its seigneur, or lord. Nearby lay his magnificent château of Vaux-le-Vicomte, the symbol of his magnificence and his former standing as one of the most powerful men in France. Now it stood as a reminder of tragedy, the hope of further glories to come fading into the winter gloom.

Perhaps it was no coincidence that Foucquet became ill at this early stage of the journey. The trauma of his already lengthy imprisonment, the stress of being kept apart from his family, the constant fear of execution, and the strain of the show trial all had taken their toll. When the news reached Paris, Mme de Sévigné wrote to a friend: "There is a rumor here that he is very ill."[9] It was said that d'Artagnan had sent a messenger to court to ask what he might do for his sick prisoner. The reply was callous: d'Artagnan was to continue the journey, no matter how ill the prisoner was.

By the afternoon of January 11, 1665, the company reached as far as Gap, the largest town in the Hautes-Alpes. The town consuls welcomed their guests and managed to find lodgings for everyone, and six bottles of wine, which had been provided by the vintner Jean Gile, were presented to d'Artagnan. At the musketeer's request, Jacques Etraud, an apothecary, was sent to attend a member of the party who had fallen ill. Who this was is not known. Certainly, Foucquet had been unwell during the early days of the long journey, but there was also a large company of musketeers, as well as valets and other servants. Any one of these men could have required the apothecary's services.[10]

D'Artagnan continued to treat Foucquet with great kindness and was attentive to his every need. Since Foucquet's personal attendants had been removed from him, the musketeer provided his prisoner with one of his own valets. In the hard Alpine winter, the air was bitterly cold, and d'Artagnan ensured that Foucquet, who was now approaching fifty, had "all the furs necessary to pass through the mountains without discomfort."[11] He made every effort to keep Foucquet's spirits up, telling him to be "cheerful and always to have courage, that all would be well."[12] Perhaps d'Artagnan, who continued to receive dispatches from the king during the long journey, secretly shared the hopes of Foucquet's friends in Paris that there would be some easing of the prisoner's ordeal. Alas, it was not to be. More than three weeks after leaving Paris, the imposing sight of the donjon of Pignerol dispelled any hopes that the plight of the ex-superintendent would find a happy ending.

Saint-Mars had arrived at Pignerol a matter of days ahead of his prisoner and had immediately set about preparing an apartment for Foucquet. He selected a suite of two chambers on the third floor of the Angle

Tower, a sizeable *D*-shaped structure set in the southeastern corner of the donjon. The larger of these two chambers measured twenty-six feet by twelve, but the second was only a garderobe measuring twelve feet by ten. This was equipped with a *siege d'aisance*: a "seat of easement," built into the thickness of the outer wall.[13] D'Artagnan inspected the arrangements, but he was not fully satisfied. Certainly, Foucquet had a living room and a proper chamber in which to keep his clothes, as well as a privy, but he did not have a bedroom. Even in prison, the rights and privileges of rank continued to be observed. Foucquet was a nobleman, holding the titles of vicomte de Vaux and marquis de Belle-Île, and the captain-lieutenant thought that a gentleman of Foucquet's quality ought to have a separate bedchamber, so he ordered Saint-Mars to assign a third room and furnish it appropriately.

Louis had set out detailed instructions regarding Foucquet's imprison-ment that Saint-Mars was expected to follow.[14] The first of these referred to the general procedures and manner in guarding Foucquet, but they gave no particular requirement except to say that Saint-Mars should look to the example set by d'Artagnan when he had been in charge of Foucquet at Vincennes, the Bastille, and other prisons. The king then turned to details that particularly concerned him. It was clear from the very beginning that the first priority was security, and Foucquet was to be subjected to a rigorous regime. The prisoner was not permitted to have any communication with anyone, nor was he to be allowed to receive visitors. He was not to leave his apartment on any pretext, not even to go for a walk or take the air.

Foucquet was an intelligent man and an intellectual, and Louis antici-pated that he would request writing materials, in which case Saint-Mars was ordered to refuse him. He could have books to read, but these were to be restricted to one at a time. As a security measure, it was imperative that Saint-Mars examine the books very carefully before giving them to Foucquet, and when they were handed back, he had to ensure that nothing had been written or hidden inside them or that they had other-wise been marked. Louis added that, whenever Foucquet required new clothes or linen, Saint-Mars was to provide them, and his expenditure would be reimbursed by the king upon submission of an invoice.

Throughout the long legal process, Foucquet had been attended by his personal physician and his valet de chambre. Now it was necessary to find someone to serve him in his new prison. While no mention of a physician was made, Saint-Mars was ordered to provide a new valet, someone he judged suitable to serve at Pignerol. It was important to bear in mind, though, that the person chosen would "be likewise deprived of all communication [with the outside world] and will be no more free to leave than the said Foucquet." To compensate for the fact that the valet would, to all intents and purposes, be a prisoner himself, Louis would pay for his board and provide 61 livres per month in wages. In case the valet should fall ill, Saint-Mars was authorized to appoint another, provided he was loyal to the king.[15]

Foucquet's valet could expect to be kept very busy indeed. His duties were wide-ranging and included helping his master to wash and dress, to shave his beard, trim his hair and nails, and look after his clothes. He would not launder the clothes, however; that was the province of laundresses who would take the ex-superintendent's shirts, bedding, and table linen to the river. The valet would also cook and serve Foucquet's meals, wash his plates and cutlery, change his bed, and generally keep his apartment clean and tidy. As though this were not enough, he was expected to act as a spy, reporting Foucquet's every word and action to Saint-Mars, who would then give an account in his dispatches to Louvois.

Foucquet had once owned elegant town houses in the center of Paris, a sumptuous manor at Saint-Mandé on the outskirts of the city, and, most famously, a magnificent château at Vaux-le-Vicomte near Maincy in the Île-de-France. Now, his world had shrunk to three modest chambers with strong iron bars on the windows. The apartment was situated so that Foucquet would be awakened each morning by the light of the rising sun as it filtered through the windows. Later in the day, as the clock of the nearby church chimed out the long hours of his lonely and empty existence, the sun would set behind the mountains, the shadows rapidly closing in, leaving him with only his valet for company in the cold darkness of the night.

The Angle Tower stood next to the barracks, where Saint-Mars's compagnie-franche was stationed. This was also where the arsenal was housed. Weaponry, including muskets, swords, and artillery, was stored there, as were the ammunition and the powder magazine. Six months after Foucquet's arrival, a summer storm crashed over Pignerol. Foucquet and his valet climbed into the window embrasure to watch as the lightning flashed and danced on the distant mountains. Without warning, a direct strike on the arsenal ignited the powder and caused a massive explosion.[16] As the walls blew out, the roof of the Angle Tower smashed down onto the ceiling, which crashed onto the floor, which gave way beneath the weight.

Nicolas Séverat, an adjutant with the Lyonnais regiment, rushed to the scene to find the bloodied bodies of soldiers lying among the rubble; the walking wounded wandered in a daze, while the shattered remains of cannon and other weaponry lay broken and scattered all about. Rushing into the donjon, he found another five soldiers, all in a state of shock, and still more dead. Looking up, he saw Foucquet and his valet. The thickness of the wall had protected them from the explosion, and both had escaped with only a few bruises and scratches. Séverat and the chevalier de Saint-Martin of the compagnie-franche found a ladder and helped them to climb down to safety.[17]

When Saint-Mars rummaged through what remained of Foucquet's apartment, he made an alarming discovery. Hidden in the back of a broken chair, he found a scorched handkerchief covered with writing. Foucquet had made pens out of chicken bones and ink by mixing soot with wine. Clearly Saint-Mars's surveillance of the prisoner had not been as close as it should have been, but there was more. Since his youth, Foucquet had shown an interest in chemistry, and he had owned several books on the subject, which he kept in his library at Saint-Mandé. Unlike some bibliophiles, however, he had not collected books for decoration or as symbols of his wealth, but he actually read them. Now, unbeknownst to Saint-Mars, he had put his knowledge to good use to manufacture sympathetic ink, which he used to write inside one of the books Saint-Mars had given him. The writing appeared when the book was warmed by the fire that had followed the explosion. Saint-Mars bundled the pens, ink, and the handkerchief Foucquet had covered with writing and sent them together with the book to Louis. The king's response was swift: "You must try to find out from monsieur Foucquet's valet how he was able to write the four lines which appeared in the book upon warming it, and of what he composed this writing."[18] After questioning the valet, Saint-Mars was to make it clear to him that he was obliged to be faithful not to Foucquet, but to the king.[19]

While the damaged buildings of the donjon were being repaired, Foucquet was transferred to the fortress of la Pérouse, some eighteen kilometers to the west of Pignerol.[20] A year later, he was returned to the newly repaired Angle Tower, and two valets, Champagne and La Rivière, were moved in with him with instructions to keep an eye on the prisoner and each other. Of these two men very little is known. It has been suggested that Champagne and La Rivière were the noms de guerres of soldiers, and that they had been seconded to Foucquet's service from their regiment.[21] However, there is nothing to indicate that either of these two men were soldiers; instead, they appear to have originally been valets in the service of Saint-Mars, who were then placed with Foucquet.

Now, three years later, the contrast between the living conditions of each of Saint-Mars's prisoners could not have been more marked. Foucquet was allowed books to read; while previously he had been given one book at a time, he could now have two. Saint-Mars was also authorized to give him news of what was going on outside. Despite these privileges, Foucquet continued to defy his jailer. He persisted in making his own writing materials and using them to record his thoughts on his fine handkerchiefs and napkins that he then concealed inside a special, hidden pocket he had sewn into the seat of his breeches. At night, Saint-Mars would quietly enter Foucquet's apartment and conduct a search, confiscating any writing he found and sending it back to the king.

For Eustache, now three weeks into his imprisonment, the empty shell of his life had fallen into a steady if desolate routine. Once each morning he saw his jailer, who brought him enough food to last until his next visit. Occasionally Saint-Mars would make a search of the cell and the prisoner, but then there would be no further contact and no conversation until the procedure was repeated the following morning. There was nothing to break the dreariness of the long hours Eustache would spend alone.

There was, however, some respite even in Eustache's unhappy existence. He was allowed the comfort of a book of prayers as well as any other book he might ask for.[22] On Sundays and feast days, he was allowed to hear mass. This would normally be said in the Chapel of Saint George in the northeastern tower of the donjon. Furnished with the sacred items and vestments necessary for the mass and other services, the chapel catered to the spiritual needs of Saint-Mars, his family, and staff as well as his compagnie-franche and other personnel attached to the garrison of Pignerol. According to Tallemant des Réaux, Foucquet was allowed to attend mass here, where the need for security obliged to him to sit on a balcony separated from the rest of the chapel behind grated and curtained windows.[23] As would be confirmed later by Saint-Mars, Eustache was also brought out of his strict confinement in order to attend mass in the chapel.[24] Like Foucquet, Eustache was allowed to make his confession three or four times a year if he wished, but he could not see a priest more often than that unless he became dangerously ill.[25]

As the heat of the Piedmontese summer mellowed into a golden autumn, both prisoners became unwell. While Saint-Mars had obtained permission for doctors to come into the donjon to attend Foucquet, no such arrangements had yet been put in place for Eustache. Despite Eustache being so ill that Saint-Mars thought he should be bled, the jailer was reluctant to act on his own initiative and asked for instructions. Three weeks later, he received his answer. He should bring in a doctor to bleed the patient, adding that, should a similar situation arise in the future, he could arrange whatever treatment was deemed necessary without asking permission first.[26]

Although the precautions that were taken with Eustache might seem excessive and indicative of his being considered a serious security risk, the prisoner Louis was most concerned about was Foucquet. Like Eustache, the former superintendent was forbidden contact with anyone except Saint-Mars; unlike Eustache, he was attended by two valets. Foucquet bore his ordeal with great fortitude and he tried to make the best of his situation. Prison though it was, Pignerol was surrounded by spectacular views of forests and mountains set against clear blue skies. The pretty town with its red roofs and beautiful churches, which filled the air with the sound of bells every Sunday, bustled below. Foucquet accepted that he would never be allowed to go outside, so he asked Saint-Mars if he could have *lunettes d'approche*, or a telescope, in order to enjoy as far as he could the beauty of the surroundings that now comprised his entire world. Louis regarded this request with suspicion, while Louvois believed that Foucquet really wanted to use the telescope "'for something contrary to His Majesty's service."[27] The request was denied.

Louis considered his cautiousness to be justified. In the days following Foucquet's arrest in 1661, a systematic search of his various properties had taken place. In the study of his house at Saint-Mandé, a document was found hidden behind a mirror. In it, Foucquet related his fears that Cardinal Mazarin would persecute him and order his arrest. The relationship between Foucquet and Mazarin was certainly turbulent at times, and Foucquet's fears were not entirely unfounded.

The *Projet de Saint-Mandé*, as the document came to be known, contained a detailed plan of action that was to be enacted in the event of Foucquet's detention.[28] It envisaged three possible scenarios and set out the measures to be taken in each case. It named people whom Foucquet felt he could rely upon to assist him, and who would agitate for his release. It identified relatives, friends, clients, and business associates, many of whom commanded military outposts or who governed towns in strategic locations. These people could provide safe havens where

Foucquet's family and friends could be protected from the royal armies. To some, the plan implied the threat that these towns and outposts, many of which were situated dangerously close to the border with the Spanish Netherlands, could be opened to the enemy in the event that Foucquet was not released.

For Louis, this was all very sinister. During his minority, when he was still too young to rule in his own right, his kingdom had been threatened by the Fronde. This was a series of uprisings initiated by disaffected members of the nobility, who were later joined by supporters from the Parlement of Paris and members of the clergy. Their aim had been to overthrow the powerful Mazarin, who was distrusted and resented as a foreigner, and to reestablish what the nobles saw as their rightful place in the government of the country. Their actions, however, posed a serious threat to Louis, who would forever be scarred by the indignity and fear to which he was exposed during those years.

Foucquet's plan reopened these still tender wounds, and while Foucquet insisted at his trial that he had written the *Projet* simply as a cathartic exercise, a way to calm his fears in a hostile situation, his enemies saw in it a blueprint for a new Fronde. Despite Foucquet having never attempted to implement the plan or even to inform those named in it of its existence,[29] the document was entered as evidence of his intent to commit lèse-majesté, a crime that would automatically have attracted the death penalty had a slim majority of the judges not dismissed it.

Throughout Foucquet's trial, it had been Louis's fear that the superintendent's powerful friends might attempt to liberate him and a new Fronde would ensue. Even when Foucquet was securely behind the impenetrable walls of the donjon of Pignerol, the king's mind was still not entirely at ease. These fears were justified when news arrived of a strange man who had been spotted in the town of Pignerol. Who he was no one could say for certain, but it was believed that he had once been in Foucquet's service. This mysterious man had not come near the donjon and had apparently made no attempt to contact his former master. Saint-Mars had ordered a search to be made, but the man was nowhere to be found.

Now, at the end of 1669, the uneasy peace of the donjon was broken once more when two men breached the security of Pignerol and managed to enter the citadel. One was Foucquet's former valet, the faithful La Forêt, who had exchanged those final unhappy words with his master in the courtyard of the Bastille. The other was the sieur de Valcroissant, who went by the name of Honneste. They were well organized and funded, and their aim was nothing less than to break Foucquet out of prison, but it is not known if they were acting on behalf of the Foucquet family or if they had formulated the plot on their own. Whatever the case, they had managed to bribe several soldiers belonging to Saint-Mars's compagnie-franche, some of whom were detailed to stand below the windows of Foucquet's apartment as lookouts. They also made contact with Foucquet's two valets, Champagne and La Rivière.

Saint-Mars was alerted to what was happening and the plot was thwarted. La Forêt and Honneste fled to Turin, the capital of neutral Piedmont, where they believed they would be safe. Unfortunately for them, men sent by Saint-Mars tracked them to their hideout, and with the help of the Duke of Savoy and the Major of Turin, the fugitives were taken under heavy guard back to Pignerol.

Once in Saint-Mars's custody, the higher-ranking Honneste was held in a cell until he could be tried. He would eventually be found guilty of attempting to carry a letter from Foucquet to his wife and sentenced to five years as a galley slave. The soldiers were interrogated and those found guilty were immediately executed. La Forêt, Foucquet's valet, who had served his master so faithfully, was questioned before being hanged on a scaffold that had been erected outside Foucquet's window.[30]

Saint-Mars was ordered to cover Foucquet's windows with a screen, which was to be so placed that it would allow in light but prevent the prisoner being able to see anything but the sky. It was also to be fitted with a covering that could be brought down and locked each night to prevent Foucquet sending out or receiving messages. This precaution, it was hoped, would prevent any further attempts by Foucquet or any of his supporters from forming any more plots.[31] As to his valets, Louis, Louvois, and Saint-Mars were well aware of how difficult it would be to replace them, given the inflexible conditions in which they were required to live. Instead of imprisoning them or sending them away, Louis deprived them of their wages as punishment for their disloyalty.[32]

If Saint-Mars thought he had put the massive breach of security behind him, he was mistaken. Louvois had learned that Honneste or one of Foucquet's valets had managed to speak to Eustache, who is here referred to as "the prisoner who was brought to you by the major of Dunkirk," and he informed Saint-Mars about it.[33] Saint-Mars must already have known, or suspected, that there was a secret spy operating inside the donjon, someone who was transmitting information back to Louvois and Louis. This had been confirmed in a letter dated September 10, 1669, in which Louvois referred to a conversation between Saint-Mars and La Bretonnière, the king's lieutenant for the government of the town of Pignerol.[34] Now this secret agent had found out that Eustache's visitor had asked him if he had anything important to say. The prisoner had refused to tell him anything; he had merely told the person on the other side of his door to leave him alone.

Quite why any of Foucquet's valets or one of the conspirators would try to question Eustache is not known. It could have been out of curiosity; he was, after all, Foucquet's only prison companion at the time, and Foucquet could have become aware of his presence when they attended mass. It remains a matter of speculation whether or not Foucquet sent someone to ask after his fellow prisoner, perhaps with a view to securing his rescue as well as his own.

What is more plausible is Louvois's suggestion: that Eustache probably thought Saint-Mars had sent someone to test him to see if he would say anything. In either case, Louvois conveyed the king's anger: "You have not taken sufficient precautions to prevent his having any communications with anyone," rebuked Louvois, "and, as it is very important to His Majesty's service that he has no communication, please inspect carefully inside and outside the place where he is held, and put it in such order that the prisoner cannot see or be seen by anyone, and cannot speak to anyone at all, nor hear those who might want to say anything to him."[35]

The revelation that the security of his donjon and compagnie-franche had been so seriously compromised terrified Saint-Mars, and he was desperate to show Louis and Louvois that he was still in full command and that no one could deceive him. "There are people who are so curious to ask me news of my prisoner," he wrote, "or the reason why I have made so many entrenchments for my security, that I am obliged to tell them contes jaunes [fairy tales] to make fun of them."[36] Even so, the events of the recent past were awful warning. Work on Eustache's special cell was stepped up, and he was installed the following April.

The exact location of the cell in which Eustache spent the first years of his imprisonment is not known for certain; but, as will be seen, there is reason to believe that the cell was inside the Lower Tower, situated midway along the southern façade of the donjon. "The Lower Tower, because of its situation, could not be seen from outside," writes Théodore Iung. It had three floors "and a rather large single room with vents, without broad daylight, on each of these floors."[37]

That August, Louvois paid a visit to Pignerol. He took with him his clerk, M. de Nallot, and the military engineer, Sébastien Le Prestre, seigneur de Vauban. Two months later, the garrison of the citadel of Pignerol was changed, with M. de Rissan, the king's lieutenant, taking the place of M. de Saint-Jacques as commander of the citadel of Pignerol.[38] The purpose of these precautions was to ensure the security of the citadel and, more importantly, the donjon, for which Rissan was ordered to liaise with Saint-Mars. Once again, the concern here was not with Eustache, but Foucquet. Louis continued to fear that the ex-superintendent might find a way to escape or that his friends and supporters might succeed in liberating him. Louis, however, need not have worried. After nine years as a prisoner, and still in shock following the execution of his faithful servant, La Forêt, Nicolas Foucquet had lost all interest in earthly matters. His spirit broken, he withdrew into himself and took solace in contemplating the next world. He requested, and was granted a Bible, which Saint-Mars was authorized to go out and buy for him. As for Eustache, shut inside the secure cell that was now his permanent home, closed in behind three sets of heavy, studded doors, he vanished from the world.

THREE

The Comte de Lauzun

One of the most challenging problems facing Saint-Mars at Pignerol was illness among his prisoners. They and their valets were frequently plagued by colds, fevers, and vague maladies that could last from a few days to several weeks. One of the main causes was their close confinement, which deprived them of fresh air and exercise. Another was the mountain climate, which left their apartments too hot in the summer and too cold in the winter.

In August 1671, Saint-Mars reported that Foucquet had a slight fever, although he was not too incommoded by it. One of his valets, however, was very ill, as was "the prisoner you sent me"; that is, Eustache.[1] A week later, Foucquet was still unwell. As he wrote, Saint-Mars was not particularly concerned, for Foucquet's "good way of life will protect him from a troublesome illness." It was a different matter for the other men under his charge, however. Foucquet's valet continued to be "extremely ill," as did "the prisoner who was brought to me."[2] Eustache, alone in his miserable cell, had scarcely enough of the bare necessities of life, and now Saint-Mars did not even deign to use his name. It is not clear whether this was deliberate, his way of showing that he was actively seeking to preserve the secrecy that surrounded his mysterious prisoner, or whether he had forgotten Eustache's name.

A month later, Foucquet had recovered from what turns out to have been an attack of sciatica. His valet and Saint-Mars's "other prisoner" were still unwell, although it appears that they had improved slightly.[3] As the first leaves of autumn began to fall, Saint-Mars was authorized to have a suit of winter clothes made for Foucquet, but his two valets had to make do with the clothes they already had.[4] With the coming of winter, Saint-Mars's tribulations were about to increase still further.

It was on December 12, 1671, when the Porte de Saint-Jacques, the secret entrance to the donjon of Pignerol, swung open to reveal two hundred musketeers assembled in the snowy wastes beyond. The musketeers were commanded by captain-lieutenant d'Artagnan. Almost six years previously, he had brought Nicolas Foucquet to this remote and melancholy outpost. Now he had returned with another prisoner.

As a small carriage rattled through the gate and came to a halt, Saint-Mars walked up to it and waited for the door to be opened. Inside sat a man in his late thirties,[5] small and fair; although not handsome, he had a certain attraction and the bearing of a man who was used to life at court and military service. A former favorite of Louis XIV, the illustrious Antonin Nompar de Caumont, marquis de Puyguilhem, comte de Lauzun, was passed into Saint-Mars's care.

Saint-Mars had been expecting Lauzun's arrival for more than two weeks, having been advised by a letter from Louvois to prepare rooms for him. By now, the jailer knew what was expected of him, but Louvois, acting on the king's orders, gave detailed instructions all the same.

The king ordered Saint-Mars to ensure that Lauzun would be guarded with "all the precautions imaginable."[6] He and the valet assigned to him must never be allowed to leave his rooms, the door to which must never be opened except in the presence of Saint-Mars, who was told to apply the same precautions taken for the security of Foucquet. Indeed, he was to be "much more alert in guarding the prisoner than has been necessary for guarding the other [Foucquet] because he is capable of anything to save himself by strength or artfulness, or by corrupting someone, than monsieur Foucquet."

If Saint-Mars deemed Foucquet's apartment to be more secure than the one he had prepared for Lauzun, then he should put Lauzun in that one and move Foucquet to the rooms currently occupied by Madame de Saint-Mars. In this case, Saint-Mars was required to place screens on the windows and chimneys and brick up all the doors except one. This door, which would serve as the only entrance into the chamber, should be the one in the *ruelle du lit*, or the small alcove in which the bed was placed. This way, Foucquet would be well accommodated and only one sentinel would be required to watch the entrances to his apartment and Lauzun's.

It was the king's wish that Lauzun should be denied writing materials; he was not to be given paper or ink even to write to Louis, unless the king gave his express permission first. He was, however, allowed to hear the mass that was said for Foucquet on feast days and Sundays, but precautions had to be taken to ensure that there was no communication between the two prisoners. Similarly, Lauzun would be allowed to make his confession at Easter if he wished, using the confessor that was provided for Foucquet. In the event that Lauzun became ill, he would be attended by the same physicians and surgeons who saw Foucquet.

Just as he did with Foucquet, Louis would bear the cost of the food provided for Lauzun, which should be of the same quality as that served to Foucquet. As members of the nobility, the quality of their food would be high, reflecting the fare that would be available to them if they were free.

Lauzun would also be provided with linen and clothes, "observing that the clothes should be clean and plain." As to furniture, Saint-Mars should provide a good bed, chairs, tables, and firedogs and other items for the fire. He should also obtain a Bergamo tapestry to break up the monotony of the bare prison walls and keep out drafts.

As befitting a man of his social standing, Lauzun was to be given a valet, perhaps one of those who were currently serving Foucquet, or one of Saint-Mars's own. This valet would be locked up with his master and would not be allowed to communicate with anyone other than Lauzun.

Saint-Mars was to make it his business to know everything Lauzun said or did, and to give a regular account of it. He was then asked to state how many extra men he would need to recruit to his compagnie-franche, for the "sure guard of this prisoner is very important."

Already there was a discernible change in the king's attitude toward Foucquet. Having been a prisoner for ten years, during which Louis's primary concern was that he should not escape, Foucquet's security remained important, but less so than that of Lauzun. Moreover, there is no mention of Eustache, all the more curious given the tight security surrounding him and the imperative that he should have no communication with the outside world.

Saint-Mars replied to Louvois's letter a few days later to say that thirty extra men would suffice to ensure the secure guard of his new prisoner. He noted that Monsieur de Nallot, Louvois's clerk, had arrived to oversee the arrangements and that, together, they had decided that the best place to lodge Lauzun was the apartment below the one occupied by Foucquet. It had two rooms with low ceilings, it was warm, and there were grills on the windows made of thick iron bars. Despite this, the rooms were considered to be light enough, at least as far as Saint-Mars was concerned. Once securely installed, the prisoner "would not be able to see or hear any living soul."[7] Louvois would remember this apartment, Saint-Mars said, for he had inspected it during his recent visit to Pignerol, and he had no doubt that the minister would be pleased with this arrangement.[8] Saint-Mars then explained that he had the keys and locks for the apartment made in front of his lieutenants, whom he relieved by turns, so that, he said, he "cannot be deceived."[9] He continued:

From what I am having done in this place, I can answer to you on my life for the safety of Monsieur de Lauzun, and for the fact that he can neither receive nor transmit any news to the outside world. I stake my honor, Monseigneur, that you will never hear news of him, except through me, while he is under my care; and I shall take my precautions so well and shall be so alert that I am running no risk in what I undertake. You have shown me so fully the will of his Majesty, on the subject of the safety of the new prisoner who is being brought to me, that I can protest to you that he will be as though "in pace." I shall treat him politely, without, however, holding any communication with him unless you command it expressly.[10]

Lauzun, Saint-Mars promised, would be as quiet as the dead: "I engage upon my honor, Monseigneur, that as long as this gentleman is under my care you will hear no further word about him, it will be as if he is already *in pace.*"

It was Saint-Mars's practice to bore holes in the walls of his prisoners' apartments so he and his turnkeys could watch their movements and hear what they said. The walls of Lauzun's apartment permitted this; but just to be certain that nothing went unnoticed, Saint-Mars assured Louvois that he would learn everything he needed to know from the valet assigned to serve Lauzun. "I have found one with much trouble, because the clever ones do not wish to pass their life in prison." In the end, Saint-Mars suggested that, as with Foucquet, Lauzun should be provided with two valets so that they could take care of each other should one of them fall ill, but also so that they could spy upon their master and each other.

Louvois ordered that Lauzun should be allowed to hear mass, but only on feast days and Sundays. Saint-Mars promised him that this order would be carried out to the letter. He added that the man who confessed Foucquet would also attend Lauzun "at Easter and at no other time, whatever may happen."

Saint-Mars signed off with this assurance: "My only desire is to carry out exactly the orders with which you have honored me. I shall always endeavor to do this with zeal, passion, and fidelity, so I trust that you may be content with my small services." No one could ever question Saint-Mars's devotion to duty and his determination to carry out his orders to the letter.

When he entered his dismal prison, Lauzun told Saint-Mars, "You have prepared a lodging for me *in secular seculorum*." Sinking into a state of depression, he took badly to his new environment. He refused to eat, which left him dizzy with hunger, and would not speak to anyone, not even his valet. When eventually he did speak, it was to tell Saint-Mars that he felt he was going out of his mind, and the jailer feared that he might be right. When he learned that Louvois had not sent Saint-Mars a message for him, he cried out three or four times, "Pignerol! Pignerol! They will have the pleasure. I shall make a tragedy of my prison, and you will be the first to see it!"[11]

Throughout the long journey from the Bastille, Lauzun had expressed his astonishment at his detention. Now, almost three weeks into his imprisonment, he asked Saint-Mars why he had been sent to jail, but Saint-Mars could only reply that he had learned nothing about it.[12] By January 1672, Lauzun's mental state had deteriorated to the point that he was threatening to kill himself.[13] He genuinely had no idea why Louis had ordered his arrest and was at a loss to understand why he should have been sent to Pignerol, so far from the glittering court of which he had been such an ornament. However, in searching for reasons for Louis's displeasure, Lauzun surely did not need to look far, for he had antagonized the king so many times that the real mystery lay in why Louis had not acted against him earlier.

On one memorable occasion, Lauzun had competed with Louis for the heart of a lady. Catherine-Charlotte de Gramont was Lauzun's cousin, and the two had largely been brought up together.[14] The comte fell helplessly in love with her, and, to his delight, his passion was reciprocated. With no prospective marriage in sight for either of them at that point, the lovers were allowed to see each other as often as they liked. Lauzun, however, was merely the younger son of an impoverished

Gascon noble, which made him an unsuitable match for the daughter of the aristocratic maréchal de Gramont. In time, Catherine-Charlotte's marriage to Louis de Grimaldi, Prince of Monaco, was arranged, and the prince traveled to France for the wedding. This took place on March 30, 1660, and Monaco returned to his principality shortly afterward, leaving his young bride at the French court. She would leave to join her husband in the late summer of the following year.

It was not until 1665, when Mme de Monaco returned to France on a diplomatic mission on behalf of her husband, that Lauzun would see her again. Any hopes he might have harbored about rekindling their romance were dashed when Louis fell for the princess's charms. Lauzun, consumed with jealousy and resentment, decided to have his revenge on the king. He bribed the princess's maid to tell him when Louis and her mistress arranged their next tryst. He did not have long to wait. As Louis waited expectantly inside his apartments for his lover to arrive, Lauzun quietly locked the door to the private back entrance, took the key, and hid inside the nearby privy to listen to the drama that was about to unfold.[15]

Mme de Monaco duly arrived with Bontemps, Louis's faithful and discreet chief valet, who saw her safely through the narrow passageways that led to the back door of the king's apartments. Bontemps reached into the shadows for the key, expecting it to be in its usual place, but, of course, it was missing. Thinking that Louis had perhaps forgotten to leave it in the lock, Bontemps lightly scratched on the door to attract the king's attention. Louis assured his valet that he had left the key outside as arranged, but still Bontemps could not find it. When, after extensive and frantic searching on both sides of the door, the key could not be found, the lovers had to admit defeat. As the disappointed princess returned to her own rooms, Lauzun gloated over the trick he had played from the safety of his hiding place.[16]

In this way Lauzun exacted his revenge on Louis, but Mme de Monaco did not escape unscathed.[17] Angry at her infidelity, the comte stormed into her rooms to confront her, but when he found that she was not there, he took out his frustration by breaking an expensive mirror. Later, he and the princess had a blazing row, in which Lauzun ungallantly threatened to show Louis letters that would compromise her. The princess preempted him, however; she went to the king to complain about Lauzun's behavior toward her.

Lauzun might have been a favorite, even a friend, but Louis was growing tired of his antics. He decided that it would be a good idea for all concerned if he sent the insolent little man to inspect the dragoons. This regiment, of which Lauzun was colonel, was currently stationed in faraway Béarn, which made the prospect of sending him to do his duty all the more attractive. Lauzun was devastated at the thought of traveling to the Pyrenees. He had no wish to go. He threatened to resign his post and then, in an extraordinary display of impertinence, he drew his sword and broke it, saying that he had no desire to put it to the service of a king who behaved as Louis did. Louis's equilibrium was such that he rarely lost his temper, but by now his anger matched that of Lauzun. He turned and went to the window, took up his cane, and threw it out "for fear that I should have to reproach myself with striking a gentleman." He then calmly left the room, his dignity, unlike that of Lauzun, intact. If, however, Lauzun thought that Louis had forgiven him his unpardonable outburst, he was mistaken. The following morning, he was arrested and conducted to the Bastille, where he would remain for the next four months.[18]

On another occasion, Lauzun coveted the post of grandmaster of the artillery, which had recently become vacant upon the resignation of its holder, the duc de Mazarin.[19] Lauzun pestered Louis mercilessly to give it to him, but his efforts were vehemently opposed by Louvois. As an ally of Colbert, Lauzun was naturally Louvois's enemy, and the war minister was adamant that the comte should not receive such a valuable appointment. With Louvois entreating him on the one hand, and Lauzun begging him on the other, Louis delayed making the final decision. Eventually, he promised Lauzun that he would promote him to grandmaster but warned him not to disclose the news until a formal announcement had been made.

When Louvois found out about the new appointment, he took it upon himself to sabotage Lauzun's good fortune. Knowing that Lauzun had been sworn to secrecy, he wrote a note to the king telling him that he had heard rumors of the comte's proposed promotion, wording it in such a way that Louis could be in no doubt that the rumors had originated with Lauzun himself. When Louis read the note, he was incensed. As he went to mass, he passed Lauzun in the corridor, but did not speak to him.

Lauzun was alarmed; clearly, something was wrong. Later that day, he approached the king and inquired when he might expect the announcement of his new appointment to be made. Louis merely replied that it would be impossible for him to make such a statement just yet, adding ominously that he needed time to consider the matter further. When Lauzun continued to press him, Louis told him coldly that since the comte had not kept his promise to remain silent, Louis was under no obligation to honor his promise. Lauzun, ever the optimist, continued to believe that the post was his, but he thought it prudent to ask someone to press the king on his behalf. His choice fell upon Mme de Montespan, Louis's charming, witty and beautiful *maîtresse en titre*.

Mme de Montespan appeared to be sympathetic to Lauzun's plight and she promised to do anything she could to help. Lauzun, however, was not as certain of the lady's sincerity as he would have liked. He bribed her chambermaid to hide him under the bed when her mistress next expected to entertain the king. At the appointed hour, Louis duly arrived and, after the couple had made love, Lauzun was treated to the pillow talk he was so desperate to hear. Just as she had promised, Mme de Montespan brought up the subject of the vacant post of grand master of the artillery, but Louis told her that he had no intention of awarding it to the comte de Lauzun. Instead of defending the comte and trying to persuade Louis to change his mind, Mme de Montespan recounted how she had duped Lauzun by promising to intercede for him. Lauzun could only listen as the couple ridiculed and laughed at him.

As soon as Louis and Mme de Montespan left the bedroom, the chambermaid dragged the still stunned Lauzun out from his hiding place. He somehow managed to maintain his composure and stationed himself by the mistress's door, waiting for her to emerge. Mme de Montespan was going to a rehearsal for a ballet, and Lauzun gallantly offered to escort her. He asked her if he dared to hope that she had found time to speak to the king as she had promised. She assured him that she had and began to recount the kind services she had rendered him. At this point, he leaned in and spoke gently in her ear, calling her a liar, a rascal, a hussy, and a piece of dog dirt before repeating, word-for-word, the conversation that had passed between her and the king. The poor lady was so shocked that it was all she could do to stagger to the rehearsal room, where she fell in a faint. That evening she told Louis the whole story of what Lauzun had said to her. The lovers were at a loss. They could not understand how he could have known what was said between them and concluded that he must have been informed by the devil.[20]

Another incident involved Louis's cousin, Anne-Marie-Louise d'Orléans, duchesse de Montpensier. Known as Mademoiselle, or La Grande Mademoiselle, she was the richest and, therefore, the most eligible princess in Europe. The daughter of Gaston, duc d'Orléans, Louis XIV's uncle, she was still unmarried at the age of forty-five when she fell in love with Lauzun, eight years her junior. Convinced that he was as much in love with her as she was with him, she proposed to him and he accepted. Mademoiselle bestowed her lucrative properties upon him, the comté d'Eu, the duchies of Montpensier, Saint-Fargeau, and Châtellerault, as well as the sovereignty of Dombes, all of which brought their owner substantial revenues.[21] She failed to take one important factor into account, however: as a member of the royal family, Mademoiselle was not free to marry whom she pleased. She required the king's permission, but, too afraid to approach him in person, she wrote a letter outlining her desire to marry Lauzun and requesting Louis's blessing.

Louis was cautious about the match and he asked his cousin to think very carefully before taking a step "which might be followed by a long and hopeless repentance."[22] Louis hoped that, given time, he would be able to persuade Mademoiselle to change her mind, but he did not reckon on her resolve. Her mind made up, she continued to press Louis to give his consent. To marry Lauzun, she insisted, would be the only thing that could bring happiness and peace to her life, while the king's refusal to allow the marriage to take place would leave her "the most miserable person on earth."[23] Seeing her pleas fall upon deaf ears, Mademoiselle and Lauzun turned to their friends, people from highest ranks of the nobility, to see what they could do to sway the king. Assailed by their arguments, Louis at last relented. Shrugging his shoulders in astonishment at his cousin's "infatuation," he said that "she was forty-five years old, and might do what she liked."[24] With the question now apparently settled, the couple set about making arrangements for their wedding.

One of the couple's allies had been Mme de Montespan, who had offered her assistance as they sought Louis's permission to marry. The royal favorite, however, was warned by her friends of the dangers to which her actions would surely expose her should her reign as royal mistress come to an end. Afraid now, Mme de Montespan went to Louis and begged him for her own sake to stop the marriage.[25]

As it happened, Mme de Montespan's change of heart was just the incentive Louis needed, for he had been against the marriage from the beginning. Moreover, his mistress's appeals coincided with a new rumor, one that greatly annoyed the king. Word had reached him that, as she received the good wishes of the court, Mademoiselle implied that she and Lauzun were marrying because the king wished it. This was untrue, and when Louis heard of it, he summoned her into his presence and, in front of several witnesses, spoke to her about her false assertion. Nervous now, Mademoiselle denied having said such a thing, adding that she had told everyone that the king had done his best to talk her out of marrying the comte. Louis accepted her protests, but he continued to hear stories that he considered to be very injurious to him. He described these rumors as:

> . . . *being to the effect that all the resistance I had shown to the affair was only a pretense and a farce, and that really I was very glad to obtain so great a benefit for the Comte de Lauzun, whom everybody*

believes that I like and esteem very much, as is indeed the case; there-
fore, seeing my reputation so deeply involved, I resolved at once to
prevent this marriage, and to have no further consideration either
for the happiness of the Princess or for the happiness of the Count, on
whom I can and will confer other benefits.[26]

Louis sent once again for his cousin and told her firmly that he would "not suffer her to make this marriage," nor would he allow her to marry any prince among his subjects, although "she might choose among all the qualified nobility of France whoever she liked except the Comte de Lauzun," and, having done so, Louis would personally escort her to the church.[27] Mademoiselle took the news badly. She burst into tears. She felt as though Louis "had stabbed her a hundred times in the heart with a poniard." When Louis visited his grieving cousin the next day, he tried to console her by reiterating his promise of "great benefits" for Lauzun.

As for Lauzun, he appeared to receive the news "with all the firmness and submission" that the king could desire.[28] Nonetheless, when he found out about Mme de Montespan's intervention, his anger knew no bounds. He abused her to her face and behind her back. So ferocious were his attacks that courtiers predicted his fall from grace: "Lauzun is a lost man," said one, "he will not remain six months at court."[29]

So far Louis was not aware of how Lauzun was abusing his mistress. Thinking all was well, he offered to make the comte a maréchal of France. Lauzun refused this favor on the grounds that his past military service did not warrant it. He did, however, accept the governorship of Berry and the fifty thousand *louis* that went with it, which would, he said, allow him to clear his debts.[30]

Lauzun continued to attack Mme de Montespan, and he even began to do so in Louis's presence, yet it seemed that nothing could touch him. As Louis made a royal progress to Flanders, Lauzun and his friend Guitry[31] sought his permission to cross into Holland. Why they went, no one knew; the visit could have been for pleasure, or it could have been a cover for some darker purpose, perhaps to do with the impending

Dutch War. It was all very secret. Some courtiers thought that Lauzun had, in fact, been sent away and that the excursion into Holland marked the beginning of his exile. This surmise was proven wrong when the two men returned a week later, upon which Lauzun took up his three-month tour of duty as captain of the king's guard.

It appears that some form of reconciliation now took place between Lauzun and Mme de Montespan, at least on his part. At this point, the post of colonel of the king's guard became available and Lauzun desperately wanted it, not least because the holder would be constantly in the king's company. As someone who greatly admired the king, this was an attractive proposition for Lauzun. One again, he was reluctant to approach Louis in person, so he asked Mme de Montespan if she would intervene with the king on his behalf. Once again, she agreed. History now repeated itself, with Mme de Montespan speaking to Louis in terms that were entirely detrimental to Lauzun. The little man had made her come to beg for the post of colonel on his behalf, she told Louis, adding that she would not award it if she were in Louis's place.

Louis could not understand why Lauzun employed such artifice when he could simply have approached him and asked for what he wanted. Mme de Montespan suggested that Louis should perhaps speak to Lauzun, to which Louis readily agreed. During the ensuing interview, Louis, pretending to be unaware that Lauzun had approached Mme de Montespan, expressed his surprise that the comte had no wish to acquire the post of colonel. Lauzun answered that he had received so many favors from the king already that he did not think to receive still more. He insisted that he had never thought of asking for the promotion, since there were so many others more worthy.

"This modesty sits well on you," Louis told him, but his manner was cold as he went on to reveal that Mme de Montespan had already spoken to him on the matter, which he did not think she would have done had Lauzun not requested her to do so. The king could not understand why Lauzun had tried to conceal his desire to be promoted to colonel of the guards, particularly as he had more right to the post than many; he added that he wished Lauzun would tell him the truth.

At this, Lauzun once again protested that he had never considered asking for the post, and at this Louis's mood turned darker. The king declared his astonishment at Lauzun's temerity in lying to him. He then informed Lauzun that Mme de Montespan had told him everything. Louis now assured the comte that he felt certain that he would never again believe anything he might have to say. He rose at that point and dismissed Lauzun, making it very clear that he had no desire to listen to any excuses. Lauzun stormed out of the room in anger and despair. He went straight to Mme de Montespan's apartment, where he vented his anger in a torrent of abuse.

Mme de Montespan later spoke to her friends about what she had suffered at Lauzun's hands, and received some advice from a close friend, Mme Scarron.[32] Knowing that Louis was deep into his preparations to go to war against Holland, she asked Mme de Montespan if she thought it would be a good idea to be left alone at Versailles while Louis was at the front, where Lauzun would constantly be at his side dripping venom about her into the king's ear. Such a prospect terrified the royal favorite, who allowed herself to be persuaded that she should go to Louis and urge him to order the arrest of this man who did nothing but mistreat and insult her.

At this point, Lauzun's steadfast enemy, the marquis de Louvois, was looking to the forthcoming war as a means of furthering his own ambitions, and he saw the virtue in clearing Lauzun from the field of rivals. He entered into an alliance with Mme de Montespan, who by now very much feared for her safety as long as Lauzun was at liberty,[33] and together they sought to bring about the fall of the insolent comte.

As it was, Mme de Montespan and Louvois already had the perfect weapon at hand. Lauzun, they reminded Louis, was beloved of Mademoiselle, who had been the heroine of the Fronde. He was too dangerous a man to be left at liberty. As Mademoiselle states in her *Mémoires*, "there are unhappy moments in which one cannot escape one's evil destiny."[34]

For Lauzun, that moment arrived on November 25, 1671, when he was arrested in his rooms and taken to the Bastille. Here, he languished for two days while arrangements were made to conduct him to Pignerol. At one point, Louvois allowed Lauzun's friend Barail to write to him, in his presence, to ask what ought to be done with his servants and property. D'Artagnan, who was guarding the prisoner at the Bastille, was told to provide the necessary writing materials and to allow Lauzun to answer his friend's letter, but only in his presence. The letter was to be handed to the courier who had brought the one from Barail.

Two days later, Lauzun was bundled into a carriage with d'Artagnan, who was now making his second journey to Pignerol. The captain-lieutenant of the first company of the king's musketeers was accompanied by his cousin, Pierre de Montesquieu d'Artagnan,[35] and his sub-lieutenant, Louis de Melun, marquis de Maupertuis. They set out at the head of an escort of one hundred musketeers.[36]

D'Artagnan and Lauzun had fallen out, but Lauzun had recently made up their differences. Perhaps he had sensed that, in the troubles that were now engulfing him, he would need a friend, or at least someone who was not openly hostile toward him. As the unhappy party clattered through the crisp winter landscape, Lauzun was so absorbed in his own misfortunes that he could not be induced to talk despite the best efforts of Maupertuis to draw him out. As the party passed Petit-Bourg, which Mademoiselle was expected to inherit, Lauzun sighed, "Alas, this house reminds me of the difference between my situation as it is now and what it was a year ago." D'Artagnan and his companions listened in silence as Lauzun continued: "That house would have been mine if I had been fortunate enough for the goodness that Mademoiselle had for me then to have taken effect." Tears sprang into his eyes as he let the memory of what had once been wash over him.

D'Artagnan and Maupertuis saw that Lauzun now seemed to want to talk, and they asked him questions in an attempt to draw him out. The tactic worked, for Lauzun began to speak of his love for Mademoiselle, his tenderness and friendship for her, and his words aroused the sympathy of the musketeers, stirring feeling of friendship within them. Lauzun then fell into a profound grief and could speak no more. D'Artagnan would ask him when he wanted to have dinner, to take his supper, or at what time did he wish to depart in the morning, but the mournful Lauzun merely replied "just as you please."

As the company retired each night in lodgings chosen for their security, Lauzun found it difficult to sleep. The ever-watchful d'Artagnan asked him, since he was not tired, if he would care to talk. Lauzun said that he did not, but d'Artagnan sensed that this was not quite true. Seeing that Lauzun often spoke about Mademoiselle, the musketeer said that he believed that she would be much afflicted by Lauzun's plight. Lauzun agreed, but he hoped she would not offend the king. He asked if d'Artagnan knew Mademoiselle, and the musketeer answered that he had been to her house occasionally. It was all just small talk, designed to distract a melancholy prisoner and help pass the long, lonely hours of the night. Lauzun, however, expressed his concern that the friends he had left behind might poison Mademoiselle's mind against him; he was not worried about his enemies, as he knew she would not listen to them. He chose his words carefully, anticipating that they would be conveyed back to her by the younger d'Artagnan.

Maupertuis spoke of war and the campaigns they had fought together. The conversation then turned to Lauzun's horses, which he loved very much, and he drew up a list of people to whom they should be given. This he entrusted to d'Artagnan. He also begged the musketeer humbly to entreat Louis not to allow his sister, Mme de Nogent, or her husband to meddle in his affairs or to touch the little money he had left, his jewels, or his plate, none of which was very considerable.[37]

At last the journey, which had taken almost a month, came to an end. The carriage stopped outside the cold, dark fortress and Lauzun disembarked. He took a last breath of the fresh winter air before disappearing into the shadows of the donjon.

Saint-Mars lived in fear of the valets who served his prisoners falling ill. In February 1672, his fears were realized once again when Lauzun's valet had an accident. He had burned his leg, and his injury had left him feverish and confined to bed.[38] Louvois authorized Saint-Mars to engage a second man, someone who would be obliged to reveal everything his master did or said during the times Saint-Mars was unable to spy on his prisoner in person.[39] Louvois, however, failed to understand the awkward position in which Saint-Mars found himself. It was almost impossible to find a replacement, he wrote to the minister. None of his own valets would do the job if he paid them a million: "They have seen that those I have placed with M. Foucquet never come out."[40]

Shortly afterward, Lauzun came down with a heavy cold, his nights disturbed by fever.[41] Saint-Mars now had a prisoner who was unwell, and a valet who was injured and too ill to do his job, and he was unable to find anyone willing to serve in prison because it was widely known that they would effectively become prisoners for the duration of their service. A temporary replacement was found, but a more permanent arrangement was required. After giving the matter some thought, he came up with what he considered to be the perfect answer. Recalling that the mysterious prisoner in the Lower Tower had been described as a valet, the best solution would surely be to put this man to work. Saint-Mars wrote to Louvois to explain his situation and how he could solve it:

> *It is so difficult to find valets here who are prepared to shut themselves up with my prisoners that I take the liberty to propose one to you. The prisoner who is in the tower, and whom you sent to me by M[onsieur] the major of Dunkirk, would be, it seems to me, a good valet. I do not think he would tell M. de Lauzun where he came from after I have forbidden him; I am sure that he will not give any information, nor would he tell me to leave him alone, as all the others have done.*[42]

Louvois's reply does not survive, but it is clear that the idea was rejected.

Saint-Mars dismissed the temporary valet as soon as Lauzun's own recovered from his accident. By this time, Lauzun had come to realize that valets can become allies if treated properly. As it was, when Saint-Mars searched Lauzun upon his arrival at Pignerol, he found thirty sequins and a golden box, but he did not confiscate these items because, as he thought, Lauzun would not use them for anything contrary to the king's service.[43] How wrong he was. Lauzun used these treasures, as well as several gold coins that he had in his possession, to bribe his valet, winning him onto his side so that he would refuse to cooperate with Saint-Mars.

The jailer was frustrated by this, but not surprised. He should have expected such behavior since Foucquet had also managed to win over his valets. A vindictive Saint-Mars wrote: "Should that sly fellow fall ill, I shall withdraw him from M. de Lauzun's apartments, with your permission, and put him in a place that I have set apart." This dreadful place "would make the dumb chatter when they have been there a month. I will know everything from him, and I am assured that he will not forget the slightest trifle to say to me."[44]

As for Lauzun, he had calmed down sufficiently to be able to take stock of his situation. In March 1672, he made up his mind to explore his surroundings. The floor of his room was covered with planks of walnut wood. This type of wood had been chosen because it is very difficult to burn, but having spent the whole night on it, he and his valet managed to set fire to one of these planks. Now there was a hole in the floor the size of a plate, and this allowed Lauzun to raise the plank to see what lay beneath.[45] Unfortunately, the sight and smell of the billowing smoke caught the attention of Saint-Mars and his staff. They rushed to the apartments and extinguished the fire. Saint-Mars understood straight away what his prisoner was up to, and he threated Lauzun that if he set another fire, he would leave him to it—the cries of Lauzun and his valet would not be heard. Lauzun protested that he was kneeling at his *prier-Dieu* next to his bed when the fire broke out, but Saint-Mars was not fooled.

Meanwhile, news of the fire reached Versailles, upon which Louvois wrote to Saint-Mars:

When monsieur de Lauzun burned the plank of his chamber, it was assuredly to see what was beneath, and if such a thing were to happen again, you must speak harshly to him, and tell him that you are keeping a watch on him. Moreover, you must pay him frequent visits, looking often under his bed to see that he has not lifted any planks to try to escape that way, and that, in addition, you must take all the precautions you can to keep him securely.[46]

"It would be a fine adventure," commented Madame de Sévigné, "if he had burned poor M. Foucquet, who bears his imprisonment heroically and is not driven to despair."[47] It was little wonder that Saint-Mars felt justified in saying: "I believed that M. Foucquet was one of the wickedest prisoners to guard that could be found, but now I say that he is a lamb compared to" Lauzun.[48]

At about this time, news arrived of the deaths of two men who were close to Lauzun: his friend Guitry and his brother-in-law, Armand de Bautru, comte de Nogent. Louvois wrote to Saint-Mars to say that he could break this news of these deaths to Lauzun, but he gave no further information regarding how the men died, or what had become of Lauzun's now widowed sister.[49] When he was told of the tragedy, Lauzun at first thought Saint-Mars was playing a cruel joke, and asked if he was saying such things to make fun of him. He then realized that his jailer was sincere. The news was true. Lauzun he fell into a profound grief. These men were not only his friend and close relation, but they were, he said, the only people who could perhaps speak to the king on his behalf. Now, he believed that everyone would use this tragedy as an opportunity to hurt him even more.[50]

This news deeply affected Lauzun and he, as Foucquet had done, retreated into religion. He asked for, and was given, a picture of the Virgin, before which he would fall to his knees and pray. He fasted, told his beads, groomed his lengthening beard, and taught his valet to read.[51] This period of calm turned out to be temporary, much to Saint-Mars's dismay, for that summer, Lauzun provided the focus for a massive lapse of security at Pignerol.

The details are sketchy, but what is known is that several persons had tried to make contact with Lauzun. They had been engaged and financed, to the tune of six hundred pistoles, by Mlle de La Motte-Argencourt, one of Louis XIV's mistresses from his youth who had entered the convent at Chaillot. Her motives behind the conspiracy have never been discerned. She engaged a certain Heurtaut, a Béarnaise who had once served Lauzun as valet de chambre, to liberate his former master. The conspiracy was coordinated locally by a Mme Carrière, an inhabitant of Pignerol. Also involved was a man named Plassot, Heurtaut's cousin, and another named Loggier, while Mathonnet, a low-ranking soldier at the barracks, offered assistance.

The moment he received news of the plot, an alarmed Louvois wanted to know how far it had reached. More important, he wanted to know whether or not the conspirators had managed to make contact with Lauzun, and if so, what had he told them. It may be suggested that the minister for war was worried that Lauzun might have passed information about his secret visit to Holland, a sensitive subject given that France was now at war with the Dutch.

The French authorities immediately got to work to discover where the conspirators were hiding out. Assisted by their Savoyard counterparts, they tracked down Mme Carrière, Plassot, Loggier, and Mathonnet to Turin, and seized them. It appears that Loggier was killed in the skirmish, while the others were taken back to Pignerol. Heurtaut was captured near Turin, and when he was searched, he was found to be carrying letters written in cipher. He too was taken to Pignerol, where, after a month, he opened his veins with a lancet he had concealed in a pocket.[52] Louvois told Saint-Mars to break the news of this turn of events to Lauzun and to watch him closely to see how he reacted to the death of his friend.[53] "Provided he does not do anything tragic, like his good valet, Heurtaut," wrote Saint-Mars, "all will be well."[54]

That autumn, Foucquet's wife, Marie-Madeleine de Castile, requested permission to send a letter and a *mémoire*—that is, a report or bill—to her husband. The task was not as straightforward as it might sound. Madame

Foucquet first had to send the documents with an accompanying letter to Louvois, who, as usual, would read them out to the king. Louis would then decide whether or not to allow them to be sent to Foucquet. In this instance, he consented, upon which the letter and *mémoire* were placed in a packet with a covering letter and dispatched to Pignerol.

Even here, there were rigorous security protocols to observe. Louis ordered that Foucquet was to be allowed him to read these documents in Saint-Mars's presence, after which the jailer could provide a copy, written in his own hand, if Foucquet wished him to do so, as well as a sheet of paper and writing materials so that "after he has thought about it for a few hours, he could set down his will in your presence." Saint-Mars would then send Foucquet's reply to Louvois, who would show it to Louis before passing it on to Mme Foucquet, should the king grant his consent.[55] Saint-Mars, of course, obeyed his orders to the letter. The strong, towering walls of Pignerol were matched by the equally impenetrable bureaucracy that kept the prisoners virtually beyond the reach of their loved ones in the outside world.

Eventually, orders were given concerning the conspirators who had attempted to free Lauzun. Mme Carrière was released in October 1672, having given birth to a daughter in prison. At the same time, arrangements were set in train for the release of Mathonnet. He would be freed under a directive dated December 20, 1672, which also stipulated that he must resign his post.[56] As for Plassot, Louvois ordered Saint-Mars to keep him in prison for now and to use whatever means necessary to force him to talk. He would be released on July 2, 1673, when it was finally accepted that he knew nothing of significance about the conspiracy to liberate Lauzun.[57] Throughout the crisis, as with the earlier one with Foucquet, Louis and Louvois were concerned with whether or not Lauzun had managed to smuggle messages out and that he should not escape. Once they were satisfied that the conspiracy had been frustrated, they ceased to worry.

There was still another piece of misfortune in store for Lauzun, however. Since the spring, there had been talk at court of who should replace him as captain of the royal guard. Lauzun had held this post with a mixture of intense pleasure and pride, not least because it brought him into constant and intimate contact with the king, whom he idolized. The captaincy was eventually awarded to Jacques Henri de Durfort, duc de Duras, and the news was disseminated in the newspapers. Later, in November, Louvois suggested to Saint-Mars that he ought to reveal the news to Lauzun, as he would be required formally to resign his post.[58] The marquis de Seignelay also sent a letter on the subject, writing directly to Lauzun:

> *The King orders me to write these lines to let you know that, as his Majesty wishes to dispose of your post of Captain of his Bodyguard. He would like you to send in your resignation; and he has already given orders to pay whoever you name the sum of 400,000 livres, as the price of the said post when resigned.*[59]

Saint-Mars brought the letter and some writing materials to Lauzun and told him to read it and send his reply. Lauzun took the opportunity to rail against his jailer, accusing him of cruelty. He refused to agree to the sale of his post. Louvois, therefore, wrote directly to Lauzun, explaining to him the orders given to Saint-Mars with regard to his imprisonment. He noted that:

> *Saint-Mars has orders to keep you in the room which has been prepared for you, with the valet whom he has provided, without allowing either you or the said valet to go out, or that you shall give or receive news by word or writing. He has orders to allow you everything necessary for life which you may require, and never fail in any way in the respect due to your birth or to the rank you have held at Court; further, to give you any books he can obtain when you ask for them. Take, if you please, the trouble to examine well what he does in the future, and what he may have done in the past contrary to what I have shown you to be the King's intentions, and tell me: I shall not fail to inform*

the King at once; and he will arrange so that the mistake shall not again happen.[60]

Louvois was a spiteful man who took delight in inflicting mental torment on the prisoners under his jurisdiction. This letter, which in the most polite terms explained to the hapless prisoner that his jailer had acted, and always would act, in accordance with the instructions laid down by the king, was intended to make Lauzun aware of the helplessness of his situation and to caution him to be grateful for the privileges that had been accorded to him by Louis.

As though to capitalize on Lauzun's vulnerability, Louvois chose this moment to authorize Saint-Mars to reveal the details of how Guitry and Nogent, respectively his friend and brother-in-law, had died. They had been involved in a major event in Louis's ongoing war against Holland: the famous crossing of the Rhine. Under heavy enemy fire, French troops had managed to ford the river, but the maneuver had not been without its casualties. "Monsieur de Guitry and monsieur de Nogent are no more," wrote Louvois, "having been killed [on] that campaign at the crossing of the Rhine, which the king crossed by swimming four-thousand horses to batter the enemies who were on the other shore." He was, however, assured that his sister was "very touched by the loss of monsieur her husband, but she is well at present."[61]

As 1672 drew to a close, Saint-Mars was in charge of four prisoners. Nicolas Foucquet, who remained in his apartments with his two valets, where he devoted his time to God, worried about his family, and became increasingly absorbed by the state of his health. The marquis de Lauzun had been the subject of a conspiracy, the aim of which had been to set him free and perhaps to help him smuggle out whatever messages he might have written to people on the outside. Having learned of the deaths of two men to whom he had been very close, and the loss of his cherished post of captain of the royal bodyguard, he was now apparently subdued and rendered obedient by the distress he had suffered over the previous months. One of the conspirators, Plassot, was also imprisoned under

Saint-Mars's care, and was undergoing vigorous interrogation in a bid to make him reveal the details of the plot and who else, if anyone, had been involved. Only Eustache had given Saint-Mars no trouble. Apparently forgotten by the world, he remained alone in his dreary cell, where he was visited once every morning by his jailer.

FOUR

The Fateful Encounter

S aint-Mars was more than satisfied with the work he was doing at Pignerol. He boasted that, for the ten years he had been guarding Foucquet, he had done his job well and that the few occasions his prisoner had tried to smuggle out messages, he had been caught by the sentinels stationed in front of his windows. As he wrote about his prisoners to Louvois, he confessed that he "much more feared M. Foucquet's sweetness and his honesty, than M. de Lauzun's pride and brusqueness." He was anxious to make it clear that he enjoyed his job, adding that he would not want, for anything in the world, to discontinue his way of doing things. "I answer you with my life, Monseigneur, that as long as I have the custody of these two prisoners, they will know no news except on your orders." Despite this, Saint-Mars was not entirely content with his lot. "I take the liberty of telling you," he continued, "that what could make me live here in health would be a little honor; I have been a sergeant for so long that I am the doyen of all." He explained that if Louvois did not "have the goodness . . . to point out my seniority to His Majesty, I will die what I am. I am so much submissive to all that pleases him that I want nothing but the honor of serving him well all my life."[1]

As captain of the donjon and keeper of prisoners of state, Saint-Mars felt he ought to be rewarded for his work in more than monetary terms. Certainly, the accumulation of wealth was important to him and he was well paid for his services, but he would also skim off a percentage of the money he received to pay for his prisoners' food and other items. In the case of low-ranking prisoners like Eustache, this did not amount to very much, but with his high-ranking prisoners, Foucquet and Lauzun, Saint-Mars could supplement his income considerably. In one year alone, 1672, the expenses for Lauzun, which included food, a stipend for his chaplain, items for a chapel, a Bergamo tapestry, items to be used by his valets, and curtains, as well as a mirror, plates, and clothes, amounted to 10,574 livres.[2]

Saint-Mars's motive was to increase his fortune for its own sake, certainly, but he also longed to enjoy the trappings that wealth could bring. Already seigneur of Palteau and governor of Sens, Saint-Mars wanted to be a man of substance, and he was well aware that money was the best means of achieving this aim. His increasing wealth and his standing as a property owner allowed him to apply for letters of nobility. He had begun the process toward the end of the previous year, and on January 10, 1673, Louvois was pleased to inform him that his application had been successful.[3]

Two weeks later, on January 25, Saint-Mars received Bernardino Butticari, a bourgeois in the service of the duc de Savoie for the province of Pignerol who had been arrested in the town under suspicion of spying. Having been held and interrogated for two weeks, he was given into Saint-Mars's care upon the orders of Louis XIV, who required the new prisoner to be held in "good and sure guard," and cut off from all communication.[4] Butticari would not be tried, but he would be held for a lengthy time under harsh conditions.

Butticari's detention was so severe that he could not cope with it and fell ill. In contrast to some of those under Saint-Mars's care, he managed to arouse his jailer's sympathy. In June, Saint-Mars was writing to Louvois to appeal for leniency. Three months later, having received no satisfactory reply, he interceded once again, asking for the unhappy spy to be pardoned. By December, the prisoner was "still waiting for your grace and your kindness." It was all to no avail. Louis and Louvois remained unmoved, and Butticari would remain in prison for a further twenty months. It would not be until August 11, 1675, that the letter Saint-Mars had been waiting for finally arrived: "I write you this letter to tell you that my intention is that as soon as you have received it, you will put the said Butticari at full and entire liberty, allowing him this time to leave the said donjon of my citadel without difficulty."[5]

That Butticari had been captured while trying to spy on the goings-on at Pignerol further provoked Saint-Mars's already suspicious nature, and he began to take note of everyone who came too close to the donjon. Anyone he considered to be paying too much attention would be arrested, held, and questioned.[6] He also ordered a list to be compiled of strangers who visited the town of Pignerol; he would then study the names in order to identify anyone who, in his own opinion, visited too frequently.[7] In this way, the comte de Donane was captured on suspicion of spying. As it turned out, his only crime had been to gaze up at the windows of the donjon as he walked past Saint-Maurice church. He was detained for two days before being released.[8]

At this point, Lauzun decided he wanted to write to Louvois about his captaincy of the king's bodyguard, which he had been asked to resign. Having received a letter from the minister toward the end of 1672, he had taken several weeks to contemplate his reply. Now, he wrote Louvois a letter in which his utter helplessness in the face of his situation could be read in every line:

I did not intend to complain of the treatment of Monsieur de Saint-Mars, nor of the amount of the food, nor did I say that the sufferings

I endure here are out of the common; I only intended to beg mercy from the King, and to know his will about my office and everything else, which I shall follow blindly, for I should be inconsolable if it were thought that in asking his Majesty for favors I wished to make conditions, for I shall never show anything but prompt obedience.[9]

Indeed, despite his insolence and his temper, which had left Louis in a rage on more than one occasion, Lauzun was and would always remain one of Louis's most devoted servants. Continuing his letter, he begged Louvois to recognize his goodwill and asked what he must do to tender his resignation of his post of captain of the guards, adding that he would be "inconsolable if the King were to think me capable of putting off my immediate obedience to his orders."

Louvois replied within a few days. Having read the letter to Louis, he could announce that the king was "very glad to learn from its contents that Monsieur de Saint-Mars has not exceeded [his] orders with regard to you." In other words, whatever cruel measures Saint-Mars decided to take were considered within the remit of his position as jailer and captain of the donjon of Pignerol.

Since it had been understood that Lauzun was refusing to tender his resignation, arrangements had been set in train to transfer the captaincy of the guard to the duc de Luxembourg. However, with Lauzun now apparently willing to cooperate, this process would now be postponed. Instead, Louvois appointed a notary to go to the donjon and receive the formal document from Lauzun, whose signature he would witness. In the event, however, Lauzun could not bring himself to resign a commission that had meant so much to him and of which he had been so proud, and the notary left Pignerol empty-handed.[10]

This elicited an immediate response from Louis, who issued a formal order to the officers and men of the royal bodyguard:

His Majesty being unhappy with the conduct of the Sieur comte de Lauzun, captain of one of the companies of the king's bodyguards, and

not wanting him to perform any function of his charge, His Majesty
expressly forbids lieutenants, ensigns, exempts and guards of the said
company to recognize him in that capacity, on pain of disobedience.[11]

Louvois, too, lost his patience with Lauzun and sent off a furious letter to Pignerol. He had, he said, hoped to please Lauzun by giving him the means by which he could resign his commission as he himself had requested, but given Lauzun's recalcitrance, no more would now be said about it.[12]

While all this was going on, the ex-superintendent Foucquet had been contemplating his situation. He felt useless. He had been a loyal servant to the crown for his entire adult life. Indeed, royal service had always been more than just a job to him, it had long been a way of life. Even now, after so many years in prison, he found it difficult to settle into the idleness that captivity imposed upon him. He was frustrated and resentful at seeing his talents going to waste; frequently ill, he took his mind off his unhappy condition by thinking of ways in which he could be of service to Louis and, hopefully, perhaps secure some alleviation of the conditions of his imprisonment.

For some while, he had been allowed to receive news of what was going on in the world beyond his prison walls, and Louvois wrote to Saint-Mars to tell him that "it was no great inconvenience that M. Foucquet knows that the king has made war on the Dutch." Indeed not, for Foucquet's knowledge of the affairs of state could prove useful to Louvois.

Following Foucquet's removal, Louis had abolished the office of *surintendant des Finances*, and taken control of his fiscal affairs himself, at least nominally. He appointed Foucquet's rival, Jean-Baptiste Colbert, as *contrôleur général des Finances*, which was really Foucquet's old office with a new title. France went on to enjoy a period of prosperity as a result of reforms that had been initiated or continued by Colbert. Now, as France entered the second year of its war against the Dutch, much of this good work began to unravel. Wars were expensive, and as the need for funds was pressing, Colbert began to fall out of favor. Louis distrusted him and often refused to listen to his advice. Although not disgraced, Colbert, his enemies saw, was walking on dangerous ground. This was the perfect time for his rivals to promote their own interests, and when the opportunity arose to be of service to the king, Louvois seized it. When Foucquet sought permission to write a *mémoire* directly to Louis setting out his thoughts "for the good and interest of the king," the war minister was only too happy to grant it.[13]

What Foucquet set out in this document is not known, but given his former post, it is safe to speculate that suggestions for a further reform of the finances formed at least part of it. The *mémoire* written, Saint-Mars duly sent it on. Two months later, however, Louvois returned the document, saying that it did not appear to contain what Foucquet had said it would. Instead, it seemed to him to be nothing more than an attempt by Foucquet to obtain some respite from his sentence. Thinking it inappropriate to show it to Louis, Louvois instead ordered Saint-Mars to take the *mémoire* back to Foucquet, to tell him that it was of no importance to the service of the king, and to burn it in front of him.[14]

In his final letter of 1673, Saint-Mars noted that Lauzun was worried about money he owed Antoine le Pautre, the royal architect who had built a house for him at Saint-Germain. As to Foucquet, he was "always very tranquil." Indeed, Saint-Mars wrote, he "appears to me even very happy." Nevertheless, Foucquet frequently asked if his news had been passed on to his family and always seemed "very concerned about the health of his wife and his family."

As to Eustache, to whom Saint-Mars referred as "the prisoner of the tower, whom M. de Vauroy had brought," he had nothing to say, but rather "lives content, like a man entirely resigned to the will of God and the King."[15] This point is as mysterious as anything else to do with Eustache's life and, especially, his imprisonment. He never asked why he had been imprisoned. He never asked, as the other prisoners had done, to be allowed to go home. He never complained about his imprisonment or the conditions in which he was held. Unlike some, particularly Foucquet and Lauzun, he never made a nuisance of himself. While Saint-Mars was under orders to try to make his prisoners speak, this directive was never extended to Eustache. At no time during his imprisonment did Eustache try to bribe the sentries, send or receive news, or escape. Was he simply accepting of his fate, or was being in prison, no matter how harsh the conditions, a more desirable option to whatever might have awaited him had he been free?

The spring of 1674 saw the imprisonment at Pignerol of a Dominican monk named Lapierre, who is frequently referred to as the Jacobin and, later, as the Mad Jacobin. Louvois felt obliged to warn Saint-Mars not to be deceived by the monk's fine orations, but rather to regard him as one of the greatest rogues in the world. He warned the jailer that Lapierre would be very difficult to guard.

Lapierre, who "although obscure, is no less a man of consequence,"[16] was taken to Pignerol by the sieur Legrain, provost-general of the Connétable and Maréchaussée of France. Louvois, as always, sent detailed instructions to Saint-Mars, who was required to send ten men of his company, commanded by one his officers, to whom the sieur Legrain would give the necessary instructions for the manner in which the prisoner was to be guarded. "You will recommend the officer conducts him, without creating a scandal, by road, and have him enter Pignerol discreetly and even without anyone seeing that it is a prisoner that your men are leading into the donjon." The last line of this letter was particularly sinister: "You will treat him in the manner as the prisoner whom M. de Vauroy brought you." That is to say, Lapierre was to be subject to a harsh imprisonment, as unpleasant as that of Eustache.

Louvois's letter, and the commands contained within it, was followed by another, written by Michel Le Tellier.[17] This was Louvois's father and predecessor at the ministry for war, who wrote that Lapierre "should be guarded with the same precautions as were used by the sieur de Vauroy, and as he is an unmitigated rascal who, in very serious matters has abused important persons, he must be treated harshly, and you must give him nothing but the absolute necessities of life, with no other solace whatsoever."

Still more instructions followed. Lapierre was not to be allowed a fire in his room unless the weather was extremely cold, and his meals were to consist of nothing more than bread, wine, and water. A *fripon achevé* (accomplished rascal), the new prisoner could not be treated badly enough, nor suffer the punishment he deserved. Despite this, he should be allowed to hear mass, with the usual caveats regarding his security, and he was to be given a breviary and some books of prayers.[18] Later, Lapierre would be allowed better food, and would be permitted to make his confession once a year to the same priest who confessed Foucquet.[19]

As for Foucquet, that spring brought a welcome change in the conditions of his imprisonment. In a letter dated April 10, 1674, Louis granted permission for Mme Foucquet to write two letters a year to her husband. The first of these was enclosed within the packet sent by Louvois, with the promise of another to come in six months' time. Saint-Mars was ordered to give the letter to Foucquet and to allow him two days to think about what he would like to say to his wife, after which he should give his prisoner ink and paper so he could write out his response. He would then take the letter, with the ink and paper, and send it back to Louvois.[20] Even though the letters had to pass through the hands of both Saint-Mars and Louvois, and would be censored if necessary, this regular contact with his wife was a great blessing for Foucquet.

Most of the letters that were exchanged between husband and wife did not survive, but one, written by Foucquet on February 5, 1675, was widely circulated among his friends in Paris and beyond, with several copies being made.[21] In it, Foucquet describes his life in prison, lists his illnesses, and laments that "forced idleness is the mother of despair, continual temptations and agitations." He found solace in his faith, but added that, since the Day of Our Lady in September, when one of his valets, the man named Champagne, died before his eyes, he had "neither mirth nor health." He very much missed Champagne, whom he described as "a diligent and affectionate man, whom I loved dearly, of whom I was fond and who comforted me." Foucquet's other valet, La Rivière, was constantly ill and more in need of care than his master. "He is sorrowful in temperament," Foucquet notes, "and thus with only the two of us to talk to each other day and night, judge how I spend my life."

Clearly, Foucquet was not being properly served. He was nobleman and one valet was not enough to serve his needs. His remaining valet, La Rivière, was often too unwell to carry out his duties. Also, while Foucquet's valets were hired primarily to attend to him, they were also expected to spy on him and each other. This could not be accomplished with only one servant living in Foucquet's prison apartments. Yet, although Foucquet had made no mention of it, a second man had already been appointed to serve him.

With the death of Champagne, Saint-Mars had once again faced the dilemma of finding another valet, a man who could stand in when La Rivière was unable to perform his duties. Previously, he had suggested he make use of Eustache, his prisoner of the tower, whom he knew to have been a valet before his incarceration. He was aware that Louis and Louvois had refused to allow Eustache to serve Lauzun, but they might agree to allow him attend Foucquet. He put down his reflections in writing and awaited the reply. This had arrived in a letter from Louvois, dated January 30, 1675:

> *I have received your letter of the 19 of this month and I have given account of what it contains to the King. His Majesty approves that you give the prisoner brought to you by the sieur de Vauroy as a valet to monsieur Foucquet; but whatever may happen, you must forbear from putting him with monsieur de Lauzun, or with anyone whomsoever than monsieur Foucquet.*[22]

Louvois had signed off at that point, but he was concerned that he might not have made his point forcefully enough and added a postscript: "That is to say that you can give the said prisoner to M. Foucquet, if his valet fails him, and not otherwise."[23]

Louvois could have had personal reasons for wanting to keep Eustache and Lauzun apart. The two men were lifelong bitter enemies. Louvois had opposed Louis's decision to appoint Lauzun to the rank of grand master of the artillery. He was unfit for the post, the minister agued, and his appointment would cause friction in the ministry.[24] Louvois was jealous of all the attention Lauzun received from Louis and his friendship with the king, but he also hated Lauzun because he was one of Colbert's allies—Louvois's ambition was to gain supremacy under Louis, which his great rival, Colbert, would be all too willing to frustrate. Louvois therefore persuaded Louis not to grant the post to Lauzun, and Louis, seeing the wisdom in the minister's arguments, succumbed to his reasoning.

The enmity between Louvois and Lauzun also extended to Lauzun's proposed marriage to Mademoiselle. Louvois opposed it primarily because Colbert was in support of it. Thus, the marriage became almost a proxy battlefield for the two factions. Later, as Louis was preparing to go to war against the Dutch, Louvois supported Madame de Montespan's campaign to bring about Lauzun's fall from grace.

If the minister had reason to deprive Lauzun of the companionship and service of a valet, Louis, too, had his reasons for wanting to keep him away from Eustache. Lauzun had once been a favored courtier, and Louis meant to release him one day. It would be safer for Lauzun if he knew nothing of Eustache and what he might have done in his past. For Foucquet, it was a different matter. Louis, at this stage at least, never intended him to leave Pignerol, so it was of no consequence if he were to learn whatever it was that Eustache knew, and so Eustache was appointed to serve him whenever La Rivière was unable to carry out his duties.

Two months later, Saint-Mars's search for a new valet for Lauzun had still not been successful. Louvois told him that, if he were to find someone suitable, he could place him with Lauzun, but he was adamant that "you must not, for any reason at all, give him the prisoner whom the sieur de Vauroy brought you, who must serve monsieur Foucquet only in the case of necessity, as I have instructed you."[25]

It was in the first days of February 1675 that Eustache was admitted into Foucquet's three-room apartment. The differences between it and the dark and miserable cell in which he had passed the previous five years were striking. Instead of bare and damp stone walls, a cold, hard floor, poor furnishings, and one meager meal each day, he beheld before him all the comforts of home. There was good food and wine, with generous meals being served throughout the day, and there was a table covered with fine linen, beautiful tableware, glasses, and a cruet set; Eustache would share in the food that went uneaten by his master. A fire crackled and burned in the hearth, filling the apartment with warmth and a welcoming glow. The tapestries on the walls and rush mats on the floor added to the overall feeling of comfort, as did the warm and friendly smile of the ex-superintendent Foucquet, whose beautiful and costly garments contrasted markedly with his own cheap clothes. Yet, the screens that covered the windows left him in no doubt that, however luxurious, this apartment was still a prison. Nonetheless, Eustache could at last enjoy the company of a master who was renowned for his kind and gentle disposition.

As Eustache embarked upon a new life in Foucquet's service, albeit intermittently, Lauzun, who had been very ill for several months, continued to languish. He had never been able to come to terms with his spectacular fall from grace, and now he had deteriorated to the point that it was expected he would not survive. A courier was dispatched to Paris bearing news of his imminent decease. Louvois wrote to tell Saint-Mars that he and Louis were assured that, while taking precautions for Lauzun's security, "you will not fail to give him every possible facility for the recovery of his health as much as they will not be contrary to the King's orders which you have in the manner of guarding him."

Lauzun's condition was such that Saint-Mars thought it prudent to request the services of a confessor. Lauzun, however, was afraid that any priest assigned to him might be an imposter sent to discover his secrets, and he declared that he would speak to a capuchin only. Even so, when the monk entered his chambers, Lauzun emerged from his bed, grabbed the man's beard, and tugged it as hard as he could to assure himself that it, and therefore the monk, was genuine.[26] By this time Lauzun's health had improved somewhat, but his convalescence was to be a slow process, and Saint-Mars would only be able to report the patient's full recovery that September.[27]

Despite his illness, Lauzun proved to be as enterprising in prison as he had been at court. Unbeknownst to Saint-Mars, he had spent several months digging a tunnel by which he hoped to escape his confinement and win back his lost favor with the king. Using any implement he could lay his hands on, he scraped away at the bricks and stones inside the chimney of his room, gradually making his way down until he reached a spot from which he would escape.

At the same time, he tunneled upward until he found his way into the apartment above. Here, Nicolas Foucquet continued to lead a relatively peaceful life with his valets and his books, his day filled mainly with acts of quiet devotion. It can only be imagined with what shock and surprise the former superintendent received the little man who suddenly and unexpectedly appeared in his chamber one dark night with soot all over his clothes and hair and staining the broad beam on his face.

Foucquet had known Lauzun in the days before his arrest, so there was probably a glimmer of recognition as he gazed at the apparition before him. This man whom he remembered as the young protégé of the maréchal de Gramont was more mature, certainly, but he had aged ungracefully, as Foucquet could plainly see, notwithstanding the grime that clung to him and obscured his features. The ever-confident Lauzun felt he had no need to introduce himself; he boldly strode toward the fallen minister and opened the conversation.

There was so much to talk about. In the fourteen or so years since Foucquet's arrest, Louis XIV had become, as the fallen minister had anticipated, a magnificent and glorious king. He was in the process of expanding his territories and securing his borders, and he had fulfilled one of his most important kingly roles when he secured his dynasty and, therefore, the safety of his kingdom, with a hale and hearty heir. As he had grown in magnificence, Louis had cast aside the beautiful and delicate Louise de La Vallière, the love of his youth, and replaced her with the dramatically beautiful and sensual Athénaïs de Montespan. He had also engaged the combined talents of artists, writers, poets, musicians, and architects to celebrate his power and glory in the splendid display of court entertainments. The culmination of this was a new palace, the magnificent creation that was the château de Versailles. Foucquet must have known where the king had taken his inspiration for this: his own beautiful château de Vaux-le-Vicomte, the setting for one of the most brilliant parties of the century.

As for Lauzun, his life had not been an empty one, for he had risen to the prestigious military posts of general of the dragoons and captain of the guards, and he had competed with the king for the affections of the beautiful Madame de Monaco.

Foucquet began to feel the first stirrings of alarm. After all these years in prison, shut up with only his valets for company and the visits of the ever-watchful Saint-Mars to break the monotony, he began to fear that fate had contrived to send him a fantasist as a companion. Any doubts he might have entertained about Lauzun's madness vanished when the young adventurer recounted the story of his relationship with the king's cousin, the much older Madame de Montpensier: how she had bestowed upon him not only her love but also her most lucrative properties, and how the king had at first given his consent when they asked permission to marry, but had then changed his mind before the wedding could take place.

It was at this point, according to the account written by Courtilz de Sandras, that Foucquet "could not refrain from turning to another prisoner of state who had come to join them and touching his forehead with his finger . . . he wanted to make him understand by that his less than good opinion of him who was speaking." In other words, Foucquet used a gesture to convey to another "state prisoner" his thoughts that Lauzun had lost his mind. Lauzun, seeing this, chose to ignore it and continued to speak of all that had happened since the former superintendent had left the world, but his words merely confirmed Foucquet in his beliefs.[28]

Courtilz de Sandras does not name this mysterious "prisoner of state who had come to join them," but it is certain that he could not have been referring to Foucquet's valet, La Rivière. This man, about whom very little is known, was not a prisoner, but a professional valet appointed to serve a prisoner. It is thought that he had originally been a member of Saint-Mars's own household and was assigned to Foucquet upon his entering Pignerol.[29] In fact, Courtilz de Sandras could only have been referring to Eustache, who at this stage was the only other person, excepting Saint-Mars and certain members of his staff, who had permission to enter Foucquet's apartment. Louvois's insistence that Lauzun and the enigmatic Eustache should not meet had been rendered irrelevant by this clandestine but, as it would turn out, fateful encounter.[30]

Precisely when this remarkable incident took place is not known, but it was almost certainly not an isolated occurrence. Both Foucquet and Lauzun naturally kept the secret of their meetings, which most probably took place at night, while their valets knew better than to give the game away and place their respective masters, not to mention themselves, in jeopardy.

By February 1676, after three years of furtive and tiring work, during which the fear of discovery hung over him like a specter, Lauzun's tunnel to the outside was finally complete.[31] His first attempt to penetrate the outer walls of the donjon had ended in frustration when he emerged from his tunnel only to find himself inside a disused room, the bars on the windows of which seemed to mock his efforts. Refusing to give up this mission, and the hope of eventual success having buoyed him up throughout the three long years it had taken him to accomplish it, he continued to scratch and scrape at the bars and eventually managed to loosen one of them so that he could slip through. Then, using a rope he had made by tying several linen napkins together, he carefully lowered himself to the ground. "It was a miracle he did not break his neck," wrote Mademoiselle, as she recounted the incident in her *Memoires*.

Lauzun finally touched ground and proceeded to scrape a hole in the wall, but, finding his way blocked by a boulder, he was obliged to find a new place to dig. Eventually he made a hole large enough to squeeze through, and he emerged to find himself in the courtyard of the citadel.

In the dim light of the winter dawn, he could see that the place was practically deserted. He slipped inside a woodshed, hoping to find someone whom he could bribe to open one of the citadel gates. Just at that point a serving woman entered to check on the wood stores. Lauzun offered her some money if she would help him, and she answered that she was engaged to one of the soldiers of the citadel and, if her fiancé wanted to help him and to escape himself, she would be happy to help. The fugitive then offered her all manner of rewards, but still she insisted upon involving her soldier. Not knowing the layout of the fortress, Lauzun had no choice but to wait anxiously inside the shed while the servant went off to find her fiancé.

Anticipation quickly turned to shock and dismay when, instead of the servant, a soldier arrived at the door of the shed accompanied by his superior officer. Ignoring Lauzun's promise of riches to come if they would assist him, they instead summoned Saint-Mars, and the three of them escorted the hapless Lauzun back to his prison rooms.

Following Lauzun's adventure, security was increased at Pignerol. Louis and Louvois sent a dispatch to Saint-Mars ordering him to make frequent visits to his prisoners' apartments and to take the unprecedented step of changing all the furniture in their rooms: "You cannot take too many precautions," Louvois warned him.[32]

More detailed instructions soon followed. Saint-Mars was to visit his prisoners' apartments at irregular hours of the day. He was to give them only whatever linen he deemed absolutely necessary, while obliging the prisoners to return each used piece to him each day. In addition, he was to allow them nothing that could be used to bore holes, while the knives he provided them were to be strong enough to cut up food and nothing else. Even the firedogs inside the fireplaces had to be fixed so they could not be torn out. Saint-Mars, Louvois suggested, should also make tours of inspection at random hours during the night to ensure that his prisoners were not working at anything they should not.[33]

While Lauzun and Foucquet were subject to increased security measures, Lauzun's valet was interrogated in an attempt to make him reveal what he knew of his master's escape plot. The valet, however, proved himself more loyal to Lauzun than to the king, for he refused to divulge any information. Since he had converted to Catholicism, he was to be allowed to hear mass on feast days and Sundays, but for his recalcitrance, he was to be put on a punishing diet of bread and water until he told all he knew about Lauzun's escape attempt.[34]

Other procedures were implemented with regard to the citadel as a whole: "You have learned by the letters he has written you," wrote Louvois, "that the king approves that before the door to the citadel is opened, you should visit your prisoners; and in fact, this precaution is very necessary." He then noted that a man named Lamy, for whom Lauzun had found a place in the King's Bodyguard, had recently transferred into the service of Mademoiselle, Lauzun's former fiancée, but had now disappeared from view. Saint-Mars was told to keep watch for him in case he should turn up at Pignerol. Similar fears were expressed for another of Lauzun's friends, Barail, who Louvois thought might come to Pignerol in order to make contact with Lauzun.[35] Louis, however, did not feel the need to appoint a fifth sub-lieutenant to augment the compagnie-franche, "the four you have being sufficient," Saint-Mars was told. Nevertheless, Saint-Mars's lieutenant, the chevalier de Saint-Martin, remained inside the donjon, doing his rounds each night.[36]

At some point prior to this, a mysterious man had gone to Louis XIV claiming to be in possession of some information about the Spanish Netherlands that the king might find interesting. Since Louis was about to embark upon a campaign in Flanders and the Franché-Comté, he certainly was interested, but it was not long before his interest darkened into suspicion. He had, he felt, reason to believe that this man was a double agent, and he refused to pursue the matter any further. Instead, he warned the man in no uncertain terms to have nothing to do with the Spanish.

This man is best known under the name Dubreuil, although he laid claim to nobility and was known to some as the comte du Breuil.[37] Following his failure to arouse the king's interest in the information to which he was allegedly privy, Dubreuil, about whom little else is known, went underground. It was not long, however, before he tried to contact

Louis again, this time claiming to be in good relations with the general of the imperial forces, Prince Raymondo Montecuccoli. The mention of Montecuccoli's name had the desired effect.

At this point, Dubreuil was living in the Swiss town of Basle, hiding out under the name of Samson. Louis ordered the prince de Condé and his adjutant, the comte de Montclar, who were currently commanding the French army on the Rhine, to make contact with Dubreuil. They were to offer him 200 pistoles and a "chiffre," or code, with which he could secretly communicate the maneuvers of the enemy troops. It soon became apparent that Dubreuil was acting against the French and was passing information to Montecuccoli.

Louis ordered Dubreuil's arrest, but because the spy was still on foreign territory, the French had to sit it out and wait patiently for him to cross the border where he could be seized. Louis had issued his order in February 1676, but it was to be a further two months before Dubreuil could finally be captured. He was taken by three officers and conducted to Neuf-Breisach before being moved on to Besançon. From there he was taken in stages to Lyon, where, he was given over to the care of the archbishop. In May, he was moved on to Pignerol.

Saint-Mars, meanwhile, had been warned to expect a new prisoner, whom he must guard securely. Louis had decreed that Dubreuil should be placed within the donjon of the citadel, where he would share a cell with the most recent prisoner. As usual, Saint-Mars was expected to keep Louis and Louvois informed about Dubreuil in regular news bulletins.[38]

The most recent prisoner referred to by Louvois was the Jacobin monk, Lapierre. This man, had, by this time, been a prisoner for some two and a half years. Kept in isolation, cruelly treated, and half-starved, he had lost his mind and was now violent and difficult to control and lived amid his own filth in his befouled cell. Dubreuil was understandably horrified at the prospect of being moved in with him. He pleaded with Saint-Mars to put him in a different cell, but the jailer had been given his orders and could not be persuaded, and so the spy and the insane monk were put in together. Dubreuil was to be allowed to hear the mass that was said for Foucquet and Lauzun on fast days and Sundays.[39]

Shortly after this, Louvois wrote to Saint-Mars enclosing a letter Dubreuil had sent to the archbishop of Lyon, and which the archbishop had forwarded to Louvois.

> *I am sending you a letter that Dubreuil has written to M. Archbishop of Lyon, by which you will see that he claims to have several important things to say for the service of the King. Since he must be in Pignerol now, please make him understand that he cannot hope to get out of prison unless we know beforehand what he has to say, and in case he wants to write it, you will give him some paper to write before you and wax to seal the package, which you will make him close in your presence; after which you will send it to me.*[40]

Louvois added the precaution: "I am obliged to warn you not to allow yourself to be diverted by his fine speeches, and that you must regard him as one of the greatest rascals in the world and the most difficult to guard."

With this in mind, Saint-Mars set about trying to discover what it was Dubreuil wished to say to the king, and with time and patience his efforts paid off. In reply to a note from the jailer, Louvois authorized him to give Dubreuil the necessary writing materials, taking care to count everything he gave him and to ensure that all items were returned at the end of each day. "It is necessary," he added, "before taking any resolution on what it contains, to see what this man will write; but whatever he may promise you, you must not relax the orders you have received from His Majesty in regard to him."[41]

As it was, Dubreuil wished to warn Louis of a plot that was allegedly being perpetrated by the bishop of Agde, who also happened to be Foucquet's brother. The purpose of the plot was to assassinate Louvois and by warning the minister of his imminent danger, the spy hoped to receive the reward of being allowed to move to a new cell, away from Lapierre. By now, the Jacobin's condition had further worsened, and he had so polluted the cell that Dubreuil was unable to eat or drink, and even found breathing difficult.[42] Nothing, however, was done and the threat against Louvois was dismissed as being of no importance. Indeed, Louvois reported that Louis "did not think there was any thought to be given to the speeches of such a great rascal as this one."[43] Louvois loved to refer to prisoners in such derogatory terms.

After six months of sharing a cell, the quality of life deteriorated still further for Dubreuil and Lapierre. Saint-Mars had evidently written to Louvois asking for advice about how to treat the monk, whose condition had declined to the point that he could no longer be controlled. For his part, Louvois was at a loss to know whom Saint-Mars meant; despite having countersigned the order for his arrest the minister now had no recollection of the monk or even his name. He replied:

> *Please tell me who is lodged with Monsieur Dubreuil, whom you say is so mad, noting his name and that by which he was brought to you; and sending me a copy of the letter that was sent to you when you received him, so that I may better remember who he is.*[44]

Once he had been reminded of who the monk was, Louvois refused to believe that he really was mad. He warned Saint-Mars not to be taken in, for the man, he insisted, was fully capable of pretending to be insane.[45] He recommended that Saint-Mars give Lapierre a good thrashing, which would encourage him to mend his ways.

Shortly afterward, Saint-Mars assured the minister that merely the threat of corporal punishment had been enough to calm Lapierre, which Louvois found satisfactory. He reminded Saint-Mars that he should not hesitate to flog him if necessary.[46] The jailer, however, was reluctant to use violence against a monk, fearing he could be excommunicated for it. In answer to this, Louvois had some wise words for him:

> *I must explain to you that it is true that those who strike a priest, in disdain for his character, are excommunicated, but it is permissible*

to chastise a priest when he is wicked, and one is charged with his behavior . . . The King leaves it to you to change his prison [cell], or, in case you think it appropriate to leave him with the sieur Dubreuil, you should have him tied down so that he can do no harm. But remember to take care with the sieur Dubreuil, who is one of the craftiest rogues that one could meet.[47]

Louvois's therapy for a man who had been seriously mentally disturbed as a result of the ill-treatment to which he was subject was to inflict still more abuse on him, to threaten him with physical violence, and to cause him to be tied down in the belief that, this way, he could not harm himself or his companion in misfortune. As for Saint-Mars, once he had overcome his scruples concerning striking men of the cloth, he was happy to acquiesce; he continued to follow his orders without question.

FIVE
Mystery

P rison life was cruel for low-ranking prisoners, even without the abuse meted out by Saint-Mars at the command of Louis and Louvois. Their cells were cold, dark, and dirty, and their everyday needs were neglected. Food was inadequate and regard to human dignity was slight to say the least. For those prisoners of high rank, conditions were better. They at least were fed well and given adequate clothing, the style and material of which was suited to their rank, and they lived in pleasantly furnished rooms with a fire and windows. Their apparent comfort, however, was merely an illusion, and it applied only to their physical needs.

What all the prisoners of Pignerol shared, irrespective of their rank, was the loneliness and anxiety of being separated from their loved ones, worrying about how their families were faring in their absence, or even if any of them had departed this life. For Foucquet, this was always a pressing anxiety. Upon his arrest some fifteen years previously, he had left a young wife, four small children, and an aged mother alone in a world where few would dare to assist them for fear of incurring the king's wrath. Lauzun, too, had a sister and brother whom he had not seen for more than seven years.

As it was, Lauzun's great uncle, Armand Nompar de Caumont, duc de La Force, had died in December 1675, leaving all his worldly goods to him. A notary was sent to Pignerol to allow Lauzun to consent to receive the inheritance and to sign the necessary legal documents.

The legal situation surrounding another death in Lauzun's family was to prove more complex, for it had a direct effect upon Lauzun as well as his family. His elder brother, Jacques de Caumont, a man of delicate health, died in September 1677, leaving Lauzun the head of the family. This change in circumstances made it crucial that Lauzun's sister, the comtesse de Nogent, and his brother, the chevalier de Lauzun, should journey to Pignerol with a lawyer to arrange the family's affairs. This was not an easy matter, given Lauzun's attitude toward his sister.

When they parted company at the entrance to the donjon, Lauzun had given d'Artagnan some letters for the king and Louvois. In them, he requested that neither Mme de Nogent nor her husband should have anything to do with his personal or business affairs and that in addition they should be denied access to his precious possessions. Distrusting his sister and brother-in-law completely, he asked that Barail and Rollinde[1] should direct his affairs instead, adding that he wished to grant power of attorney to Rollinde. These requests were refused, and Lauzun's affairs were entrusted to Mme de Nogent upon her promise not to help Lauzun to freedom without Louvois's orders.[2]

The comtesse had no difficulty in obtaining permission to travel to Pignerol with her brother and a lawyer, Isarn; but, as always when it came to prisoners of state, there were strict procedures to follow. The family was required to meet in Saint-Mars's own room and in his presence. Loyauté, the current commissioner for war at Pignerol, was also to attend. Isarn, Lauzun, and Lauzun's brother and sister were to conduct their private family business in loud voices, and no papers other than those directly relating to the business at hand were to be allowed into the room. For reasons that were not explained, the name of Mademoiselle de Montpensier was not to be mentioned under any pretext. The interviews were to be held on four consecutive days, with each session to last two hours: a total of eight hours in all.[3]

In the event, the first interview had to be delayed because Lauzun was too ill with a fever to attend. Mme de Nogent, the chevalier de Lauzun, and Isarn were given comfortable lodgings in the town until Lauzun was sufficiently recovered.

The first interview took place on Friday October 29, 1677. On that day, the three visitors went up to the citadel with Commissioner Loyauté, with whom they were to have dinner. Before they sat down to eat, Saint-Mars took them into the room where the interviews were to be held and showed them the king's written orders. He begged Isarn to conform to the king's demands, and the lawyer, having read the document, assured him that he would. With the formalities completed, the small group went to dinner.

The meeting was scheduled to begin at two in the afternoon, and when the appointed hour arrived, Lauzun was brought into Saint-Mars's room, where his visitors awaited him. What they saw shocked them. Lauzun was in a dreadful state. Isarn described him as being so weak, "either because of the coldness of the air, of the bright light, or a weakness caused by his illness," that he had to be supported by Saint-Mars.[4] "I admit," he continued, "that at the sight of him we were touched by pity." The dashing young man who had both amused and annoyed the court with his antics had clearly succumbed to the ravages of illness, his condition compounded by six years of rigorous imprisonment. His face, or what could be seen of it beneath his unkempt beard and long moustaches, was pale; his eyes were filled with sadness and languor "that it would have been impossible not to be moved to compassion; I cannot express to you the distress of madame his sister and monsieur his brother."

Lauzun was given a chair by the fire, the weak autumn daylight streaming in from the window falling upon him, but he moved it, saying in a low voice that the light hurt his eyes and the fire hurt his head. He looked at Isarn and told him he did not know who was talking to him or who had sent him. Isarn explained his reason for coming to Pignerol, but Lauzun was unable to understand. Instead, he told him in a somewhat cold tone "that having been six years and now beginning the seventh in strict imprisonment, not having heard any business talk for so long, and not having seen a single person, his mind was so narrow and his intelligence so darkened that it was impossible for him to understand anything that I had said."

During all this time, Lauzun's only occupation had been to "brood over and to deplore his own trouble, without thinking at all of his special affairs or of those of his family." Indeed, "everything had slipped so thoroughly out of his memory that unless he were allowed to confer privately and intimately with his sister, whatever art I might bring into play with the purpose of helping him to understand, and of inducing him to decide on a course of action, he confessed to me candidly that he would never understand anything that I said." Of course, his request to speak in private with his sister was refused. Lauzun nevertheless expressed his gratitude to Louis for allowing him to see her, adding that he felt great joy at the sight of her, "the person he loved most in the world and in whom he had the most confidence, that he was much obliged to her for having consented to undertake so long and painful a journey from love of him." He was in the greatest anguish, he said, "not for the harshness of his imprisonment, but because he had displeased the King," whose pardon and pity he still hoped to receive. Lauzun, "thereupon becoming affected and his eyes filling with tears, he covered them with his handkerchief, and remained like that for a long time."

Mme de Nogent was distressed as much at the sight of her brother as by his words, as was Monsieur the chevalier de Lauzun, and it was clear that no further business would be conducted that day. Brother and sister were conducted back to their lodgings in the town, where they both, having been upset by the encounter, retired to their beds.

The following day saw the interview resume. Lauzun granted power of attorney to his sister, telling her that he had "entire confidence in you, and only intending to benefit my brothers and the rest of my family through your advice, and wishing to enrich your family, specially Mademoiselle de Bautru, my god-daughter, of whom I am very fond." Mademoiselle de Bautru was Mme de Nogent's daughter, and Lauzun made special mention of her in a bid to ensure that his sister, whom he still did not fully trust, would carry out her power of attorney with due diligence.

He then issued instructions as to how the revenue from his inheritance was to be used. Occasionally, he would be shaken by a coughing fit, but he assured his brother and sister that they should not be concerned about his state of health, even though "he suffered from such bad air in his prison, which was so cold and wet that everything in it became rotten, even bread if it was left there for twenty-four hours, that he had no hope of ever coming out alive."

The third meeting, which took place on Sunday, October 31, saw Lauzun more like his usual self. When shown the document that granted power of attorney to Mme de Nogent, he refused to approve it and demanded that another should be drawn up. This new one he did approve, for it was written in accordance with his own instructions, to which he had applied himself with great clarity of thought.

On the fourth and final day, Lauzun once again expressed his desire to speak privately with his sister, and just at it had been the first time, his request was refused. Having little choice but to speak to Mme de Nogent before witnesses, he addressed his words to his sister, but it was clear that his message was really for Louis:

I beg you to see the King, and to tell him that I never have been nor shall be opposed to his decrees, that I shall always be a very faithful subject, that I have never been mixed up in any Court intrigue, that I have, and shall be, all my life the bitter sadness of having displeased him; that my trust is in his goodness, forgiveness, and pity, that he has overwhelmed me with benefits and honors, that I now only require his forgiveness; that he gave everything, and has the right to take away everything. I beg his Majesty very humbly to have pity on me and to allow me to serve him in any capacity he pleases [even] if it were only with spade in hand. Tell him that I find it difficult to believe that he wishes to crush a poor gentleman whose affairs, as well as those of his house, are absolutely ruined, that nevertheless I am submissive to his will and orders, that I have given you power of attorney to give the resignation of all my offices into his hands, that if he wants anything more definite I will give it, and shall all my life obey his commands with respect and humility, and in short that I shall count myself only too happy if he will have the goodness to leave me my post.

He asked her also to speak to the marquis de Louvois, to assure him that Lauzun was his humble servant and that he craved his pardon if he had offended him. He asked Louvois to found three beds for the poor and to ensure that his debts were paid. When he had finished, Mme de Nogent asked Lauzun if she could kiss his hand, but he told her that this would not be allowed. At this, he rose abruptly and, praying again that God would be with her, he bowed to all present and left the room.

Lauzun, it appeared, was looking beyond his prison walls to a time when he might be freed and allowed to return to court and into the service of the king he so worshipped.[5] That eventuality appeared to come a step closer when Louis's attitude toward his two highest-ranking prisoners, Foucquet and Lauzun, underwent a remarkable change. In November 1677, he granted them permission to leave their prison apartments and go outside and take the air.[6] Initially they were to be allowed "to walk three times a week on the ramparts which are opposite their apartment." They were to be accompanied by Saint-Mars, but their walks were to take place at different times of the day so that they could not communicate with each other. In addition, Saint-Mars was warned to ensure that his prisoners could not communicate with anyone either by word of mouth or by written message.

This was a tremendous boon to Foucquet and Lauzun. Their apartments may have been luxurious, as far as prison accommodation went, but being confined indoors every day of their lives was not healthy. Each of them suffered a succession of illnesses, mainly colds and vague fevers. Now Louis desired them to take the air for two hours every second day, as long as Saint-Mars had the time. Elsewhere in his letter, Louvois wrote that if, in order to save time, Saint-Mars would prefer to allow the two prisoners to go out at the same time, Louis would permit this, provided that the jailer was always present and could hear the conversation that passed between them, and that he ensured that they could not speak privately to each other.

Later that same month, Louvois wrote again. Louis had not addressed the question of what to do with the valets who served Foucquet and Lauzun while their masters were walking the ramparts. Now he ordered that "their valets should walk with them, that is to say with monsieur de Lauzun the one that he has, and with monsieur Foucquet one of his; each time he goes out, and he can have them take it in turns." He added that Louis approved of Foucquet and Lauzun taking their walks at different times rather than together. This contradicted Louvois's earlier statement that the two could walk together if Saint-Mars's time was short. In a letter that is now lost, the jailer asked for clarification on this point, only to be told that Louvois had "nothing to add" on the subject. Moreover, Saint-Mars was told that he could do what he judged most appropriate regarding the "two valets of monsieur Foucquet, whom you propose to go on the walk with him."[7] This statement makes it clear that Eustache, who was originally meant to serve Foucquet only when his usual valet was indisposed, had now become a permanent member of Foucquet's prison household.[8]

Louvois finishes his letter to Saint-Mars with the enigmatic phrase: "I beg you to thank monsieur Foucquet on my behalf for all his honesty." What does this mean? Possibly, Saint-Mars's request for a clarification in the matter of what to do with his valets as he took the air had come from Foucquet himself, and Louvois was simply acknowledging this and expressing his gratitude to Foucquet for ensuring that all was done in accordance with the king's orders.

Although Foucquet, Lauzun, and their respective valets were allowed to go no further than the ramparts of the donjon, they could not have been oblivious to the beauty of Pignerol and the surrounding countryside. It was one thing to look upon it from their windows, although in Foucquet's case he had to peer out through the mesh that obscured the view, it was quite another to go out into the dizzying fresh air and feel the cool breeze on their faces. It was now late autumn, almost winter, and Pignerol was swept by the crisp, chill air that blew from the snowy mountains on biting winds, while the torrents raged with icy waters far below, their roar competing with the everyday sounds of the nearby garrison.

It must be wondered: What caused Louis to soften his attitude toward these two prisoners? Perhaps it was because no further attempts had been made to rescue either Foucquet or Lauzun from prison, so both men could now be considered low risk. This was all the more so because each prisoner appeared to have abandoned his attempts to slip messages to the outside. Moreover, Louis was in good humor as the result of the successful progress of the Dutch War.[9] Louis himself claimed that his change of heart was in response to a request from Lauzun to go out and take the air. As has been seen, Lauzun was ill with fever at this point, and, having asked this concession from Louis, the king was happy to grant it to his former favorite; but was there more to it?

Several months earlier, Louis's mistress, Mme de Montespan, had traveled to the spa at Bourbon to enjoy the curative waters. Here, she met one of Foucquet's brothers and his youngest daughter, who had also come for the water cure. Mme de Montespan took the time to chat with them "about the most delicate topics," that is to say, Foucquet's imprisonment, the separation and exile of his family and the hardship they were facing as a result.[10] The following day, Foucquet's wife arrived at Bourbon, and she was received with great kindness by the royal mistress. Mme de

Montespan took the time to speak with the unfortunate lady, listening with "sweetness and an appearance of admirable compassion."

Mme Foucquet expressed her hopes that God would grant her dearest wish, which was to be allowed to share her husband's imprisonment as was her right as his wife, and that "Providence would give Mme de Montespan on occasion some remembrance and some pity for her misfortune." This was no idle wish because, at that time, Foucquet's mother was looking after Mme de Montespan's son, who was staying with her in the country while the boy's father was conducting business in Paris. As Mme de Montespan listened to Mme Foucquet's sad story, she could not help but be deeply touched by it, and so it is perhaps no coincidence that, within a few months, Louis began to show a small but significant degree of clemency toward his state prisoners. However, while Louis had considered the needs of his aristocratic prisoners, he remained indifferent to those of lower rank. Of these, he had little concern as long as they continued to be held securely and that they gave as little trouble as possible to M. de Saint-Mars.

A year after granting Foucquet and Lauzun the liberty to walk on the ramparts, Louvois sent Saint-Mars the following letter:

> *I send you a letter from me, for Monsieur Foucquet, that the intention of the King is that you give it to him closed as you find it; that you carry ink, paper, a seal, and Spanish wax to his room, and leave it there for him to answer at his leisure, and that you address to me the sealed letter that he will give you for me. As the King finds it well that he should write to me from now on when he wishes it, you will give him as much ink, paper and wax as he asks you for. You will leave him the stamp which he used to write to me the first time; and when he gives you letters either closed or open for me, you will send them to me in the state he gives them to you.*
> *This is the intention of the King,*[11]

Enclosed with this letter, which was dated December 23, 1678, was one that Saint-Mars was to deliver unopened to Foucquet. It concerned another of the prisoners of Pignerol, Eustache, and its contents make for interesting reading. Addressing himself directly to Foucquet, Louvois wrote:

Monsieur, it is with great pleasure that I satisfy the order which it has pleased the King to give me to advise you that His Majesty is in a position to grant, in a short time, considerable amelioration to your imprisonment; but as he wishes to be informed beforehand if the man Eustache, whom you have been given to serve you, has not spoken, before the other valet who serves you, of how he has been employed *before coming to Pignerol. His Majesty has commanded me to ask you this, and to tell you that he is waiting for you to notify me of the truth, without any consideration, so that he may take the measures that he finds most appropriate regarding what the said Eustache might have said about his past life to his companion. The intention of His Majesty is that you answer this letter in person, without indicating its contents to M. de Saint-Mars, to whom I am writing that the King desires he should give you some paper and [lacuna]. I sincerely share the joy that the beginning of this letter must give you.*[12]

In this letter, Louvois originally spoke of what Eustache had seen before being sent to Pignerol, not how he had been employed. Rather than having committed a crime, Eustache appears to have become privy to sensitive and secret information, or had perhaps encountered someone or witnessed or otherwise learned something he ought not to have done. For this, he was captured, perhaps having been lured into a trap, and imprisoned on the very edge of French territory in order to ensure his silence.

The letter, with the erroneous phrase crossed out, was duly handed to Foucquet, who was provided with the necessary writing materials and given as much time as he needed to compose his answer. Having done so, he sealed his letter according to Louvois's instructions and gave it to Saint-Mars, who then sent it unopened to Louvois.

Foucquet's reply, which is dated January 6, 1679, does not survive, but another from Louvois, written in answer to it, does. In it, he wrote that Louis was satisfied with the information Foucquet had given. Clearly, the former superintendent had been able to assure Louis and Louvois that Eustache had not spoken of this secret to his colleague, La Rivière. As a result, Foucquet was to be granted certain privileges. Within a short time, he would be allowed to write to his wife and other members of his family as often as he liked. His letters were to be sent directly to Louvois, who would ensure that they would be passed on to the addressee. Louvois then added that, as Foucquet would already have learned from Saint-Mars, Louis expected him to take whatever steps he deemed appropriate to ensure that his valet, Eustache Danger, would have no communication with anyone other than himself; specifically, Eustache was to speak to no one in private. Indeed, Louis expected Foucquet's cooperation in this matter because, as Louvois wrote, the former superintendent was aware of how important it was that no one should know what Eustache knew.[13]

Louvois's letter suggests that Louis and he accepted that the former superintendent was aware of at least some aspects of Eustache's past, with Louvois openly stating that Foucquet understood how important it was that no one should find out what Eustache knew. This could be interpreted as a veiled threat to Foucquet, warning him to keep a close watch over Eustache and guard his secret, or the king would make life hard for him again.

As Petitfils points out, however, this letter is important for several reasons.[14] It shows that Louvois, the king, or both had renewed their interest in Eustache, a prisoner who has hitherto been almost forgotten. It suggests that what Eustache knew had to be hidden. It reveals that Eustache was privy to a secret that appears to be of great import, perhaps connected with something he had seen—a secret, moreover, that Foucquet knew prior to his imprisonment, or that he had subsequently learned from Eustache after he had entered his service as his valet. Foucquet was able to assure the king and Louvois that Eustache had not spoken about what he had seen prior to his arrest. He understood the importance of his valet's secret, and his own silence was guaranteed.

Marcel Pagnol has argued though that Louis could simply have hanged Eustache rather than spend good money to maintain him in prison.[15] However, executions did not just happen in the ancien régime.[16] Not even Louis was above the law, and he was not able to break the law. Had this not been the case, Foucquet would never have been sent to Pignerol, but would have been executed on the Place de Grève instead.

Louvois followed up this letter with a reply to one from Foucquet, dated February 3. In it, the privileges that were to be bestowed upon Foucquet and Lauzun were summarized. They were, however, explained more fully in a lengthy document entitled *The way in which the King desires Monsieur de Saint-Mars to guard, in the future, the prisoners who are in his charge.*[17]

Foucquet and Lauzun were granted permission to write to their families whenever they liked; their letters, which would be addressed to Louvois, would be read out to the king before being passed on to their respective addressees. It was imperative, however, that they should not try to receive any news from outside other than through Saint-Mars. They were forbidden to receive or send letters other than through Louvois. They were, however, to be provided with any books and newspapers they wanted.

They were allowed to socialize any time they wished. This meant that they could spend their days together and take their meals together. Moreover, if they liked, Saint-Mars could eat with them. Here we see one of the niceties of the prison system: the preservation of rank. Saint-Mars the jailer, although recently ennobled, was of lower rank than either Foucquet or Lauzun. Even in a prison setting, in order for him to share their table, the two aristocrats had to invite him. They could also, if they desired, socialize with officers from Saint-Mars's compagnie-franche.

While, previously, the prisoners had been allowed to walk on the ramparts of the donjon opposite their apartments and at limited times of the day, now they could walk whenever they liked. In addition, the space in which they could walk was widened to include the citadel, but only as long as certain security precautions were applied.

For Foucquet, this meant he could walk in the citadel as long as he was with one of Saint-Mars's officers and accompanied by some of the sergeants or soldiers of lower rank. Lauzun, however, could not leave the donjon without Saint-Mars, two officers, and six armed sergeants or other-ranking soldiers. Louis was well aware that Lauzun was more capable than Foucquet was at making an escape attempt, and so Saint-Mars was told to make him understand that these men would kill him if he tried to get away.

The officers and soldiers of the compagnie-franche were allowed to converse with the prisoners, provided Saint-Mars or an officer could hear what was being said. Also, any officer of the citadel could accept invitations from Foucquet and Lauzun to visit them in their apartments, again on condition that there was always one of Saint-Mars's officers present.

Louis expected that Foucquet and Lauzun would not deviate from this procedure: if they did, their privileges would be withdrawn and the security measures that were imposed upon them in the earliest days of their imprisonment would be reinstated. As usual, Saint-Mars was required to give the king a weekly account of everything that happened with regard to his prisoners.

Louis attributed his munificence, as before, to "compassion for the long punishment of these gentlemen," whose imprisonment he wanted to alleviate. He held out the hope for more favors to come, promising that within a few months he would allow people from the town of Pignerol to spend time with Foucquet and Lauzun, and even that Foucquet's wife and children would be allowed to visit him.

Louis, however, had not forgotten that Foucquet had been entrusted with the security of the imprisoned valet, Eustache. With so many people being allowed to enter his master's apartment, as well as Foucquet being granted the freedom to go out into the citadel, the problem arose as to what do to with Eustache during these times. Louvois sent Saint-Mars Louis's solution:

Whenever monsieur Foucquet goes down into monsieur de Lauzun's
chamber, or monsieur de Lauzun goes up to monsieur Foucquet's
room, or some other stranger, monsieur de Saint-Mars will take care
to withdraw the man named Eustache and will not put him back
into monsieur Foucquet's room until there is no one but him and his
old valet.

Similar precautions were to be taken whenever Foucquet took a walk in the citadel. Eustache had to remain inside Foucquet's apartment, although La Rivière, who was not a prisoner, was allowed to accompany his master.

This was such good news that Madame Foucquet could not quite believe it when she was told her husband had been granted these privileges. Louvois wrote to her to confirm: "It is true," he assured her, "that M. Foucquet is at liberty to see M. de Lauzun, to eat and to walk with him."[18]

Two weeks later, Louvois wrote again to clarify several points.[19] Louis, who had evidently been giving much thought to the security of Eustache, reiterated his wish to leave it to Saint-Mars to arrange with Foucquet "as you judge appropriate, regarding the security of the person named Eustache Danger, recommending you above all, to see to it that he speaks to no one in private." In an astonishing turn of events, Foucquet, a state prisoner, was now placed in charge of another state prisoner, Eustache.

Regarding the visits Foucquet and Lauzun could make to each other's apartments, Saint-Mars was ordered not to leave the doors of their apartments open so that they could move freely from one to the other; instead, Saint-Mars or one of his officers was required to escort them. They should then be left locked in together until an agreed hour, at which time they would be returned to their own apartment under escort.

By a similar arrangement, the officers of the citadel who wished to keep company with either Foucquet or Lauzun would have to be accompanied by another officer, presumably of Saint-Mars's compagnie-franche, who would withdraw until an agreed time. Most important, during the time that the prisoners were out walking, the wickets of the citadel were to be kept firmly closed.

Within a month of these new orders being issued, it was discovered that Foucquet had received and answered a letter from his friend Gourville. This breach of security, however, brought none of the penalties that had been threatened earlier. Instead, Louvois merely sent a note to Saint-Mars warning him not to forward any correspondence to Foucquet that had not been sent in one of the minister's own packets and that was not accompanied by a letter from him.[20]

In a further gesture of largesse, Louis authorized the removal of the screens that had been placed over the windows of Foucquet's apartments. Once again the prisoner would be allowed to enjoy the warmth and light of the sun that streamed into his rooms, and to delight in the sight of the town and the mountains beyond the close confines of the donjon.[21] As conditions were improving for Foucquet and Lauzun, and even for Eustache to a large degree, life continued in the usual way for Saint-Mars, who was preparing to receive yet another prisoner.

SIX

Matthioli

Lying on the banks of the Po some seventy-seven kilometers east of Turin was Casale, the capital of the marquisate of Montferrat, a dependency of the dukedom of Mantua.[1] Like Pignerol, Casale held strategic military importance and was coveted by the Savoyard court at Turin and by Louis XIV. It was the key to Milan, a city-state held by the Spanish, who had wrested it out of French hands in 1652 and held it ever since.

Louis had long been uncomfortable with the thought that one set of his enemies was in possession of such an important stronghold, and another was in such close proximity to it; but, while he had taken an interest in Casale, he had so far made no attempt to retake it. Instead, he had contented himself with expanding his territories to the north and east, sharing his father's reluctance to be seen to be meddling in the affairs of the Italians, which could send them running into the arms of the Spanish.

On the other hand, Jean-François d'Estrades, abbé de Moissac, who was Louis's ambassador to Venice, thought that the time had come for his master to acquire Casale. He saw the stronghold as a useful platform from which Louis might launch an attack on Milan whenever he saw fit to use it. At the same time, Casale provided d'Estrades with a means by which he might regain the king's favor, after having recently incurred his displeasure. D'Estrades knew that the Duke of Mantua was short of cash. He also knew that if the duke could be persuaded to grant the French the right to occupy Casale in exchange for a significant sum of money, the ambitions and desires of all three men could be satisfied.

Ferdinand Charles de Gonzaga, who was perhaps better known as Charles IV, duke of Mantua, was twenty-five years old and had inherited the dukedom of Mantua from his father at the age of only thirteen. Intelligent and cultured, he nevertheless preferred to spend his time in Venice, where he indulged his love of women and the theatre, and performing charitable works, all of which drained his purse. The business of governance he left to his mother, the regent Isabella Clara, who lived at the ducal palace in Mantua and was assisted by her lover, the comte Carlo Bulgarini, a Dominican monk.[2]

The court of Mantua, which was situated in Lombardy in Northern Italy, was a domain of the Holy Roman Empire and was riven by factionalism, a situation that had not gone unnoticed by the French. As d'Estrades observed in a letter to Louis, the council that was headed by the regent and the monk acted wholly in the interests of Spain. Still, the young duke "was not so abandoned to his pleasure, but that he still had some ambition," and he was very unhappy about the state to which he had been reduced by the ambitions of his mother and his suspicions of the Spanish.[3]

The enterprising ambassador had conceived a project that would detach the duke from his mother, her lover, and his hated council, and induce him to enter "into the views" of Louis XIV, and in turn to come to some arrangement with France respecting Casale.[4] The major difficulty in d'Estrades's plan lay in establishing contact with the Duke of Mantua. Having studied with great care those in the duke's entourage, he identified a man he felt would be the best person to act as intermediary. His name was the comte Ercole Antonio Maria Matthioli.

Born on December 1, 1640, in Bologna to an aristocratic family, Matthioli was the son of Valerian Matthioli and Girolama Maggi. A distinguished scholar in civil and canon law, he had become a professor at the University of Bologna but left to enter the service of Charles III, Duke of Mantua, the father of Charles IV, as a secretary of state. Upon the death of Charles III in August 1665, the young Charles IV retained Matthioli, creating him supernumerary senator of Mantua; this post had once been held by Matthioli's grandfather, but its only real advantage was to confer upon the holder the title of count. At some point, Matthioli fell out of favor with the regent and her lover, upon which he resigned his office and retired to Verona with his wife and two children, although he maintained his links with the young Duke Charles.[5]

While d'Estrades recognized Matthioli's good qualities, he nevertheless had his suspicions. As he explained, Matthioli "had been much in the Milanese, and had had a good deal of access to the Spanish ministers, I would not put any confidence in him, till I had first tried him."[6] For this task, d'Estrades employed the services of a man known for his pro-French views, Benedetto Giuliani, to observe Matthioli closely.

As someone whose job it was to gather and disseminate news throughout different parts of Italy, Giuliani could come and go without arousing suspicion. Once d'Estrades was satisfied that Matthioli was "much discontented with the Spaniards, who had always amused him with hopes, and afterward abandoned him," he sent Giuliani to Verona on the pretext of engaging Matthioli in private business, but in fact to represent to him the dangerous state the Duke of Mantua was in: that it was a matter of great affliction to all who saw that the young duke was still under the thumb of his mother and her ambitious lover, that he had no money, and who passed his life "with actresses and women of the town."

It was whispered abroad that the duke would have no children by his wife, and that his want of an heir encouraged the Spanish to foment the divisions in his court so that they could profit from them and try to obtain Casale and the whole of Montferrat for themselves. Others looked to take possession of parts of Mantua, while the king of Spain[7] sought to establish himself as the rightful heir to the throne of Mantua. Giuliani had to persuade Matthioli that only by placing himself under Louis's protection would Duke Charles find complete security.[8]

Giuliani's words resonated with Matthioli, who "had long, with grief, seen the truth of it," and who knew that the Duke of Mantua "had more talent and ambition than he was thought to have." Matthioli promised that he would find out the duke's feelings about the proposal, upon which "he would charge himself with whatever negotiation" d'Estrades wished to pursue.[9]

Matthioli, therefore, agreed to act as intermediary between d'Estrades and Duke Charles, and arrangements were made for a meeting in Venice. In this, the duke's favorite city, the duke, the ambassador, and the intermediary "might see each other conveniently and without being observed, on account of the Carnival, during which, all the world, even the Doge, and the oldest senators, go about in mask."[10] Charles, however, was anxious that the negotiations should be held in the strictest secrecy and would be concluded as quickly as possible. He did not want to arouse the suspicions of the Spanish, he explained, fearing that they would ruin him before he could receive any assistance from Louis, who, in turn, would "lose all hope of getting possession of Casale."[11] D'Estrades reluctantly agreed to this condition.

D'Estrades wrote to Louis, giving an account of his dealing so far with the Duke of Mantua. He enclosed in his packet a list of the duke's demands and a letter addressed to the king by Matthioli, who declared: "I bless the destiny, which procures me the honor of serving so great a monarch, whom I regard and revere as a demigod."[12] Louis was appreciative of Matthioli's devotion to his interests and he did not hesitate to say so in a letter dated January 12, 1678: "You cannot doubt but that I am much obliged to you for it, and that I shall have much pleasure in giving you proofs of my satisfaction upon every occasion."[13]

Louis was also very pleased about the terms of the agreement, although he felt that the negotiations were going too quickly, and he urged d'Estrades to prolong them in order to allow him time to make preparations to send troops to occupy Casale: "I am reduced to be sorry that I cannot find any difficulties," wrote d'Estrades.[14] There was, however, one area of contention, and it lay in the sum of money Louis was requested to pay to Duke Charles. The duke had asked for 100,000 pistoles, which Louis felt was too much. In the end, d'Estrades managed to persuade Charles to accept 100,000 crowns, which would be payable when both Louis and Duke Charles had signed the treaty.[15]

The conference between Duke Charles and d'Estrades took place amid the colors, sounds, and festivity of the Carnival of Venice at midnight of March 13, 1678. Charles wanted to send Matthioli, in whom he had "a blind confidence," to France to acquaint Louis with the facilities he would find "in conquering the Milanese, the intelligences that may be established there, and the detail of the whole negotiation."[16] For his part, Louis was eager to "receive the Count Matthioli favorably, and to listen willingly to his propositions, as soon as he shall be arrived at the Court."[17]

Matthioli, however, became ill with a fever, and his departure for France had to be delayed by several months. It was not until at the end of November 1678 that he finally arrived in Paris, following a lengthy journey by way of Switzerland. Shortly afterward a treaty was agreed, under the terms of which the Duke of Mantua would undertake to receive French troops in Casale; should Louis send an army into Italy, Duke Charles would be in command of it; immediately upon the execution of the treaty, the Duke of Mantua would receive a cash payment of 300,000 livres, to be paid in two installments.[18] Matthioli was then received by Louis in a private audience, which was held in Mme de Montespan's apartments. The king gave him a ring, the diamond of which was valued at some 2,000 écus in louis d'or, and a sum of money as a personal gift, with the promise a much larger gratification once the treaty had been ratified. He promised that Matthioli's son would come to court as a royal page, while Matthioli's brother, a clergyman, would receive a good benefice.[19] With his mission concluded, Matthioli returned to Italy with detailed instructions for the application of the articles of the treaty.

On the French side, preparations for the occupation of Casale and the installation of troops were already well in train. Nicolas de Catinat, brigadier of the infantry and future maréchal of France, was appointed to command the new garrison when it was established. His men were already assembling at Briançon while they waited for the treaty to be finalized. Catinat, meanwhile, moved into the donjon of Pignerol so he could be close at hand for the takeover of Casale. In order not to arouse suspicion should Spain or Austria learn of his presence, he masqueraded as a prisoner under an assumed name, Richemont. The pretense was carried to the extent that he was allowed to walk incognito in the donjon precincts with the other prisoners; that is, with Foucquet, Lauzun, and their respective valets. He was also permitted to visit them in their chambers and "to converse with them, which will assist in enabling him to pass the time of his stay."[20]

At the same time, Alexis Bidal, Baron d'Asfeld, a colonel of the dragoons, had traveled to Venice to oversee the ratification of the treaty. These maneuvers, as well as the movement of French troops, although supposedly secret, did not escape the notice of either Emperor Leopold or Carlos II of Spain, who remonstrated with Duke Charles of Mantua. He calmly dismissed their fears. With Louis now impatient to conclude the treaty, the Duke of Mantua drew up a plan in which Matthioli would meet d'Asfeld at the Church of Notre-Dame-d'Incréa, in a village close to Casale. This would take place on March 9, when the treaty would be finalized. The duke would go to Casale the following week and formally hand over the town and its fortress to Louis's troops.

With these arrangements in place and everyone ready to go, Matthioli fell strangely silent. A letter written to him on February 21, 1679, by Louis's secretary of state for foreign affairs, Arnaud de Pomponne, provided the first intimation that the French authorities had become suspicious of Matthioli. In it, Pomponne assured the diplomat that Louis "is willing to promise himself a good success in it [French possession of Casale], and will not entertain any doubt of the promise which has been so solemnly given to him being kept."[21] The letter received no response, and a second one, written two weeks later, also went without reply.

The French now became very concerned, but the answer to the mystery was about to reveal itself in the most surprising way. D'Estrades, who has been transferred from Venice to Turin to await the conclusion of the treaty, was approached by Jeanne-Baptiste, princesse de Nemours, duchesse de Savoie. At the end of December, three weeks after his reception by Louis XIV, Matthioli had gone to the duchess and confided to her all that had taken place with regard to the transfer of Casale to the French. He had shown her all the original documents, including a letter from the Duke of Mantua to Louis XIV, the full powers Matthioli had been granted for the purpose of negotiating the treaty, the treaty itself, the ratification signed by Duke Charles, and a letter from the duke to the governor of Casale ordering him to receive French troops in accordance with the terms of the treaty.[22]

These revelations had plunged the duchess into a dilemma. She was pleased to have been made privy to the negotiations but was undecided as to what to do with the information, particularly as Louis's occupation of Casale posed a threat to Piedmont. In spite of this, she was reluctant to launch armed resistance against Louis; for one thing, she lacked sufficient forces to meet his superior power, but she was also afraid of rousing him to anger. Yet, she had to act: there was every chance that Matthioli would offer his information to Spain or Austria, an equally undesirable prospect.[23] After weighing her options for several weeks, the duchess finally decided that her best and safest strategy was to inform Louis that Matthioli had betrayed him, and she did so through his ambassador, d'Estrades.[24] The news not unnaturally came as a shock to Louis. He had trusted Matthioli, welcomed him to Versailles, and generously rewarded him. At this stage, however, he thought he could salvage the situation and mitigate the damage by applying pressure on the duke of Mantua and threatening Matthioli.

Then, on March 9, as d'Asfeld was making his way to Incréa to meet Matthioli, he was arrested on the orders of the Count of Melgar and held for a short time as a prisoner of Spain.[25] The French were informed of the incident by Matthioli himself, who claimed to have received the news from a valet he had met on the road. Pinchesne, who was acting as the French chargé d'affaires in the absence of an ambassador, expressed his doubts when he reported news of the incident to Pomponne, saying that it had been impossible for him to verify it.[26] Even so, d'Asfeld's mission had to be accomplished, so Catinat was dispatched to Incréa, where he was to meet up with Matthioli. He set off under cover of darkness with Saint-Mars, who was disguised as an officer of the Pignerol garrison, and a man belonging to d'Estrades's entourage.

Catinat and his companions arrived at Incréa, but Matthioli failed to meet them. They soon learned that their presence had been discovered, that the local peasantry were up in arms, and that a detachment of cavalry were on their way to take them. Saint-Mars and the other companion escaped, as did Catinat, who arrived in disguise at Casale. With the governor of Casale in sympathy with the French, Catinat passed an agreeable evening, but he was glad to return to the safety of Pignerol the next day.[27]

As it turned out, Matthioli had returned to Venice, where he had several interviews with Pinchesne; already suspicious, the chargé d'affaires now discovered to his alarm that Matthioli had spent some days in Milan. Uncertain as to how to proceed, he suggested that Matthioli should go to Turin to speak with d'Estrades, while warning him of the danger he would be in should the transfer of Casale fail as a result of his activity.[28] Matthioli duly traveled to Turin, where he spoke to d'Estrades as instructed. "It is impossible to conceive the insolence of his daring to show himself," wrote Pomponne when he received the news update from Pinchesne, "at a moment when all Italy rings with his perfidy."[29]

In the meantime, Louis had decided that enough was enough. It was time to make an example of Matthioli and show the world what became of those who dared to betray the confidence of the king of France. He instructed the marquis de Louvois to write to Saint-Mars and, in a letter dated April 27, 1679, to alert him to the imminent arrival of a new prisoner:

> *The King has sent orders to the Abbé d'Estrades, to try and arrest a man, with whose conduct His Majesty has reason to be dissatisfied; of which he has commanded me to acquaint you, in order that you may not object to receiving him, when he shall be sent to you, and that you may guard him in a manner that not only may he not have communication with anyone, but that also he may have cause to repent of his bad conduct; and that it may not be discovered that you have a new prisoner.*[30]

Those ominous words: "he may have cause to repent of his bad conduct" and the secrecy surrounding his imprisonment did not bode well for Matthioli.[31]

The following day, April 28, 1679, Louis wrote to the abbé d'Estrades ordering him to arrest Matthioli and take him to Pignerol in secret. Louis was insistent that d'Estrades must ensure that no one would find out what became of the man who had betrayed him.[32]

As it happened, Matthioli had crossed into territory belonging to the duchesse de Savoie, and although she agreed that he ought to be arrested, she did not want it to take place on her land. A solution to this difficult situation presented itself when Matthioli, always short of funds, requested cash in compensation for the expenses he had incurred during the negotiations for the treaty. D'Estrades, still anxious to capture Matthioli in order to remain in the king's favor, told him that a man named Richemont, who commanded the troops that were to garrison Casale, could provide him with the required funds. All Matthioli had to do was meet Richemont on the frontier toward Pignerol, a meeting at which d'Estrades would also be present, and the money would be handed over to him.[33] The proposition naturally appealed to the unsuspecting Matthioli. He met up with d'Estrades, who was accompanied by one of his relatives, the abbé de Montesquieu, in a church near Turin. The three men climbed into a carriage and embarked upon their journey to the frontier.

The small party was within three miles of the rendezvous point when they found their road flooded. A river had burst its banks in the recent spring rainfall and partially brought down a bridge. Matthioli assisted in the repairs, and the three continued on foot until they came upon Catinat, who was accompanied by the chevaliers Saint-Martin and de Villebois of Saint-Mars's compagnie-franche, and four soldiers from the Pignerol garrison. D'Estrades, in the presence of Catinat, asked Matthioli to confirm that he had possession of all the original documents concerning the transfer of Casale. When he replied that he had, Matthioli was arrested and taken to Pignerol. "He is in the chamber which the individual named Dubreuil occupied," Catinat wrote, "where he will be treated civilly, according to the request of the abbé d'Estrades, until the wishes of the King, with regard to him, are known."[34] Catinat ended his letter by announcing that he had given Matthioli "the name of Lestang, no one here knowing who he really is."[35]

D'Estrades thought it a matter of urgency to obtain the original documents pertaining to the negotiations and the treaty concerning the transfer of Casale to France. At first, Matthioli had said that they were kept in a box at Bologna, in the hands of his wife, who had retreated to the convent of the Nuns of Saint-Louis. Catinat explained that he had not yet had a chance to question Matthioli about these documents, but "two hours hence I will go to his room, and do not doubt the menaces I shall make to him, which his criminal conduct will render more terrific to him, will oblige him to do all that I wish." Meanwhile, Blainvilliers, Saint-Mars's lieutenant, was sent to Bologna to retrieve the papers.[36]

As it turned out, Blainvilliers had been sent on a false errand; he returned with some papers, certainly, but they were not the vital ones connected to the negotiations. Under questioning by Catinat, Matthioli divulged that the documents were in fact at Padua, "concealed in a hole in the wall of a room, which is in his father's lodging, and which he says is known to him alone."[37] Meanwhile, the abbé d'Estrades had tracked down Matthioli's valet and brought him to Pignerol along with Matthioli's clothes and "all his papers."[38] Catinat inventoried these documents and found ciphers and the odd letter, but nothing of any substance. The servant, a man named Rousseau or La Rousseau, or Russo in Italian, was retained at Pignerol, where he would continue to serve his master.

Matthioli was ordered to write three letters to his father. In the first, he required his father to hand over the documents he had in his keeping to Giuliani, who was on his way to see him. In the second, he was forced to acquaint his father with "the real state in which he is, and that it is important, as well for his life as his honor, that his papers should be immediately delivered into the hands of the Sieur Giuliani." The third letter was to be used in case the first two failed. In it, Matthioli instructed his father to meet him at the house of the abbé d'Estrades. During the ensuing interview, Matthioli would be required to persuade his father to hand over the documents. "I have inspired him with so great a fear of the punishment due to his bad conduct," writes Catinat, "that I find no repugnance in him to do all that I require of him."[39]

At first, Matthioli was treated "very kindly in all that regards cleanliness and food," but as with all the prisoners of Pignerol, vigorous efforts were made to prevent him having communication with anyone.[40] This situation was not to last for very long; within a few weeks Saint-Mars was ordered to treat the new prisoner with severity: "It is not the intention of the King that the Sieur de lestang [Matthioli] should be well-treated, nor that, except the absolute necessities of life, you should give him anything that may make his time pass agreeably."[41] This terrible order appears to have been questioned by Saint-Mars, who asked for clarification. Louvois wrote to say that "I have nothing to add to what I have already commanded you respecting the severity with which the individual named Lestang must be treated."[42] Two days later, Louvois provided further details. Saint-Mars was to "keep the individual named Lestang in the severe confinement I enjoined in my preceding letters, without allowing him to see a physician, unless you know he is in absolute want of one."[43]

Matthioli requested writing materials, but what he wanted to say is not known. Louvois, nevertheless allowed Saint-Mars to "give paper and ink to the Sieur de Lestang, with the understanding that he is to put into writing whatever he wishes to say; which you will send to me, and I will let you know whether it deserves any consideration."[44]

Unlike Saint-Mars's other two high-ranking prisoners, Foucquet and Lauzun—both Matthioli and Lauzun were counts, while Foucquet was a marquis—Matthioli was treated with the strictest severity and was denied the privileges and comforts deemed necessary for a man of his rank. He was given no books, was deprived of all contact with anyone other than Saint-Mars or his lieutenants and his own valet, and he was even denied medical treatment unless Saint-Mars deemed it absolutely necessary that he should be attended by a physician. In short, his treatment was similar to that of the low-ranking prisoners, with the exception now, of course, of Eustache, who enjoyed the comforts that came with being employed as Foucquet's valet.

In time, the ill-treatment received by Matthioli took its effect. Saint-Mars wrote to Louvois informing him that it had made the prisoner "like the monk I have the care of,"[45] that is, Matthioli was now mentally ill. He is "subject to fits of raving madness," continued Saint-Mars, "from which the Sieur Dubreuil also is not exempt." Matthioli complained that he was not being treated with the respect due to "a man of his quality and the minister of a great prince ought to be."[46] Saint-Mars assured Louvois, however, that he was following his orders regarding his newest prisoner to the letter, adding, "I think he is deranged by the way he talks to me." Matthioli spoke to God and his angels every day, and they had told him that the both duke of Mantua and the duke of Lorraine had died; "and as an additional proof of his madness," Saint-Mars continued, "he says that he has the honor of being the near relation of the King, to whom he wishes to write, to complain of the way

I treat him." Naturally, Saint-Mars did not consider it appropriate to allow Matthioli to do this, and he refused to give him the paper and ink he had asked for, especially as the prisoner was not "in his right senses." Such was the fate and the punishment of those who dared to betray the trust of Louis XIV.

SEVEN
Stat spes

Many years previously, when Nicolas Foucquet was still awaiting trial, he was held for a short time in the tower of the Château de Moret while the court stayed at nearby Fontainebleau. His troubles were such that he came to understand that hope would not always spring eternal, and yet, as he was led out of the door to begin the return journey to Paris, had he looked up at the lintel, he would have seen the words carved into the stone: *Stat spes*, hope remains.[1]

Now, after so many years in prison, that promise looked close to being fulfilled. On April 18, 1679, Foucquet was given the freedom to write letters whenever he wished. They were still to be sent to Louvois, who would pass them on to their respective addressees, but this newfound freedom was significant. No longer was his correspondence subject to the scrutiny of officialdom. Instead, Saint-Mars was told to provide Foucquet with Spanish wax so that he could seal the letters before handing them over to his jailer to be sent on to Louvois.[2]

Now, barely a month later, Louvois wrote to Saint-Mars to inform him that Louis had granted permission for Foucquet's family—his wife, Madame Foucquet, their children, and Gilles Foucquet, Foucquet's brother—to come to Pignerol to visit Nicolas. During this visit, the entire family was to enjoy an extraordinary level of freedom. Mme Foucquet could see her husband any time she liked, and she would be allowed to stay in his chamber and even sleep there whenever she wished to. The whole family was allowed to keep Nicolas company and to talk freely with him without Saint-Mars or his officers being present. The one caveat was that, if they were to walk in the citadel, the usual security precautions were to be observed while Foucquet was out of his chamber.[3]

In the same packet of letters was another in which Louis gave permission for a man named Louis Gervais de Salvert to accompany the Foucquet party to Pignerol. Monsieur Salvert was described as "un homme d'affaires," a businessman. Madame Foucquet had been left to look after the family's affairs alone following the arrest of her husband. This included administering Foucquet's debts and running the estate of Vaux-le-Vicomte, which had been returned to the family once Louis had taken as much as he wanted from it. One of Mme Foucquet's priorities was to protect her own fortune from her husband's creditors, thereby preserving as much of it as possible for the couple's eldest son and heir. He was to be permitted to speak to Foucquet as necessary.[4]

Louvois announced the news to Madame Foucquet in a letter dated May 20. She was told that she could embark upon her journey without first stopping off at Saint-Germain to thank Louis, as she had initially proposed to do.[5] As the party made its slow and winding way toward Piedmont, Foucquet's eldest son, Louis Nicolas, vicomte de Vaux, rode on ahead carrying letters from the king to Saint-Mars.[6] How proud Nicolas must have been when he saw this young man enter his chamber, his eldest son and heir to the Foucquet name. The vicomte had been only eight years old at the time of his father's arrest. Now here he was, an officer in the royal army, handsome and smiling in his bright uniform, taking his weeping father in his arms. Father and son had so much to talk about.

Soon they were soon joined by Madame Foucquet. Now aged forty-three, the fear, the worry, and the hardship of the past eighteen years had all made their mark on her still beautiful face. Marie-Madeleine, Foucquet's daughter by this second marriage, was twenty-three and unmarried, her life put on hold by her family's circumstances. Foucquet's youngest son, Louis, future marquis de Belle-Isle, had been only two months old when disaster had struck his family, and was now a handsome eighteen-year-old, but there were two members of the family missing. Foucquet's second son, Charles Armand, was, at the time permission was given to journey to Pignerol, preparing to join the Oratorians, a congregation of secular priests whose spiritual life centered upon the human aspect of Jesus. Charles Armand would travel to see his father in the autumn. Foucquet's mother, Marie de Maupeou, was eighty-nine and too old to make the journey, but there is no record that she had been given permission to go.

According to Saint-Simon, Foucquet spoke to his family about Lauzun, "whom he had left young and with so good a footing at Court for his age." Lauzun, said Foucquet, "was now crazy and put away to conceal his madness in that very prison." However, he was shocked to learn that everything Lauzun had told him had, in fact, been the truth. Astonished, Foucquet "could not get over it, and was inclined to believe the brains of all were deranged; it took some time to convince him" that this was not the case.[7]

The Foucquet family was not alone in its good fortune, for Lauzun also was the recipient of the royal clemency. His sister, Madame de Nogent, and his brother, the chevalier de Lauzun, arrived at Pignerol shortly after the Foucquet party. However, Lauzun's request to see his old friend Barail was denied, at least at first.[8] It would be several months before Barail would be allowed to visit, but when he received permission, he stayed for eight days. During this time, the two men were free to see each other whenever they liked, but their meetings were personally supervised by Saint-Mars.[9]

In contrast to Foucquet, Lauzun had not been granted permission to write letters freely, and all his correspondence was to pass unsealed through Saint-Mars's hands before being sent on to Louvois. Any breach of the regulations would result in Lauzun's writing privileges being rescinded.[10] Moreover, Lauzun's windows were still screened at this point despite earlier permission to open them up, although Saint-Mars was granted permission to open the screens during the day, as long as the usual precautions were observed. This suggests continuing fears surrounding Lauzun's security, a concern that could only have increased given the great number of people who were now coming and going through the doors of the donjon.[11]

In an additional act of grace, Louis gave permission for Foucquet and Lauzun to have dinners brought in from the town if they wished it,[12] a concession they would have embraced eagerly. The prison apartment of Nicolas Foucquet in particular had now become a cheery place that spring. Along with the good food and the flowing wine was the sparkling conversation of happy people. Foucquet's two valets, La Rivière and Eustache, mingled with his sons and daughter, his wife and her businessman, his brother, soldiers from the garrison, and well-heeled visitors from the town, as well as their servants, and even Madame de Saint-Mars came to socialize with Madame Foucquet.[13]

It was virtually open house, despite Saint-Mars's best efforts to preserve security and keep track of people who slipped through the gate leading from the town to visit his illustrious prisoners. One unexpected but very welcome visitor was André Le Nôtre. Arguably the greatest landscape gardener of his age, Le Nôtre had designed the parks and gardens of Foucquet's magnificent Château de Vaux-le-Vicomte and had since gone on to design the sumptuous gardens of Versailles. He had been traveling in Italy and decided to call in to see his old patron before making his way home to France.[14]

When Louis and Louvois found out about this, they expressed their disapproval, and although they allowed that Le Nôtre's stopover was of no consequence, they warned Saint-Mars sternly that he was not at liberty to allow such visits. Instead, other than their families, prisoners should be allowed to entertain only the officers of the citadel and inhabitants of the town.[15] This restriction was even applied to the abbé d'Estrades, who had apparently requested permission to see Foucquet and Lauzun during an impending journey to Pignerol. Louvois advised him, however, that the two prisoners were allowed to see their families and no one else. He added that, since they were free to walk within the confines of the donjon, d'Estrades should avoid going there.[16]

Louis and Louvois were clearly nervous about the number of people entering and leaving the donjon at will. When, in October, Madame d'Herleville, the wife of the governor-general of Pignerol, called on Foucquet and Lauzun, her visit was strictly supervised by Saint-Mars, who was required to ensure that no one present should be allowed to speak in a whisper.[17] Two days later, the jailer was reminded that no one, with the exception of their respective families, should be allowed to speak to Foucquet and Lauzun except in his presence or that of his officers.[18] Toward the end of October, Louvois wrote to say that, while Foucquet and Lauzun were allowed visitors other than members of their families, certain restrictions were to be imposed. Specifically, Monsieur d'Herleville and his wife were allowed to visit no more than three or four times a year.[19]

The constant reiteration of the rules suggests an apprehension that they were being, or might be, broken. Saint-Mars, however, was not the man to be found wanting when it came to obeying orders. He had noticed a Jesuit priest who was taking an interest in his prisoners, and he regarded him with suspicion. Louvois agreed that this priest should not to be allowed to enter the donjon at all, and if he insisted upon trying to come inside, Saint-Mars was ordered to turn him away, as he was to do with anyone else he distrusted.[20] Saint-Mars would assure Louvois that he followed this order to the letter, pointing out that some strangers from the town of Pignerol had tried to pay a visit to the prisoners but he had sent them on their way.[21] The security of the donjon would always remain a concern, and Saint-Mars would later be reminded to ensure that the doors to the citadel were firmly closed during the hours of darkness.[22]

As the summer began to mellow into autumn, Mme Foucquet left Pignerol to attend to her private affairs, taking the vicomte de Vaux with her. By this time, the couple's second son, Charles Armand, had arrived, and he now remained at Pignerol with his father and his sister, Marie-Madeleine.[23] Foucquet barely had time to lament their absence, however, because he was soon joined by another brother, Louis, bishop of Agde. This younger brother, who was permitted to visit "for the sake of his business,"[24] was also Foucquet's godson. He was granted leave to remain for four months, during which time the two of them would be free to see each other whenever they chose. At this point, Louvois passed on the order that Foucquet's brother, Gilles, was not to be allowed to lodge in the donjon. Such were the security fears that continued to trouble the king and his minister.[25]

This point raises the question of where the Foucquet family lived during their stay at Pignerol. Only Mme Foucquet was permitted to spend the night in her husband's prison apartment. It is probable that the rest of the family stayed in the lodgings taken by Gilles in the town. Mademoiselle Foucquet, however, wanted to be close to her father, who had never been robust, but was now increasingly unwell. She wanted to take care of him, but it was not convenient for her to travel between the town and the donjon every day, especially now that winter, with its bitter winds and long frosty nights, was setting in. Saint-Mars, however, came up with a helpful solution. A staircase could be built into the antechamber of Foucquet's apartment, allowing Marie-Madeleine to move into the rooms above. With free access to her father, she could attend to him whenever he needed her. Louis and Louvois approved of this arrangement and Saint-Mars was granted permission to proceed. With the usual stipulation that the prisoner's security must be guaranteed, work began immediately.[26]

It was at about this time that Lauzun, never an easy man to guard, took to behaving very badly. An exasperated Saint-Mars wrote that his prisoner insulted people "who have no other fault with him but to execute the orders of His Majesty," in other words, Saint-Mars and his turnkeys.[27] As Lauzun displayed increasingly volatile behavior, Saint-Mars wrote to inform Louvois of the situation. Louvois wrote back saying that Louis would be informed of his madness, which message Saint-Mars passed on to Lauzun.[28]

If the threat that the king would find out about his bad conduct was expected to make Lauzun behave, it failed in its objective. At the beginning of October, Louvois was obliged to inquire of Saint-Mars how it was that Lauzun managed to get hold of some money. He had fifty pistoles at least, a not inconsiderable sum. Saint-Mars was ordered to take it away from him.[29] The money could have been given to him by soldiers of the citadel, perhaps won in gambling games, but however he acquired it, he should not have been in possession of money.

As it happened, Lauzun was not the only prisoner to have money, for Saint-Mars was paying Foucquet the wages of his valets. This included La Rivière but not Eustache, who was still a prisoner; however, it turned out that Foucquet was also receiving wages meant for Champagne, his favorite valet who had died in 1674. As a result of this bureaucratic oversight, Saint-Mars had been paying Foucquet this money for some five and a half years. A horrified Louvois hastily informed Saint-Mars that "the intention of the King is not that you pay to monsieur Foucquet the wages of his valet who is dead."[30]

At the same time, Lauzun's valet was taking advantage of the greater liberty afforded to the prisoners to slip out of his master's chamber and was holding conversations with various people.[31] Who they were Louvois did not say, but presumably they were soldiers and officers of Saint-Mars's compagnie-franche, or perhaps visitors from the town; either way, the valet's behavior constituted a major breach of security.[32]

In time, however, Lauzun changed his ways. Apparently on his best behavior now, he was finally allowed to seal his own letters before they were sent off to Louvois,[33] but still Saint-Mars had to ensure that his prisoner did not receive any correspondence that did not first go through Louvois.[34]

During the autumn of 1679, a new topic of conversation had begun to appear in the correspondence that passed between Saint-Mars and Louvois: the two men had become fascinated by a change in the relationship between Lauzun and Foucquet. The uneasy friendship that had developed between the two prisoners had turned decidedly frosty. Clearly, they had fallen out, but neither the jailer nor the minister knew the reason why. Intrigued and eager for news, Louvois urged Saint-Mars "to get [Foucquet] to write to me without, however, telling him that I asked you to talk to him about it."[35] Either Saint-Mars failed to persuade Foucquet to open up or Foucquet was vague in his replies, for, as Christmas and New Year faded into a bitter January, Louvois and Saint-Mars were still at a loss to explain the antipathy between their two most illustrious guests. Once again, Louvois pressed the jailer to see what he could find out,[36] but his curiosity was to remain unsatisfied.

What had happened to destroy the fragile harmony that had made life bearable for Foucquet and Lauzun will probably never be fully understood. Saint-Simon thought that it had to do with Foucquet's having dismissed Lauzun as a madman.[37] According to the memoirist, Lauzun had been deeply offended by his companion's belief that the stories he had told about his life at court were exaggerations, if not downright lies. This certainly was the case, but timing alone would preclude this as an explanation for their sudden enmity. Instead, Lauzun's former fiancée, Mademoiselle, was almost certainly correct when she attributed it to what she called "*des galanteries*"—an intrigue or a love affair, with the object of Lauzun's affections being none other than Foucquet's daughter, Marie-Madeleine.[38] This lady, in the full bloom of youth and beauty, who had moved into cramped lodgings at the fortress in order to take care of her father, had proved too much of a temptation for the man who had been deprived of feminine company for so many years.

At forty-six, Lauzun was no longer a young man by the standards of the day, but he was filled with a renewed energy. He began to take an interest in his appearance, and where he had once refused to shave or look after himself, he was now well-groomed and immaculately turned out. He even asked for new silver buttons for his doublet.[39] He requested, and received, permission to exercise four of the young horses belonging to Saint-Mars's stables. As she walked in the precincts of the citadel with her father, Marie-Madeleine would be treated to the spectacle of this gallant as he rode in the courtyard of the citadel and the bastion for several hours each day.[40]

Marie-Madeleine, Foucquet, and Lauzun would eat together, served by Eustache and La Rivière, and when Lauzun returned to his rooms each evening, he would slip through the hole he had made by the chimney each night and pay court to the fair Mademoiselle Foucquet. Foucquet, constantly unwell by now, did not at first notice the antics of this insolent man. When he did, he was deeply upset and insulted by such blatant disrespect. From that point on he refused to allow Lauzun to visit his apartment or to walk with him in the citadel grounds. As to the hole by the chimney, it was neglected and then forgotten. Saint-Mars and Louvois puzzled over the acrimony that now existed between the two prisoners, at a loss to explain what might have happened.

Of course, the families of Foucquet and Lauzun remained unaware of this unhappy turn of events. For them, the king's softening attitude toward the imprisonment of their loved ones led them to hope that the next step would be freedom, that Louis would show clemency and release his prisoners, who had suffered too long under such harsh conditions. Fate, however, was not to be so kind, and what happened next would destroy the cherished hopes of one of these unlucky families.

EIGHT

La Tour d'en bas

Everything changed on March 11, 1680. Louvois's secret informer at Pignerol had discovered that Foucquet and Lauzun had been communicating without Saint-Mars's knowledge, and therefore without his permission or supervision, and he reported this fact to his master. The minister immediately sent orders to Saint-Mars to look into the matter. Louvois was anxious to know if the report had any substance, and if so, Saint-Mars was to let him know what he discovered.[1]

Saint-Mars, who was angry at the thought of having been taken for a fool by his two highest-ranking prisoners, men he thought he could trust, set about his investigation, determined to show he was no dupe. Overturning furniture, pulling up mats and carpets, and tearing down tapestries, he searched Foucquet's apartment and Lauzun's rooms. No corner was left undisturbed until, at last, he came to the chimney. Surely no one could dig in there, not with all the soot, the ashes, and the heat of the fire, but then he discovered the hole that Lauzun had made.

He confronted his prisoners, demanding an explanation. Lauzun's reaction is unrecorded, but for Foucquet, the consequences of such a turn of events were devastating. He had reached the point where he could reasonably have nurtured the hope that Louis might at least be contemplating allowing him to go free; in the face of Saint-Mars's discovery, he must have realized that such a longed-for dream must now be out of the question. Already in ill health, it is believed by some that the shock of this confrontation and the realization of what it must mean hastened Foucquet's death.[2] The ex-superintendent went into a rapid decline, and he died on March 23.

So it was that on a spring day in early April 1680 that Madame de Sévigné wrote to her daughter to make an unhappy announcement: "My dear child, the poor M. Foucquet is dead, I am touched."[3] These pithy, unemotional, and somewhat distant words of the lady who had once been one of Foucquet's closest friends, and who had recorded the events of his trial in a series of deeply emotional letters, are in marked contrast to the flurry of activity that now took place in faraway Pignerol.

Within the shadowy confines of the donjon, much was going on. Foucquet's son, the vicomte de Vaux, had returned some time earlier, and now he and Mlle Foucquet moved unchecked and unsupervised in and out of their late father's apartments. More seriously, they sorted through and removed some of his effects.

Saint-Mars, meanwhile, made arrangements for his deceased prisoner to be laid to rest in the Church of Saint Clare. This was to be only a temporary measure, for the vicomte de Vaux had written to Louvois on behalf of his mother to request the king's permission to remove her husband's earthly remains from Pignerol. Louvois assured him that Mme Foucquet would have no difficulty in doing so; indeed, Louis had already issued the necessary orders.[4]

Saint-Mars had also taken up his quill and, in a letter dated March 23, had informed Louis and Louvois of the death of Nicolas Foucquet. This letter no longer survives, but its contents can be constructed from the reply Louvois sent several days later.[5] It must have been with some trepidation that Saint-Mars confirmed that the minister's informant had been correct and that a hole had indeed been carved out in the chimney that had granted Lauzun access to Foucquet and facilitated their clandestine nighttime conversations.

This was bad enough, but it was not the worst of it. The jailer adjudged "that Monsieur de Lauzun knows most of the important things that M. Foucquet knew and that the man named La Rivière is not unaware of them." There is one name missing here: that of Eustache. The "important things" spoken of by Saint-Mars comprised Eustache's secret: something Foucquet had already known, or that he had come to learn from Eustache, a secret he may have been made to swear to keep when Eustache was first appointed to serve him as a valet. Now, as a result of his visits, it was assumed that Lauzun had also become privy to the secret, while La Rivière, who shared his master's living space, could not have avoided hearing it mentioned in conversation.

Louvois relayed Louis's order that the hole in the chimney should be so well sealed that anyone subsequently working in the spot would never know that it had ever existed. Likewise, the staircase leading to the rooms used by Mademoiselle Foucquet was to be dismantled.

Lauzun, Louis decreed, must be moved into Foucquet's old apartment on the floor above his own. This was more secure, and he would be subject to even stricter surveillance than before. Saint-Mars was required to make frequent visits to Lauzun, to search his rooms even to the point of shifting all the furniture in order to make sure this devious man was not doing anything he should not. Most importantly, Lauzun was to be persuaded "that the men named Eustache d'Angers and the said La Rivière had been set free." Saint-Mars was expected to repeat this story to anyone who might inquire after the two men.

In reality, Eustache, a prisoner who had served as a valet, and La Rivière, who had never been a prisoner but had been employed as a valet, were ordered to be shut up together in one chamber. Their imprisonment was to be strict: Saint-Mars had to take care that they could have no communication with anyone, either by word of mouth or in writing. He also had to ensure that Lauzun would never be able to find out that they were still at Pignerol; it was vital that he should believe that Eustache really had been nothing more than a valet employed to look after Foucquet and that anything he might have heard to the contrary was pure fantasy.[6]

The furniture in Foucquet's apartment officially belonged to the king; purchased for the use of a man of Foucquet's rank, it was of good quality and was certainly not cheap. Now Louis simply told Saint-Mars to dispose of it as he saw fit. What became of the various pieces is not known, but it is probable that the wily jailer sold them for a reasonable price and pocketed the proceeds. He regarded it as one of the perks of his job to skim off a percentage of the money that was sent to him for the purchase of food, clothing, and whatever furnishings were deemed appropriate for each of his prisoners. In this way, he boosted his already considerable income. No sum was too small, and even the low-ranking prisoners, who were allocated 4 livres each day for their maintenance, would inadvertently make their own contribution to Saint-Mars's revenues.

Louvois noted that the chevalier de Lauzun had been granted permission to visit his brother once again. This was to be a longer visit this time, but Saint-Mars was warned to ensure that the chevalier passed no weapons to his brother, or any implements that could be used as tools in an escape attempt.

The chevalier had also been given permission to eat in his brother's apartment, but Saint-Mars was required to instruct him on how he was expected to behave before he would be allowed inside. Specifically, there was a strict timetable to which the chevalier must adhere. He could enter Lauzun's apartment at eight in the morning on condition that he left at eleven. He could then return at two in the afternoon and remain until six in the evening during winter, or seven in summer. Such a rigid timetable could not have been comforting to Lauzun, who must have despaired at the thought of his imprisonment continuing for several months at the least. The brothers could walk together outside if they wanted to, as long as they remained within the view of Saint-Mars. If he wished, Saint-Mars could accompany them, a safety precaution to discourage Lauzun from attempting to slip away. Louis and Louvois also suggested that, while Lauzun and the chevalier were out walking, Saint-Mars should take the opportunity to search his prisoner's apartment to ensure that there were no concealed weapons or tools. Quite how Saint-Mars was expected to do this while he was also walking the courtyard and ramparts of the donjon the king and his minister did not elaborate; fortunately, Saint-Mars could rely on the assistance of his lieutenants.

Lastly, Louvois cautioned Saint-Mars not to enter into any discourse or confidence with Lauzun regarding what he might have learned during his conversations with the late Foucquet, adding the warning: "The more pliant and obliging he is to you, the more care you must take to guard him, because no man in the world in more capable of dissimulation than he."

For a time, despite the king's orders to the contrary, Lauzun continued to live in his own apartment, on the second floor below the rooms that had been occupied by Foucquet. Now a new directive arrived, reiterating the previous order that the prisoner must be moved, but there was a problem. The defiant Lauzun stubbornly insisted that he wanted to remain where he was. This surprised Saint-Mars, who noted that Lauzun's apartments were damp. He asked Louvois for more men for his compagnie-franche to help him guard his most difficult prisoner. Louvois replied that Louis felt that there were already enough personnel to cope with Lauzun.[7]

A month came and went and Lauzun still proved reluctant to move into Foucquet's old apartment. By way of compromise, he asked if he could have Mlle Foucquet's old rooms instead, a request that was emphatically denied. Perhaps Lauzun feared that Foucquet's old rooms were too secure and that he would never be able to mount another escape attempt. Whether or not this was the case, Saint-Mars had to force him to vacate the rooms he had occupied for more than eight years and move upstairs. As compensation, he was allowed to choose which of the rooms he would use for his bedroom. However, within weeks, Saint-Mars requested permission to change Lauzun's valet.[8] As he had done before, it is probable that Lauzun had won over his servant, and now Saint-Mars worried that the two might be plotting another escape. He received permission to withdraw the valet, who was to be made to understand that, should he ever approach within ten leagues of Pignerol, he would immediately be arrested and sent to the galleys.[9]

Saint-Mars's problems were far from over. It was well known that Foucquet had passed some of his time writing. He had produced many poems and works of devotion, and had translated passages of the Bible, particularly Psalm 118.[10] Louvois made reference to these writings, many of which, so Saint-Mars had told him, had been taken away by the vicomte de Vaux. Louvois soundly rebuked the jailer for having allowed this to happen, and ordered the papers to be confiscated and the young man to be locked up inside an apartment within the donjon.[11] Saint-Mars obeyed, but as he cleared away the late prisoner's remaining effects, he discovered some more papers hidden inside one of the dead man's pockets. Perhaps fearing another reprimand, he hesitated to inform Louvois of this latest discovery but, in the end, he had no choice. Louvois duly told him to send the papers in a packet to the king, along with those he had removed from Vaux.[12] Saint-Mars sent only one sheet of paper and had to be reminded to send the rest a few days later.[13]

By the third week in June, with the papers found in Foucquet's pocket still not forthcoming, Louvois once more asked Saint-Mars to send the documents to him: "As regards the loose sheet, which accompanied your letter of the 8th, you were wrong not to inform me of its contents from the first day that you knew of it. Moreover, I pray you to send, in a packet, what you have found in the pockets of monsieur Foucquet, so that I can present it to His Majesty."[14]

What Saint-Mars found in Foucquet's pocket and what might have been written on the loose sheet must remain a mystery. As has been seen, Foucquet was adept in making invisible ink, so Louis might have feared that his former minister had written secret messages on the paper. Yet, surely after the many years he had been in prison—four years during his interrogations and trial and a further fifteen at Pignerol—whatever secrets Foucquet knew were no longer of any worth. Perhaps Louis and Louvois feared that any message left by Foucquet, whether or not it was written in invisible ink, might have concerned Eustache.[15] As tempting as it is to speculate, there is simply no way of knowing what was written on the loose sheet Saint-Mars found in Foucquet's pockets, but from what is known about Foucquet's character as an honest and loyal servant to Louis, and the innocent and devout nature of his prison writings, it would be surprising indeed if he left anything that would be detrimental to the service of the king.

On July 10, 1680, Louvois wrote to Saint-Mars concerning "the prisoners in the lower part of the tower"[16] who were to be allowed to confess once a year. Matthioli was also mentioned under his prison name of Lestang. He was clearly still very ill, but Louvois had little sympathy. Indeed, he wondered at Saint-Mars's patience "and that you should wait for an order to treat such a rascal as he deserves, when he is wanting in respect to you."

This letter, as with the others he sent to Saint-Mars, was actually written by a secretary at Louvois's dictation. Once complete, it was handed back to Louvois, who would sign it in the usual way before sealing it and handing it to his courier. On this occasion, however, the minister wrote one final paragraph in his own hand: "Send me word how it has happened that the individual named Eustache has been able to do what you have sent me word of, and where he got the drugs necessary for the purpose, as I cannot think you would have furnished them to him."

This mysterious passage has been taken to indicate that Eustache had poisoned Foucquet.[17] This theory is informed by inconsistencies surrounding the reports of the death. Specifically, there appears to have been some disagreement about the cause of death. Memoirist Bussy-Rabutin stated that Foucquet had died of apoplexy,[18] an opinion that is supported by the official account as published in the *Gazette*.[19] Mme de Sévigné, on the other hand, wrote that "there would be much to say" about Foucquet's final illness, the symptoms of which she described as "convulsions and sickness without being able to vomit."[20] Even though she did not say so openly, she certainly appears to be speculating that the cause of death might have been poisoning.

This is hardly surprising. The fear of poison was ever present. Many years previously, as Foucquet was making his way to Pignerol, some of his friends expressed fears that he might be poisoned; indeed, the news that he had taken ill on the journey provoked cries of "What, already?"[21] The physician Gui Patin believed that this had, in fact, been Louis's prime motive in choosing the fortress at Pignerol as Foucquet's jail; "When we are between four walls," he wrote, "we cannot eat what we want, and sometimes we eat more than we want." He noted that the countryside surrounding Pignerol produced truffles and mushrooms, which, when mixed into sauces could be "dangerous to our Frenchmen, when they are prepared by Italians."[22]

More recently, a consignment of tea was sent to Foucquet, but before it was given to him, Saint-Mars was required to decant the contents of the box into another container to ensure that the prisoner received only tea and nothing else.[23] No doubt Louvois was more concerned that a weapon might have been hidden among the tea leaves, but there was always the fear that the tea itself might have been laced with poison. Saint-Mars, whose considerable experience as a jailer had taught him not to be surprised at anything, would have been alive to this possibility since one of his earlier prisoners, Plassot, was discovered to have had a supply of poisons among his belongings upon being released in July 1673.[24]

Patin was right to imply that no precaution would afford complete protection to a prisoner if someone were determined to murder him, but who would want to kill Foucquet and why? A clue might be found in a letter written by Bussy-Rabutin to a friend: "You know, I think, about the death from apoplexy of M. Foucquet at the time he had permission to go to the waters at Bourbon. This permission has come too late; bad fortune has advanced his years."[25] That Bussy-Rabutin thought that Foucquet was to be allowed to take the healing water treatments at Bourbon was as remarkable as it was unexpected, for it would almost certainly have marked the first steps of the former superintendent's journey to freedom.

Bussy-Rabutin, however, was not the first to speculate upon Foucquet's imminent release; rumors of it had circulated for some time, most notably when Lauzun was arrested in 1671. Many had thought that Lauzun's ruin would have occasioned Foucquet's recall, even though the two events had no connection whatsoever.[26] Although the rumor mill had quieted since that time, it had been given a new lease of life in recent days. The ever-vigilant Bussy-Rabutin noted in a letter dated March 4, 1680, that he had heard that someone had been sent to fetch Foucquet out of prison.[27] Five days later, he wrote of a strong rumor that insisted that Foucquet was to leave Pignerol and return to Paris, much to the excitement of his friends, who longed to see him set free and returned to them. In the event, one of the Foucquet brothers did return from Pignerol; it was not Nicolas, but the bishop of Agde, who had received permission to attend the reading of the will of another brother, Basile, who had died some weeks earlier.[28] At that point, Nicolas Foucquet remained in his apartment at Pignerol attended by his two valets, La Rivière and Eustache.

On the other hand, there were those for whom the return of Foucquet could spell disaster, and for this reason some have speculated that Foucquet was murdered in order to ensure that such an eventuality could never come to pass. Foucquet was once described as "the most vigorous actor at court" by a former colleague, Guillaume de Lamoignon, first president of the Parlement of Paris.[29] According to Maurice Duvivier,[30] Foucquet was murdered by Eustache, who had been persuaded to poison his master by either Colbert or Lauzun, both of whom had promised him freedom as his reward.

Colbert's motive was clear. Not only had he taken over Foucquet's office as superintendent of finances, albeit under a different title, he had also been influential in bringing about his downfall. He, more than anyone, had much to gain by preventing Foucquet's return; he therefore persuaded Eustache to poison Foucquet. Yet, it has to be asked, how could Colbert have communicated with Eustache, who had no means of corresponding with anyone? Moreover, there is nothing to suggest that he knew who Eustache was, let alone where he was. While Eustache's name is given in the letter that had been sent to Saint-Mars in July 1669 to warn him to expect a new prisoner, it is omitted from the register of Ministry for War.[31] Whether this was a bureaucratic oversight or an attempt to conceal what had become of him is a matter for conjecture.

As to Lauzun, he and Foucquet had fallen out shortly before the latter's death. In this scenario, Lauzun would have asked Eustache to murder the only man to have treated him with kindness and civility, and in whose service he had found relief from the harsh and lonely conditions to which he had been subjected for several years. In favor of this theory, Lauzun would have been able to gain access to Eustache had he so wished, so it is not impossible that the two could have conspired to poison Foucquet. Lauzun, however, was in no position to promise Eustache his freedom or anything else, and Eustache would surely have known that. He was, after all, an exemplary prisoner, who lived "like a man entirely resigned to the will of God and the King."[32]

To Duvivier's short list of suspects might be added Louvois. As the son of Michel Le Tellier, another of Foucquet's implacable enemies who had worked alongside Colbert to bring him down, he might not have welcomed the prospect of the former superintendent's recall. Although relations between Foucquet and Louvois had become relatively genial of late, this apparent cordiality was nevertheless subject to a significant imbalance of power between the two men. While Louvois was the master, he could afford to be friendly, while Foucquet, as the prisoner, was in no position to antagonize the man who held jurisdiction over the prisons of France and who worked so closely with the king. Should Foucquet be pardoned and recalled, this balance might well shift markedly in Foucquet's favor, and the former superintendent just might decide to take out his anger on the son of one of the men responsible for his ruin and lengthy incarceration. Although Louvois obviously knew who Eustache was and where he was, again it must be asked how he could have communicated the order to poison Foucquet to Eustache without Saint-Mars finding out about it and intervening to save his prisoner's life.

Another theory, this one put forward by Marcel Pagnol, suggests that Saint-Mars had administered the poison on the direct orders of Louis XIV, although he offers no motive for the crime. Pagnol points out that Saint-Mars would have had no need to go out and procure the poison; he had found some in the belongings of Plassot several years earlier and, rather than disposing of it, he had kept it.[33] In Pagnol's view, Eustache and La Rivière were secretly imprisoned together in the Lower Tower to ensure their silence, for they knew that Foucquet had been poisoned. Saint-Mars had once spoken of a place where mutes would talk after having been there for a month;[34] that same place could equally serve to keep silent those who should not speak.

In fact, Foucquet had posed no threat to anyone, least of all Louis XIV. The king had authorized the gradual alleviation of his imprisonment in a slow but steady course that must have allowed his friends and family to hope that he would soon be released. Should such an event occur, it is highly unlikely that Foucquet would have returned to court; Louis, after all, still believed him to have been guilty not only of mishandling the finances, but also of high treason. Had Foucquet left prison, it would have been so that he could live quietly as a private person, and his liberation would have been an act of compassion on the part of the king to an old man who was broken in every way.

Foucquet had been unwell for quite some time. In his first surviving letter to his wife, dated February 1675, he gave a list of his ailments: problems with digestion, with his liver, swelling and inflammation in his legs, sciatica, colic, and stones. He was seriously ill in July 1677 and again in August of the following year, when he was allowed to consult Vézou, who had formerly attended Mazarin. More recently, in December 1679, Foucquet wrote asking permission to leave Pignerol and withdraw to a place where he could take care of himself. This request, as he must have anticipated, was denied.[35] A short while later, he wrote directly to Louvois to ask to be allowed to have a change of air for health reasons.

Louvois replied that he had put the request to Louis, but that the king had not yet responded.[36] Two months later, Louvois sent some packets of remedies to Foucquet. The prisoner also required the services of a surgeon, who would apply the standard remedy of the day, bleeding, and who would receive 320 livres for his services.

Moreover, Foucquet's condition had worsened over the last few weeks of his life, exacerbated by depression. He was unhappy about his quarrel with Lauzun. Salvert, Mme Foucquet's homme d'affaires, was doing the work that Foucquet ought to have been doing for his family. Lauzun's behavior toward Mademoiselle Foucquet was an insult to the former superintendent and his family. Then there was the death, in January 1680, of his brother, Basile. The two had once been very close, but had become enemies prior to Nicolas's arrest, with Basile siding with those who wished to do his brother harm. Basile had not accompanied the rest of the family to Pignerol, but the two had exchanged letters. In the end no real reconciliation was reached, and therefore no closure to the bitterness that had tainted their relationship had been achieved.

Foucquet died at a time when Paris and the court were gripped by a series of scandals that came to be known as the Affair of the Poisons. It is little wonder, then, that Mme de Sévigné should have been influenced by events going on around her. Certainly, there were discrepancies in reports of Foucquet's death, but these can easily be accounted for by unawareness of the true facts, guesswork, and the influence of ongoing events closer to home.

Several sources attest to the death of Nicolas Foucquet on March 23, 1680: Madame de Sévigné's letter to her daughter; Bussy-Rabutin's letter to a friend; the official account published in the April 6, 1680, issue of the *Gazette*; as well as the correspondence between the vicomte de Vaux and Louvois. No one at the time suggested that Foucquet had died of poisoning, or indeed that he had been murdered. In fact, Foucquet's decline can be tracked in documents that passed between Saint-Mars and Louvois. Following Foucquet's seizure, Lauzun had gone to his room where he asked for, and received, the dying man's forgiveness for the wrongs he had done him. A rumor circulated that Foucquet had died in his son's arms. Since young vicomte de Vaux was present at Pignerol at the time, as was his sister, this is entirely possible.[37]

What, then, were the drugs found in Eustache's possession? There are several possible explanations, none of which include murder. The drugs may have comprised the ingredients of sympathetic ink or indeed the finished product, which Foucquet was known to have made and some of which he might have given to Eustache or were perhaps stolen by him. It is not impossible that Foucquet taught his valets to make this ink, although it is difficult to imagine that so sensible a man would do something so irresponsible.

More probably, the drugs were a compound or tincture manufactured for medicinal use. The word can refer to a remedy prepared by an amateur or charlatan, that is to say quack medicine, such as Eustache might have made.[38] It could also have been a medicine made for Eustache by Foucquet, who was considerably more knowledgeable about pharmacy than was Eustache. He was known to have made medicines in prison, such as Queen of Hungary water, bitter chicory water, and syrup of peach flowers.[39] It is known that Eustache had been ill. On September 13, 1679, for example, Louvois asked for news of his health.[40] It is conceivable that Foucquet provided him with medicines and nursed him through his illness, as he had previously done with his valet Champagne.

Eustache was imprisoned in the Lower Tower weeks before the drugs were found in his possession. His imprisonment, therefore, did not increase in severity because it was thought he had poisoned his master; he was simply being returned to his cell now that he was no longer required to serve as a valet. For La Rivière, the situation was entirely different. Under normal circumstances, a man who had been employed as a valet, even if he had served a state prisoner, would have been retained for several weeks or months before being set free, his accumulated wages in his pocket, to continue his life as he chose. The detention was a simple but effective security precaution, devised so that any news or information his master might have passed to him would be old or useless by the time he returned to the world. Unfortunately for La Rivière, the circumstances were anything but normal. Not only was he suspected by Louis and Louvois of having learned Eustache's secret, but he was also aware of the secret hole in the chimney through which Foucquet and Lauzun had communicated and had failed in his duty to reveal it to Saint-Mars. Under these circumstances, his imprisonment would have been justified, and he was sent to the Lower Tower alongside Eustache. From this point onward, Eustache and La Rivière lost not only their freedom, but also their identities. Their names would no longer appear in the official correspondence.

Louis XIV as a young man. The king was thirty-one years old when he ordered the arrest of his famous prisoner. *Photo: Wikimedia Commons.*

François Michel Le Tellier, marquis de Louvois, minister for war. He oversaw every detail of the daily life of the prisoners under his jurisdiction. *Photo: Wikimedia Commons.*

Bénigne Dauvergne de Saint-Mars was initially the only one to have direct contact with Eustache.

ABOVE: Nicolas Foucquet, Saint-Mars's first prisoner at Pignerol. Foucquet would play a major part in the story of the mysterious prisoner. *Photo: Wikimedia Commons.* BELOW: Antonin Nompar de Caumont, comte de Lauzun. It was vital that he had no contact with Eustache whatsoever, a directive that would be invalidated by Lauzun's own activity. *Photo: Wikimedia Commons.*

Lettre de cachet sent to Captain de Vauroy. The letter gives the prisoner's name as Eustache Dauger, but the *u* in Dauger could be a badly formed *n*. Compare this with the *n* in *Captain* two lines above and *Pignerol* three lines below.

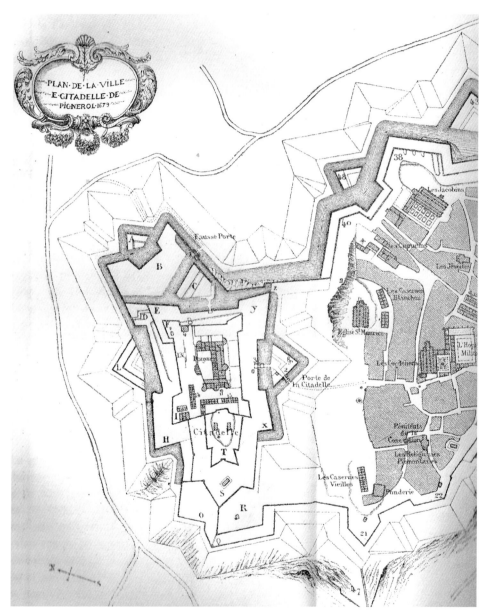

The citadel of Pignerol and part of the town.

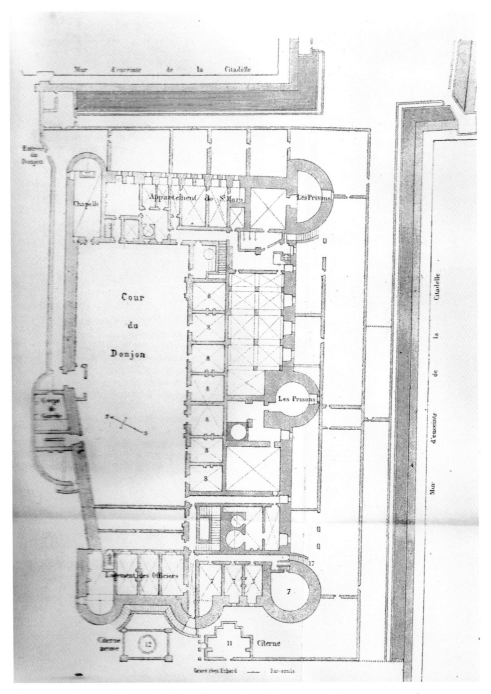

Plan of the donjon of Pignerol. Angle Tower, where Foucquet and Lauzun occupied apartments, is the *D*-shaped structure in the northeastern corner of the donjon. The Lower Tower, where Eustache's cell was, is in the tower below that, in the center of the eastern curtain wall. Saint-Mars's apartments run along the north wall, and the chapel of Saint-George is in the northwest corner.

LEFT: Dramatic image of Pignerol being struck by lightning. BELOW: Letter dated July 10, 1680, showing Louvois's handwriting at the foot. He asks Saint-Mars to "send me word how it has happened that the individual named Eustache has been able to do what you have sent me word of, and where he got the drugs necessary for the purpose, as I cannot think you would have furnished them to him."

LETTRE DE LOUVOIS À SAINT-MÂRS DU 10 JUILLET 1680.

Archives nationales, K 120 A, Cartons des Rois, n° 313.

The Château d'Exilles. The Tour Grosse can be seen on the right behind
the smaller tower. Here, Eustache shared a cell with La Rivière.

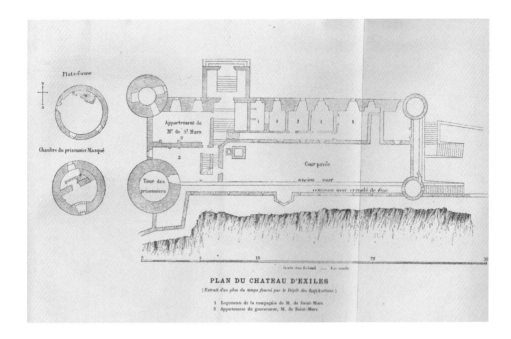

PLAN DU CHATEAU D'EXILES
{ Extrait d'un plan du temps fourni par le Dépôt des fortifications. }

1 Logements de la compagnie de M. de Saint-Mars
2 Appartement du gouverneur, M. de Saint-Mars.

ABOVE: Floor plan of the Château d'Exilles. The Tour Grosse is the larger of the two towers situated on the southwest corner. Saint-Mars's apartment is situated on the northwest corner. BELOW: The prison buildings on the Île Sainte-Marguerite.

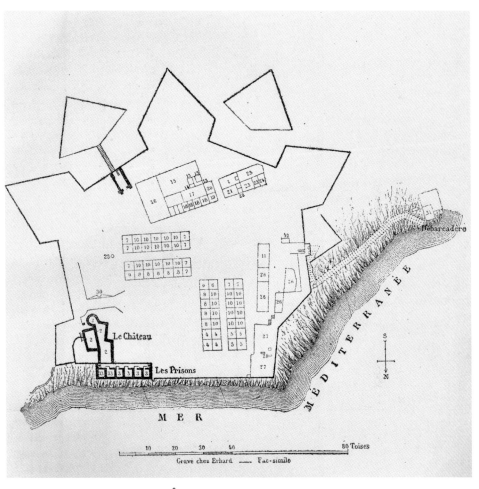

Floor plan of the buildings on the Île Sainte-Marguerite. The cell occupied by Eustache is on the left-hand side of the block overlooking the sea. Saint-Mars's apartments run above at right angles to the prison block.

Ste-Marguerite Island. – "Dungeon of the Iron Mask".

ABOVE: The inside of the cell showing the barred windows. In fact, there is evidence that the cell walls were more highly decorated than this. BELOW: The Bastille, Paris, the fourth and final prison in which Eustache was held.

Du mesme Jour lundy -19- me de
nouembre 1703 — le prisonnier
Jncoñeu touiours masque d'un masque
de uelours noir que monsieur de
St mars gouuerneur a mene auec
que luy en uenant des illes St margueritte
quil gardet depuis Contamps lequel
setant trouue hier un peu mal en
sortant dela messe il est mort —
se Jourduy sur les dix heures du
soir sans auoir eu unne grende
maladie il neseput pas moins
en girant nottre homonier le
comfessa hier soir puis desamort
il napoint reseu les sacremens
et nottre homonier la exorte un
momant auend que de mourir
et seprisonnier Jncoñeu garde de
puis silontamps aeste enteve
le mardy a quattre heures dela
pres midy -20- me nouembre dans
le semetiere St paul nottre pa

Je apris du voisse ou sur le registre mortuel
depuis contant on adonne un nom ausy Jnconu
nome sur le registre que monsieur derosarges maior
mr de mareffiel et ur veil hieurgien qui sont
que on apaie et
40 ht dante
venant signe sur le registre

Page from Du Junca's register describing the death and burial of the
prisoner. Note the reference to the velvet mask in lines 3–4.

ABOVE: Romantic image of the Man in the Iron Mask being attended by Saint-Mars. BELOW: Romantic image of the Man in the Iron Mask with a musketeer standing guard.

Romantic image of the Man in the Iron Mask, shown here
with a ball and chain attached to his ankle.

Liebig card showing the Man in the Iron Mask being handed a book by Saint-Mars. Another man, possibly Jacques Rosarges, stands in the background with more books for the prisoner.

NINE

Exilles

Saint-Mars had come to Pignerol in January 1665 with the specific purpose of guarding one prisoner, Nicolas Foucquet. Since that time, he had taken in several others, some of whom left after a short time, and others who were still under his care. Following Foucquet's death on March 23, 1680, Saint-Mars was left with seven prisoners. In order of their entry into Pignerol, they were Eustache, who was described by Louvois as a valet and a "wretch," and who had later been allowed to serve Foucquet in prison. Butticari, a spy working for the duc de Savoie, who was freed on Louis's orders on August 11, 1675, but rearrested four years later. He was released before December 1680. Lafleur, about whom almost nothing is known, was possibly a soldier attached to the Pignerol garrison who had been arrested on a minor charge. Imprisoned in November 1678, he, too, was free by December 1680.

Lauzun was one of Louis XIV's favored courtiers, and the official reasons for his imprisonment remain a mystery. He had been moved to more secure accommodation higher in the Angle Tower. Lapierre the Jacobin was kept under such terrible conditions that he had gone insane. Dubreuil had also gone insane as a result of the harsh treatment to which he was subjected. Lastly, there was Matthioli, referred to in official correspondence as Lestang, who shared a chamber with his valet, Rousseau. There was now a secret eighth man, however, La Rivière, who had lost his freedom because he was believed to have learned something he should not know and because he failed to report a major breach of security caused when Lauzun made a hole in the chimney.

For a time, life carried on as normal behind the cold stone walls of the citadel. That summer, the comtesse de Nogent came to see her brother, Lauzun. Saint-Mars was required to observe the same precautions as he had done when the chevalier de Lauzun had visited. He was also asked to report anything that passed between brother and sister that might be of interest to the king.[1]

During the long, weary years that Lauzun had been a prisoner, one person continued to hold a special place for him in her heart: his former fiancée, la Grande Mademoiselle. She had never stopped campaigning for his release. At every opportunity, she would appeal to Louis, but her pleading availed her nothing. Now, it looked as though her dearest wish was about to be granted.

Years earlier, on March 31, 1670, to be precise, Lauzun had waited in a darkened corridor while Mme de Montespan gave birth to her first child with the king. Taking the baby, a boy, in his arms, he carried him to Mme Scarron, who looked after the king's brood of illegitimate children. Louis loved all his children, but this child, now the duc du Maine, ten years old, with the face of an angel and endowed with the razor-sharp wit of his mother, was his favorite. Although the king had legitimized him, he wanted to shower him with yet more marks of favor, but there was a limit to what he could do for a child born out of wedlock.[2] He turned to someone who was in a position to help, a lady whose wealth was immense and who had no child of her own to inherit it: his cousin, la Grande Mademoiselle. Mme de Montespan, encouraged by Louis, began to flatter her.

"Think of what you might do that would be agreeable to the King," said Mme de Montespan, "that he may grant you that which you have so much to heart."[3] Just in case Mademoiselle failed to take the hint, the point was pressed more firmly by a gentleman named Pertuis, a great friend to Lauzun, who nudged her: "If you could only lead them to hope that you would give your wealth to M. du Maine!"[4]

Of course, what Mademoiselle had so much to heart was Lauzun's freedom, but now she knew that the price for this would be to hand over a substantial portion of her estates and the titles and revenues that went with them, as well as a generous cash endowment; all this she would relinquish in favor of the duc du Maine.

As it was, Mademoiselle was very fond of children, and she liked to spend time with Louis's sons and daughters. A childhood illness had left the duc de Maine crippled in one leg, and his condition had been made worse by the attentions of a Dutch doctor who had boasted that he could straighten out the limb. Madame Scarron would often take the child to Barèges to take its curative waters, from where the little duc would write charming letters to Mademoiselle.

Despite her love for the boy, Mademoiselle was understandably reluctant to hand over so much of her property. It took several months of persuasion, and always the promise of Lauzun's freedom was dangled before her as a reward. In the end, she knew she had no choice but to comply with Madame de Montespan's wishes. On February 2, 1681, in a special ceremony, Mademoiselle signed away the sovereignty of Dombes and the earldom of Eu, the combined income of which amounted to 50,000 écus. The signature was witnessed by the king's minister Colbert, Lauzun's friend Barail, and Mme de Montespan, who held the king's power of attorney for the occasion.

Everyone praised Mademoiselle's actions and tried to convince her that she had done the right thing, but she was not so sure. Returning to her chamber after the ceremony, she accidentally dropped her looking glass, which was made of thick rock crystal: "I am terrified," she said; "perhaps it is an omen, and I shall repent of what I have done."[5]

Louis expressed his pleasure at the outcome of the transaction, as well he might, but Mademoiselle's desire to secure the release of Lauzun showed no sign of being granted. Several weeks were to pass, during which she fell from hope to despair. All the time, Mme de Montespan assured her that she was doing everything possible to help Lauzun, until one day she invited Mademoiselle to take a promenade with her, saying she had something to tell her. Mademoiselle did not want to go and ignored more than one summons, but in the end she gave in to the royal mistress's demands and agreed to see her.

"You have not been in haste," chided Mme de Montespan when the two ladies met in the garden. "The King has desired me tell you that he will allow M. de Lauzun to leave Pignerol, to go to Bourbon." Mademoiselle felt cheated; she wanted Lauzun to come to her, not to go to Bourbon, so many miles away. Worse was that Lauzun would still be a prisoner. "The King leaves the choice to you to select whom you please to guard him," continued Mme de Montespan, adding that Louis "wished it still to have the appearance of an imprisonment."[6]

This was bad enough, but there was worse to come. Later, as the two ladies walked together in the garden of Saint-German, Mme de Montespan turned to Mademoiselle and said: "The King has told me to inform you that he does not wish you to think of marrying M. de Lauzun." Mademoiselle was devastated. The tears began to flow. She had been led to believe that she would at last be allowed to marry Lauzun, and she told Mme de Montespan so. The royal favorite merely told her coldly, "I have promised you nothing."[7] All Mademoiselle would receive in return for her sacrifice was Lauzun's release from Pignerol.

For Saint-Mars, this eventuality could not come quickly enough. In the autumn of 1680, Lauzun, never the easiest of prisoners to guard, had become even more difficult, his behavior surely forgivable in a man who had been subject to the harshest imprisonment without trial and without understanding what he had done to deserve it. He had taken to abusing Blainvilliers and Villebois, both lieutenants in Saint-Mars's compagnie-franche. In reality, there was little Saint-Mars could do except point out to Lauzun that his men were not at Pignerol to be ill-treated by him and that, should he persist in this abuse, Saint-Mars would be obliged to lock him inside his room because these men no longer wished to accompany him on his walks in the citadel and he could not entrust the job to anyone else.[8] Nevertheless, attempts had been made to placate Lauzun. He had enjoyed the visit from his sister. On one occasion he asked to see Père des Escures, the superior of the Jesuits of Pignerol. This request was granted, and he and the priest were allowed to converse as and when they wished for as long as they wished providing the usual security precautions were applied.[9]

Lauzun also received a visit from his friend Barail, who had come on the pretext that Lauzun had injured his arm. Barail brought a surgeon with him in order to maintain the pretense. In fact, he had secretly been tasked to prepare Lauzun for his imminent release. During the negotiations that had taken place between Mademoiselle and Mme de Montespan, it emerged that Mademoiselle had sold her earldom of Eu to Lauzun, and now, with thoughts of freedom being too tempting to resist, he announced that he was willing to discuss terms by which the earldom would pass to the young duc du Maine. Louis, satisfied with how things had turned out, issued orders on April 22, 1681, for Lauzun to be taken to Bourbon. Mademoiselle had selected Maupertuis, who had formed part of Lauzun's escort on the journey to Pignerol almost ten years earlier, to lead him on to the next stage of his captivity.

That September, Mme de Montespan made her way south to Bourbon, where she entered into discussions with Lauzun about the terms under which he would surrender Eu. She initially offered him lands worth 40,000 livres a year, but he wanted more. No doubt thinking about adequate compensation for his years in jail, the loss of his posts and the humiliation he had suffered as a result of his disgrace, he asked to be restored as captain of the guards, a gift from the treasury of 200,000 livres, and the back payment of the pension he had missed during his imprisonment. His aim as usual was high, but in this instance, it was to fall short of expectation. His request was never going to be granted and, in the end, he had no choice but to settle for the barony of Thiers, the estate of Saint-Fargeau, and 10,000 livres to be provided by Mademoiselle and Mme de Montespan.[10] With the business of the duc du Maine's inheritance accomplished, Lauzun's slow journey to freedom began.[11] The bright sunlit spa of Bourbon, with its clear air, healing waters, and glamorous clientele, made a sharp contrast to the brooding darkness that clung to the walls of the citadel of Pignerol.

In August 1680, Saint-Mars was granted permission to accommodate Matthioli and Lapierre together in the same cell "in order to avoid the necessity of having two almoners."[12] While Louvois's comment is sometimes taken to indicate that Matthioli was in holy orders, he simply meant that one chaplain could attend both prisoners, thereby saving Saint-Mars the time and effort of finding one for each of them.

For Matthioli and his Jacobin companion, their already harsh imprisonment had become a living hell. Both of these men were mentally ill, and Matthioli could not understand why Lapierre had been put into his cell beside him. As Saint-Mars writes, Matthioli was "four or five days in the belief that the Jacobin was a man that I had placed with him to watch his actions."[13] It is interesting to note here that Matthioli is referred to by his own name, rather than his prison name, Lestang; Lapierre, on the other hand, is now only ever referred to as "the Jacobin."

Saint-Mars continues: "Matthioli, who is almost as mad as the Jacobin, walked about with long strides, with his cloak over his nose, crying out that he was not a dupe, but that he knew more than he would say." For his part, Lapierre remained seated on his bed watching his companion "gravely, without listening to him." Matthioli was convinced that the monk had been put in his cell to spy on him, but was "one day disabused, by the Jacobin's getting down from his bed, stark naked, and setting himself to preach, without rhyme or reason, till he was tired." The sight of these two very disturbed men provided a source of amusement for Saint-Mars and his lieutenants, who watched their "maneuvers" through a hole they had bored over the door.

That autumn also saw the strange affair of the diamond ring, which Matthioli had given to Blainvilliers. The story of its changing hands in Pignerol is somewhat mysterious. As Saint-Mars explains it,[14] Matthioli gave it to the lieutenant out of fear. Matthioli, the jailer reminded Louvois, had been using violent language and writing abusive sentences on the walls of his cell with charcoal. In the face of such behavior, Blainvilliers had felt obliged to threaten him with a sound beating if he did not mend his ways. Matthioli was then joined by Lapierre, upon which, following direct orders from Saint-Mars, Blainvilliers showed Matthioli a cudgel and told him that it was the means by which unruly prisoners were rendered manageable. If Matthioli did not behave, Blainvilliers warned him, he would have no choice but to use it. Several days later, Blainvilliers was serving dinner when Matthioli held out the diamond ring to him and said, "Sir, here is a little ring which I wish to give you, and I beg you to accept of it." Blainvilliers took the ring, but made it clear that he did so only to hand it to Saint-Mars "as he was not allowed receive anything himself from the prisoners."

Saint-Mars did not know what to do with the ring; while it was not unusual for prisoners to try to bribe their guards, none of them had ever offered anything so valuable. He noted that he thought the ring must be worth fifty or sixty pistoles, and it has been speculated that it might have been the one given to Matthioli by Louis XIV as a reward for his part in the negotiations concerning Casale before his betrayal. Unsure of what to do, Saint-Mars asked Louvois for advice: "I will keep it, till it shall please you, Sir, to give me orders what to do with it."[15] Louvois's answer arrived several weeks later: "You must keep the ring, which the Sieur Matthioli has given to the Sieur de Blainvilliers," he said, "in order to restore it to him, if it should ever happen that the King ordered him to be set at liberty."[16]

As winter fell, Saint-Mars had little to exercise him. There was some concern about brambles growing in the walls of the citadel, a matter that was taken care of by Louvois, who sent the commissary, Channoy, to see to them. The minister advised Saint-Mars to wait until the spring before he uprooted the brambles, "because that will make them die more certainly, and then at the same time the mortar might be inserted into the fissures."[17]

A breach of security broke the monotony when it was discovered that a gentleman named Quadro, who had visited the donjon to explain the fortifications to one of Saint-Mars's nephews, had drawn up a plan of the donjon and passed it on to the governor of Milan. Louis was alarmed and ordered Louvois to write to Saint-Mars:[18] "As it is important for the service of His Majesty, that the Italians should never have any communication with the citadel of Pignerol, nor with the prison there. His Majesty has commanded me to let you know that he wishes you not to allow anyone to enter there, without his express order." This meant that should anyone wish to enter the donjon, they would not be allowed inside unless they carried the necessary papers issued by the king; alternatively, they would be obliged to wait until a courier carried their application for permission to enter the donjon and to return with the document bearing the king's approval.

Saint-Mars was commanded to dismiss any Piedmontese, Savoyard, or Italian soldiers and staff working at the citadel and to "get rid of them as quietly as possible, under pretext of their not serving you well." While Saint-Mars was content to comply in the matter of documentation for visitors to the donjon, he was unhappy with this order. There were three foreign servants on his staff who had served him for seven years, and he could guarantee their fidelity. He appealed to Louis to be allowed to retain them. His request was granted, but Louis was adamant that no Piedmontese, Savoyard, or Italian national should serve in the compagnie-franche.[19]

During this time, M. de Rissan, the king's lieutenant in the government of the citadel of Pignerol, was on a lengthy leave of absence due to illness. By May 1681, he was still unable to return to work and Saint-Mars was temporarily promoted to take his place. The post was well rewarded, for he was paid 6,000 livres in addition to the revenues he already received from his regular job and whatever he could make by creaming off funds assigned to subsidize his prisoners. There was a downside to this temporary promotion, however. The new posting placed Saint-Mars under the direct authority of the crabby marquis d'Herleville, and the two men did not get along. It was understandable, therefore, that when Louis offered to make this posting permanent, Saint-Mars was reluctant to accept it. In fact, reluctance was putting it mildly. Louvois wrote of the jailers "extreme repugnance," in the face of which Louis revised his offer. Instead, Saint-Mars would become governor of Exilles.

Situated on a mountaintop overlooking the splashing white waters of the Dora Riparia, the ancient fortress of Exilles was about ninety kilometers from Pignerol, deeper within the Alps and at a higher elevation. It watched over the road that led from Briançon to Turin, one of the major thoroughfares between France and the duchy of Savoy. Every bit as dark and imposing as the citadel and donjon of Pignerol, the rectangular-shaped fortress of Exilles lay along a roughly east-west axis.

Exilles had been a state prison since the 15th century. It boasted two small towers at its eastern side and two much larger ones at the west, and it was in the largest and strongest of the western towers, the *Tour Grosse*,[20] that Eustache and La Rivière were to be lodged.

Exilles was, at this date, part of the Dauphiné, the governor of which was the duc de Lesdiguières. The duke had recently died at the age of only thirty-six, upon which Louis appointed Saint-Mars to take over his post. The commission was dated May 12, 1681, and Louis required Saint-Mars to take with him only "those of the prisoners who are under your care, whom he shall think it important not to entrust to any other hands but yours."[21]

The salary that came with the governorship was less than 4,000 livres, so Louis arranged for Saint-Mars to continue to receive the 500 livres a month that he was paid at Pignerol. This gave him a salary "as considerable as those of the Governors of the great places in Flanders," that is, those who were in charge of fortresses Louis had captured during his wars, places that were vulnerable to attack.

Before he could transfer his prisoners to Exilles, suitable accommodation had to be prepared for them. Saint-Mars and the Sieur de Channoy traveled to the fortress to assess what repairs should be made in order to render it secure. During his absence from Pignerol, Saint-Mars was required to take every precaution to ensure that the prisoners he left behind met with no accident and that they could have no contact with anyone.

Louvois next asked Saint-Mars to send him a list of all the prisoners under his care, "and to write opposite each name all that you know of the reasons why they were arrested."[22] Considering his position as minister for war, surely Louvois ought to have known who was in his prisons and why. However, it is possible that he was testing Saint-Mars to see if the jailer was interrogating his prisoners, or perhaps he wanted to know if the prisoners had spoken to Saint-Mars about their crimes. Whatever the case, when it came to La Rivière and Eustache, there were special orders. "With regard to the two in the lower part of the tower, you need only designate them by this name without adding anything else." The *messieurs de la tour d'en bas* were being pushed deeper into the shadows where, so Louvois appeared to hope, they would be forgotten.

Louvois sent Saint-Mars his grants as governor of Exilles the following month, as well as further instructions for the transfer of the two prisoners. As soon as Saint-Mars judged the chamber at Exilles fit to hold them securely, he was to "send them out of the citadel of Pignerol in a litter, and conduct them there under the escort of your troop"—that is, Saint-Mars's compagnie-franche. Louvois had enclosed orders for the march, so there would be no further delay.

The minister continued: "Immediately after the departure of the aforesaid prisoners, it is His Majesty's intention that you should go to Exilles, to take possession of the government, and to make it, for the future, your residence."[23] The journey taken by the prisoners would be slow. The litter was a type of wheel-less chair carried by four men who bore the weight on their shoulders, or perhaps by beasts of burden. In this case, it was men from the compagnie-franche who had the responsibility of carrying the two prisoners through unforgiving mountain terrain in the heat of summer.

With only two prisoners to watch over, Saint-Mars's compagnie-franche was now reduced to forty-five men. Despite this, Louis still expected him to guard them "with the same exactitude you have made use of hitherto," and to send Louvois "intelligence respecting them" from time to time.[24] As to Matthioli, Saint-Mars was to take his belongings with him to Exilles so that they would be given back to him should Louis decide to set him free.[25] This letter has led many to think that Matthioli was one of the two prisoners selected to accompany Saint-Mars to Exilles. However, Saint-Mars wrote to the abbé d'Estrades to tell him about his transfer, adding: "I will have two *merles* that I have here, who have no other name than the gentlemen of the lower tower; Matthioli will remain here with two other prisoners."[26]

Upon the departure of La Rivière and Eustache, therefore, three prisoners were to remain behind at Pignerol: Lapierre the Jacobin monk, Dubreuil the spy, and Matthioli, who had been placed beside Lapierre. There was no mention of Rousseau, Matthioli's valet, but he was not a prisoner as such, only the servant of a prisoner. They were to be left in the care of the sieur de Villebois, who was promoted to governor of the citadel of Pignerol until such time as M. de Rissan or his permanent replacement should arrive. Channoy, meanwhile, was ordered to arrange for Villebois to be paid two crowns a day for the upkeep of the prisoners.[27]

The preparations for the transfer were going well. By mid-May, Saint-Mars had completed the list of repairs he wanted to make at Exilles, and Louis granted him one thousand crowns to cover the cost of the work to be done on the tower and his living quarters. Once the money arrived, the work could begin; once it was completed to Saint-Mars's satisfaction, he could transfer his prisoners, leaving the command of Pignerol to Villebois.[28]

A letter written by Louvois a month later gave details of the work Saint-Mars wanted to be done. He had proposed furnishing the tower with new doors, which he suggested should be taken from Pignerol. These were the three sets of doors he had been ordered to install in order to isolate Eustache during the early years of his imprisonment. Louvois agreed that secure doors should be installed, but felt it was unnecessary to carry them all the way from Pignerol. He told Saint-Mars to have them made at Exilles instead.[29]

Saint-Mars was keen to inform Louvois of the measures he intended to take for the security of his prisoners once they were established at Exilles.[30] "In order that they would never be seen," he wrote, "they would not be allowed to leave their chamber when they heard mass." One of his lieutenants would sleep in the chamber above theirs, while two sentinels would be stationed outside to watch "the whole round of the tower," but they would be so placed that they would not be able to see or speak to the prisoners and vice versa. These sentinels would be handpicked from the compagnie-franche.

A confessor had already been appointed, although Saint-Mars had his doubts about him. He suggested instead that he engage the curate of Exilles,

> who is a good man, and very old, whom I will forbid, on the part of
> His Majesty, to enquire who these prisoners are, or their names, or
> what they have been, or to speak to them in any way, or to receive from
> them by word of mouth, or by writing, either communication or notes.

With such precautions, it must be wondered how the curate would be expected to accomplish his task of confessing the prisoners, if he is not allowed even to speak to them.

Although apparently ready to set off for his new posting, Saint-Mars's departure was delayed for several weeks because the repairs had not yet been completed. This, however, was less of a problem than it might have seemed. Nicolas de Catinat, who had hidden at Pignerol under the name of Richemont during the negotiation surrounding Louis's acquisition of Casale, was due to return to the fortress under the same guise. "As the service of the King will perhaps require you to remain [at Pignerol] all the following month, it would be well that you should advance the aforesaid repairs of Exiles [sic] as little as possible." This way, Saint-Mars had the perfect excuse should anyone inquire why he had not yet left to take up his new posting, and he was told to "act in such a manner, that your continuing to remain there may not appear to be the result of voluntary delay."[31] Catinat, as before, was lodged in an apartment within the citadel. He was met by Saint-Mars, who conducted him to his apartment as though he were a genuine prisoner. His visit this time was expected to last three or four weeks.[32] On this occasion he would be successful in purchasing Casale for Louis XIV, and the transaction would be completed by the autumn of 1681.

On September 20, 1681, Louvois wrote a mysterious letter: "The King will not disapprove of your visiting, from time to time, the last prisoner who has been placed in your charge, after he shall have been established in his new prison, and shall have left that where he is at present confined." The Victorian historian, Ellis, identified this prisoner as Matthioli: "It is rather curious to observe from this document," he writes, "that St. Mars was permitted to visit his prisoner at Exiles [sic], but not while he continued at Pignerol."[33] Barnes,[34] on the other hand, suggests that Louvois was referring to Catinat, whom he called a "sham prisoner under the name of De Richemont [sic]." In this case, the "new prison" was Casale, the government of which Catinat would take up upon its secession ten days later.

In fact, the prisoner referred to was a man named Videl, a protestant from the vallée du Queyras, who was guarded by the king's lieutenant, Du Prat de la Bastie, and of whom neither Ellis nor Barnes were aware.[35] Stationed at Exilles for several years, Du Prat de la Bastie, who knew Saint-Mars from the time they had served together in the first company of the musketeers under the command of d'Artagnan, would stay on at Exilles. Nothing further is known about Videl, why he was imprisoned, or even the date of his entry into Exilles. The limited correspondence regarding him reveals only that he had been lodged in the Tour Grosse but was to be moved out to make room for Eustache and La Rivière upon their arrival. Louvois was simply telling Saint-Mars that Louis did not object to his visiting Videl from time to time.

Saint-Mars, his family, his reduced compagnie-franche, and his two prisoners arrived at Exilles in October 1681. The soldiers' barracks and living quarters sprawled along the northern wall overlooking the paved courtyard. Saint-Mars and his family took up lodgings in a narrow building between the two towers at the western end of the citadel. Here, he was well placed to keep a watchful eye on the prisoners in the towers as well as his men as they went about their maneuvers and duties.

In the plan of Exilles dating from the time Saint-Mars knew it, the Tour Grosse was, like the other towers, circular. Accessed by a door that opened onto the courtyard in front of Saint-Mars's lodgings, it featured a spiral staircase, which ran up the inside of the wall. The chamber itself, which Eustache and La Rivière were to call home, had a window that overlooked the village, but the wall in which this was set was so thick that very little light came in.[36] Since it faced west, the chamber was dismal for much of the day, brightening up only for a short time when the setting sun reached it in the evenings.

One of Saint-Mars's earliest surviving letters from Exilles is dated December 4, 1681. In it, he speaks of his prisoners, one of whom is always ill, and who gives him "as much occupation as I have ever had with any of those I have hitherto guarded."[37] This unfortunate captive, although afflicted with illness, was considered to be more of a problem to his jailer than Foucquet, who was also frequently ill and who gave Saint-Mars great concern over his invisible ink, and Lauzun with his escape attempts. Fortunately for the prisoners, Saint-Mars had already engaged a doctor to attend to them whenever they had need of medical care.

Winter, with its frosts, snows, and bitter winds, seemed to fall harder at Exilles than it had at Pignerol, and by December Saint-Mars recognized that Eustache and La Rivière were both in need of warmer clothes. He wrote to Louvois asking permission to shop for the various items the men needed. Louvois wrote back to remind Saint-Mars that clothes for "these sorts of people" should be expected to last for three or four years.[38]

The presence of new prisoners and, more especially, the compagnie-franche attracted attention in the village of Exilles. People were naturally curious, and some even ventured out to peer at the fortress in a bid to see who might be inside and what they were doing. Louvois was informed of this activity from his mysterious source who had followed Saint-Mars to Exilles. This was not the first time Louvois had learned of what the villagers were getting up to, and he had already written to Saint-Mars about it, warning him to ensure they could not discover anything. Now, Louvois felt the need to write again, to remind the jailer that:

> As it is important to prevent the prisoners who are at Exiles, who were called at Pignerol "of the Lower Tower," from having any dealings [with anyone], the king has ordered me to command you to guard them so harshly and to take such precautions that you can answer to His Majesty that they cannot speak with anyone, not only from outside but even from the garrison of Exiles.[39]

Under the circumstances, this was a perfectly reasonable order, but Saint-Mars was piqued at the implication that he was neglecting to perform his duty as well as might be expected.

He replied, thanking Louvois for taking the time to write to him, but he was anxious for Louvois and Louis to know that he was well aware of what was required of him and that he was doing everything in his power to maintain the security of his prisoners: "Since the last time you, Sir, gave me this order, I have guarded these two prisoners, who are under my care, as severely and exactly as I formerly did Messieurs Foucquet and Lauzun, who could not boast that they had either sent or received any news, while they were in confinement."[40]

Here, Saint-Mars is being more than a little disingenuous, for he knew full well that both Foucquet and Lauzun had successfully sent and received messages despite Saint-Mars's best efforts to stop them. He went on to explain that his two prisoners could hear the people speaking as they passed along the road that ran by the foot of their tower, but they were unable to make themselves heard. At the same time, they could see people on the mountain, but they could not be seen because of the bars that were placed across their windows.

Saint-Mars had stationed two sentinels, who were on duty day and night, at either side of the Tour Grosse, but at a reasonable distance from it. They watched the prisoners' windows from an oblique angle and were under orders to ensure that no one spoke to the men within and that the prisoners did not cry out from their windows. Any passersby who wanted to stop on the footpath or on the mountainside were made to move on. Moreover, as Saint-Mars explained, his own room adjoined the tower, and his own windows overlooked the path below. From this vantage point, he could hear and see everything, even his two sentinels, "who are by this means always kept alert."

Security within the tower also received due attention. Saint-Mars had arranged things so that the priest who came to say mass for the prisoners could not see them, "on account of a curtain I have made, which covers their double doors." At mealtimes, servants would carry the food and utensils to a small table outside the chamber door. Saint-Mars's lieutenant would then take the items inside. Saint-Mars assured Louvois that "No one speaks to them except myself, my officer, M. Vigneron [the confessor], and [the] physician from Pragelas, which is six leagues from hence, who only sees them in my presence." He added that, with regard to linen and other necessities, "I take the same precautions which I did with my former prisoners."

The two sentinels stationed at the foot of the tower must have further aroused the curiosity of the local population. It is little wonder that they should amble along the path or linger on the side of the mountain gazing eagerly at the forbidding tower that had suddenly become more interesting of late. Security, however, remained tight and no news leaked out about the two new prisoners. It was as though Eustache and La Rivière had vanished from the face of the earth.

Louis read Saint-Mars's latest letter with satisfaction, but one item gave him cause for concern. Louvois duly sent off a note to inform the jailer that only the lieutenant who was accustomed to speaking with the prisoners was to have any dealings with them.[41] This was Jean de La Prade, a musketeer and lieutenant of the compagnie-franche.[42]

With only three prisoners to guard, time lay heavily on Saint-Mars's hands. He had hoped to fill it with the occasional visit to Casale, but he complained that he dared not leave Exilles in case Louvois sent him a packet of correspondence for the marquis de Pianesse, a minister of the court of Turin.[43] Not only was Saint-Mars a jailer, he was now a messenger acting as a postman between the courts of France and Turin, but it was also dawning on him that he was a virtual prisoner at Exilles. That April, he sought permission to go to pay his respects to the duc de Savoie. Louis raised no objection as long as the security of the prisoners was not compromised, and they could have no contact with anyone other than Saint-Mars's appointed lieutenant and that nothing could befall them during his absence.[44]

A month later, Saint-Mars asked permission to leave the fortress once again, this time on personal business. "I cannot see the king allowing you to absent yourself from the command he has been pleased to give you," wrote Louvois. "Therefore, you must put your affairs in order without leaving the place where you are."[45]

The next surviving letter, which dates from June 1683, shows that Saint-Mars had revised the arrangements regarding the confession of the prisoners. Where previously they were allowed to confess once a year, they were now to be allowed to see a chaplain only following a direct order from the king or unless they were in imminent peril of death; "that is what you will observe, please," wrote Louvois.

This change had come about as a result of the death of the abbé Antoine Rignon, the chaplain who had attended the prisoners in the donjon of Pignerol. He had traveled to Exilles once each year to provide his services to Eustache and La Rivière. Upon his death, in the late spring of 1683, he appears not to have been replaced. Saint-Mars regretted the death of the old chaplain, but Louvois had told him bluntly that such sentiments were unnecessary. The minister had long harbored doubts about Rignon's fidelity toward the king and believed that he had betrayed the trust of Saint-Mars, particularly with regard to Foucquet and Lauzun.[46]

Up to this point, Saint-Mars had written very little about the prisoners under his care. "It is a long time since you have mentioned your prisoners," wrote Louvois. "Please send me word of how you manage them and how they are." Louvois was particularly interested in La Rivière, and wanted to know under what circumstances he had been placed into Foucquet's service.[47] This letter provides confirmation that the two gentlemen of the Lower Tower, whom Saint-Mars took with him to Exilles, were indeed Eustache and La Rivière, two of Foucquet's former valets who had been hidden away together.

With another reminder from Louvois to keep him apprised of what went on with his prisoners, Saint-Mars took to writing even if he had little to say. "The letter written in your own hand on the 21st of this month has been handed to me," Louvois wrote at the end of January 1685. "I see from its contents what your prisoners have said to you, which is of no consequence."[48]

Saint-Mars was now approaching sixty years old. Exilles was damp and unpleasant, and he longed to get away for a time. That January, he asked permission to travel to Paris in order to deliver a message he claimed was too sensitive to place into the hands of a courier. Louvois, however, was having none of it. He cast doubt on the likelihood of Louis granting the jailer's request and told Saint-Mars instead to place the message inside two envelopes, the inner one of which would be marked that it was confidential and for Louvois personally. The outer envelope would have the usual address.[49]

Undaunted, Saint-Mars tried again. This time, he asked if he could leave the fortress for a short while so he could recover his health. Louis was amenable and agreed that he should "take the air where you judge it suitable for your health." The usual precautions had to be taken for the security of the prisoners, particularly to ensure that no one could communicate with them during his absence.[50] Such measures were standard.

Where Saint-Mars spent his precious time away is not known, but he had returned to Exilles by the end of May. He was refreshed but he had unsettling news for Louvois: one of his prisoners wished to write his will. The minister asked for details of the prisoner's intentions. He assured Saint-Mars that all would be treated with due confidence: "If you put on the letter that it is to be handed to me, no one will open it."[51]

Although neither Saint-Mars nor Louvois mention the name of this prisoner, there is every reason to believe that the man in question was La Rivière. The valet-turned-prisoner had come to terms with the reality that he would never be allowed to return home. He now knew that he would die in prison.

La Rivière's wages had initially been paid to Foucquet, who had kept the money until such time as the valet might leave or be dismissed. At the time of the failed attempt to rescue Foucquet from prison, the valet's wages had been suspended,[52] but they appear to have been reinstated. Following Foucquet's death, La Rivière should have received this money; but, of course, fate had intervened. Once a prisoner, he would never be in a position to spend the money, a significant sum that he now wished to dispose of in his will.[53]

By the end of 1685, Saint-Mars wrote to say that the prisoners of Exilles were ill and had been put on a course of medicine.[54] He does not specify if all three of his prisoners were unwell, or whether it was La Rivière and Eustache, who continued to share a chamber. A doctor, Stéphane Perron, attended the patients, but he lived at Pragelas, which was some forty-two kilometers away by the shortest route. The man had to travel the rough mountain roads in deep snow and biting winds, but his services were appreciated by the prisoners, who, despite their afflictions were reported to be "perfectly tranquil."[55]

This situation was not to last, however, for within the year, La Rivière had taken a turn for the worse. He had developed dropsy, and a deeply concerned Saint-Mars wanted to clarify procedure regarding his confession. "It is right that you should have the one of your prisoners who has dropsy confessed when you see that he is approaching death," Louvois wrote in November 1686. "Until then, neither he nor his companion should have any communication [with anyone]."[56] Within a few short weeks, La Rivière's torment came to an end. Saint-Mars announced the death on January 5, 1687. Louvois's letter, in which he acknowledged news of La Rivière's death, mentioned no name. La Rivière had become nothing more than "one of your prisoners."[57]

La Rivière's death left Eustache alone in the Tour Grosse and without a companion for the first time in many years. Cut off from the world, the grinding monotony of his days was broken by infrequent visits from Saint-Mars or La Prade, neither of whom was truly sympathetic to his plight.

The cold loneliness of Exilles was cruel indeed, but it was not only the prisoners who were affected: Saint-Mars felt it, too. As much a prisoner as those he guarded, he had tried to alleviate his boredom and sense of isolation with the occasional visit to Turin and the court of the duc de Savoie, but he longed to leave Exilles and return to the world. As impossible as it must have seemed to him at that point, his wish would be granted, and much sooner than he could ever had imagined.

TEN

The Île Sainte-Marguerite

The island of Sainte-Marguerite basked in golden sunshine, its shores washed by the gentle warm waters of the Mediterranean. The scent of pine trees filled the air, blending with the perfumes arising from the eucalyptus, orange, and olive trees. Myriad flowers carpeted the woodland floor. It was an island paradise, the beauty of which concealed its mundane function as a military outpost and, when necessity called, a prison.

The governor of this idyllic garrison, Guillaume de Pechpeyrou-Comminges, comte de Guitaut, had recently died of a fever while traveling to Paris. His post was currently being run by a captain-major, Pierre de Bussy, seigneur de Dampierre, but this was a temporary arrangement. Very soon a new governor would arrive: M. de Saint-Mars.

It was in early January 1687 that Saint-Mars received news that he had been appointed governor of the Îles de Lérins, which comprised the islands of Sainte-Marguerite and its smaller companion, Saint-Honorat. Louvois instructed Saint-Mars to journey to Sainte-Marguerite to make an assessment of the work necessary to enable him to guard his prisoners securely. Once he had surveyed the buildings, he was to draw up a plan and an account of the costs involved. He was then to return to Exilles to await the king's orders concerning the conducting of the prisoners to the islands. Louvois added: "I believe it is unnecessary for me to recommend that you take such measures that, during the time that you will be going to the Île Sainte-Marguerite, and returning from there, the said prisoners will be guarded in such a manner that nothing can befall them, and that they have no dealings with anyone."[1]

Louvois also wrote to the clerk of the post at Grenoble, enclosing another letter for Saint-Mars. The instructions were to have it sent by express delivery, and for the reply to be handled with the same urgency.[2] This letter crossed one from Saint-Mars, in which the jailer informed him of the death of La Rivière. In his reply, Louvois again refers to "one of your prisoners" but does not name him.[3]

Saint-Mars was very happy about his new position. For too long the inclement weather and unpleasant conditions at Exilles had undermined his health, and he had asked several times for a new posting. He wrote to Louvois to express his gratitude that his dearest wish was being fulfilled and he would be leaving the dreary fortress of Exilles for good.[4] He was already looking forward to beginning the next stage of his career on Sainte-Marguerite and had begun to plan the route he would take as he prepared to embark upon his fact-finding mission. "I would request to be permitted to take the road through Piedmont," he said, "on account of the great quantity of snow that there is between here and Embrun." As for his return journey, "which shall be as quick as I can make it," he hoped Louvois would approve of his making a detour on the way out so that he might pay a visit to the duc de Savoie, "from whom I have always received so much kindness."

Saint-Mars reassured the minister, and through him the king, that his prisoner would be well guarded during his absence. The security surrounding Eustache was such that he was forbidden even to converse with Saint-Mars's lieutenant, who, of course, obeyed his orders precisely. As for transporting Eustache to the island, Saint-Mars had given that some thought, too. In his opinion, "the most secure conveyance will be a chair covered with oil cloth, in which there would be a sufficiency of air, without its being possible for anyone to see or speak to him during the journey, not even the soldiers whom I shall select to be near the chair. This conveyance will be less embarrassing than a litter," he explained, "which can often break."

Louvois's response was that Saint-Mars could indeed follow the route to Sainte-Marguerite that he had identified as being the most appropriate as long as he made it his priority, once he arrived on the island, to examine the buildings and identify the work that needed to be done in order to ensure his prisoner's security. As to the means by which the prisoner was to be transported, Louis wanted Saint-Mars to use a wheeled chair covered over in a manner suggested by the jailer, or any other method he might deem appropriate providing he could answer for it.[5] With his arrangements in place, Saint-Mars set out on his long journey a week or so later. As he had planned, he made a detour to Turin, where he paid his respects to the duke before going on to the islands. He arrived on February 19.

Situated some two kilometers off the coast of Cannes, then a small fishing village,[6] Sainte-Marguerite, its new governor saw, was so secure that prisoners could be held there without fear of escape. It boasted an already established garrison, and its agreeable climate made a sharp contrast to the icy winds and cruel snows of the Alps. He was greeted by the acting governor, Dampierre, who showed him the island's facilities and introduced him to the personnel stationed at the fortress. There was an officer who looked after the artillery and stores, a captain of the post, four gunners, an almoner, and a surgeon assisted by *fraters*, or barbers.[7]

The troops stationed on the island, which Saint-Mars would inherit, comprised 180 men and two small companies of seventy men each.

Occasionally, infantrymen would quarter on the island. These men were in addition to Saint-Mars's own compagnie-franche.

The fortifications had been established in 1560 by Charles IX on the ruined foundations of Roman buildings, with a tower being added some forty years later by a liegeman of Charles de Lorraine, duc de Guise. The new fortress had then been taken over by the Spanish, who occupied the island in the mid-1630s and strengthened it with demi-lunes, moats, bastions, and defensive walls. When it was returned to French hands shortly afterward, the new governor, the comte de Guitaut, reinforced these defenses. Now, as Saint-Mars prepared to transfer to the island, Vauban suggested further modification,[8] although nothing came of these plans.

Saint-Mars observed that the fortress had been intended primarily as a military installation, not a prison, so it had no purpose-built cells or chambers fit for guarding state prisoners. This, however, did not prevent prisoners from being held on the island from time to time, some of whom had been arrested on charges so obscure that Louvois was unaware of why they were there. Several years earlier, in a letter dated April 4, 1674, he had written to the commissioner and administrator, Lenfant, saying that he had been advised that Guitaut and Dampierre had custody of three or four people in the prisons of Sainte-Marguerite "without any legitimate motive." He asked Lenfant to explain the presence of these people.[9] Clearly, prisoners could, and did, become lost in the system. Of the captives of Sainte-Marguerite, only one remained upon Saint-Mars's arrival on the island. This was the chevalier Benoît de Thésut, who had been held since September 1685 under a lettre de cachet issued by the king at the request of his family.

For the next two weeks, Saint-Mars knocked on stone walls, rattled heavy wooden doors, and stamped on the floors of the fortress. He walked all over the island in a bid to identify areas that might be vulnerable to intruders or from which a prisoner might mount a successful attempt to escape. Eventually he set out his findings and recommendations in a note to Louvois. In his estimation, the most urgent consideration was to construct a new building, one specifically designed to serve as a prison, and which would include secure lodgings for Eustache. This work, he reckoned, would cost 5,026 livres.

At Versailles, Louis and Louvois read Saint-Mars's note with satisfaction. The cost was approved, and Louis issued a directive giving Saint-Mars leave to depart Exilles and take up his new posting as soon as he was ready, adding that this should be done as soon as possible after Easter.

Louvois expressed his confidence that Saint-Mars had found a way to guard his prisoner securely while the new prison was being built. Just in case the jailer needed reminding, the minister outlined the precautions that had to be observed. As usual, the prisoner was to have no dealings with anyone, and Saint-Mars was to ensure that nothing could befall his charge while he was in the temporary prison. In other words, Eustache was to be prevented from talking to anyone, giving or receiving messages, escaping, or being liberated by anyone.

As to the journey to the island, Louvois felt he did not need to remind Saint-Mars to watch over his prisoner very carefully, but he did so anyway. He was confident, he said, that Saint-Mars would not fail to do everything necessary to guard the prisoner on the road.[10]

If Louvois expected events to run smoothly, he was about to be disappointed. Saint-Mars wrote back within the week to say that he had been on Sainte-Marguerite for the past thirty days, twenty-six of which he had spent in bed with a "continual fever." He was eventually cured of his illness by taking powdered quinquina bark. Now that he was recovered, he had sent for his litter and he planned to leave the island in three days' time. He awaited only Louvois's command, upon the receipt of which, he assured the minister, "I shall set forth again with my prisoner, whom I promise to conduct here in all security, without anyone seeing or speaking to him. He shall not hear mass after he leaves Exilles, till he is lodged in the prison which is prepared for him here, to which a chapel is attached." The letter is torn at this point, and only the words "I pledge my honor to you for the entire security of my prisoner" can be read.[11] There was still concern to ensure that Eustache had no commerce with anyone except Saint-Mars or his appointed and approved lieutenant.

With Louvois's blessing, Saint-Mars set out from Exilles with Eustache in tow on April 18, 1687, just as the winter snows were beginning to give way to the delights of the Alpine spring. As Louis had decreed, the prisoner traveled in a chair covered with oiled or waxed cloth. This was carried by eight porters who had brought the chair from Turin. Saint-Mars paid them 203 livres, which included the hire of the chair; he was careful to point out to Louvois that he had paid this money out of his own pocket.

The journey took them through Briançon, Embrun, Grasse, and on to Cannes, where a boat carried them the short distance to Sainte-Marguerite.[12] Upon disembarking at the landing stage on the western shore of the island, a short and winding path took them to the new buildings Saint-Mars had ordered to be built.[13] It had been a relatively pleasant journey, at least for Saint-Mars, but it had not been without incident. The cloth that swathed the chair had been so tight that its unhappy occupant did not have "as much air as he wished," with the consequence that he was frequently unwell. As a result, the party spent twelve days on the road and arrived on Sainte-Marguerite on April 30.[14]

As he wrote to Louvois upon his arrival on the island, Saint-Mars could not resist indulging in a little self-congratulation on his success at concealing the identity of his prisoner: "I can assure you, Monseigneur, that no one has seen him, and that the manner in which I have guarded and conducted him during the journey makes everybody try to conjecture who he is."[15]

Louvois must have read these lines with dismay. Surely, the whole object of carrying the prisoner inside a covered chair was to hide him from prying eyes, yet here was Saint-Mars, who ought to have known better, gloating over the attention his prisoner had attracted on their lengthy journey. Not only had the mysterious prisoner roused interest in the local populace through whose towns and villages he passed while encased in his makeshift portable prison, but word of his existence was already beginning to spread far and wide.

Among those who were intrigued by this mysterious man in Saint-Mars's custody were four people who were touring France's Mediterranean coastline that spring. Louis de Thomassin-Mazaugues, a counselor of the Parlement of Aix, was traveling in a felucca with his wife, his sister-in-law, and a friend, the abbé de Mauvans. Happily, the abbé kept a journal of their expedition, which took them in stages from Saint-Tropez to Genoa, hugging the coast all the way.

The small group had decided to stop overnight on Saint-Honorat, the smaller of the Lérin islands, and disembarked at the landing stage on Sainte-Marguerite to request the necessary permit. This was duly granted by Dampierre, who went on to show them the new fortifications that were being built at the direction of Saint-Mars. He explained that the new governor had just left the island to collect an unknown prisoner, who was to be escorted with so many precautions, and to whom it was made known directly that if ever he was weary of life, he had only to say his name, because there were orders to shoot him in the head immediately if he did so. Dampierre added that they were providing lodgings for this prisoner, which would match those of Saint-Mars. It had been arranged, moreover, that the new governor would be the only person to see the prisoner, that he would give him his food himself, and he would be almost his only jailer and his guard.[16]

Within five months, the mysterious Eustache had become a talking point among the Jansenist clergy in Paris. They were even able to read all about him in their handwritten gazette, a document that was copied and circulated among them with impressive speed.[17]

The text in question is a short article attributed to Louis Foucquet, bishop of Agde, who had been exiled for being a Jansenist, and who was one of half a dozen or so editors of the gazette. The article[18] noted that Saint-Mars, here erroneously referred to as Cinq-Mars, had taken a state prisoner to Sainte-Marguerite from Pignerol on the orders of the king. No one knew who this prisoner was who was forbidden to speak his own name and would be killed if he did so. It noted that the prisoner traveled in an enclosed sedan chair with a mask of steel on his face. All that anyone could get out of Saint-Mars was that the prisoner was for many years at Pignerol "and that all the people one believes to be dead are not."

This is a fascinating article. It is the first historical document to claim that Saint-Mars's prisoner wore a mask—and it was not an iron mask, but steel. As such, it would be useful to look at this a little more closely to see what can be made of it.

The most obvious observation is that the article is not based on eyewitness testimony but relates a secondhand story from an anonymous source. It contains several discrepancies: it mistakenly refers to Saint-Mars as Cinq-Mars, but this could be a simple spelling error because both versions could sound very similar. More seriously, it states that the mysterious prisoner was taken to Sainte-Marguerite directly from Pignerol, completely omitting the six years he had spent at Exilles. This may be accounted for by Saint-Mars's apparent assertion that the prisoner had been at Pignerol for many years, with the anonymous writer thinking it unnecessary to make mention of Exilles. The article mistakenly asserts that the prisoner had been forbidden to speak his name. As to the steel mask, we recall Saint-Mars, in his letter to Louvois, said that the prisoner did not have as much air as he had wished. We might infer that this was owing to the oiled or waxed cloth that was tightly wound around the chair in which the prisoner was carried. Saint-Mars, it is important to point out, said nothing of his prisoner wearing a mask of any material. Having said that, it could be argued that Saint-Mars might have forced his prisoner to wear a mask on the journey from Exilles to Sainte-Marguerite to ensure none of the soldiers or others in the entourage would recognize him. Some of them would have seen him in Foucquet's company, and they had been told that he had been released upon the death of his master.

The article then speaks of someone who was believed to have died while in Saint-Mars's care, but who may not be dead after all. The most recent death among Saint-Mars's prisoners was La Rivière. As a valet from an obscure background, the public would not have been acquainted with this man and so would probably not have formed a belief about him one way or another. The only dead prisoner who had been well known to the public was Nicolas Foucquet. However, in a letter to Louvois, Saint-Mars noted that he did not carry his prisoner's few possessions to Sainte-Marguerite as he had intended because of their condition. "My prisoner's bed is so old and worn out," he explained, "as well as everything he had used, such as table linen and furniture, that it was not worth the trouble of bringing it here; they sold for only thirteen écus."[19] Since the furniture and linens used by Foucquet had been supplied by the king and were of a quality appropriate for a man of his social rank, it is clear that these items could not have belonged to the former superintendent. Nevertheless, that this speculation is mentioned at all lends poignancy to the article because of its attribution to Louis Foucquet: the bishop was the late Nicolas Foucquet's younger brother and godson; if he was the author of the article, it is possible that there was some speculation or wishful thinking on his part regarding Nicolas's possible survival.

What this document really amounts to is a buzz of excitement surrounding a high-security prisoner, originating with a jailer who teased local townsfolk about a mysterious man under his guard. It may have originated with, or been informed by, the abbé Mauvans or one of his party. His journal contains snippets of information concerning Saint-Mars's mystery prisoner, which originated with the staff on Sainte-Marguerite who were awaiting their exciting new guest and who mentioned "so many precautions" under which he was being escorted. The gossip then spread, acquiring new and more imaginative details as it went. The prisoner, whom we recall was wrapped up so securely in oiled or waxed cloth that he found it difficult to breathe, had no need of a mask to conceal his features. Indeed, had Saint-Mars thought of using such a device, he would probably have boasted about it to Louvois in his letter. It is telling that he did not.

As soon as he arrived on Sainte-Marguerite, Eustache was lodged in temporary accommodation, the security of which Saint-Mars could confidently vouch. The Mediterranean climate had not proved beneficial to him, however, for he remained unwell. As the year 1688 dawned, the new prison building was declared ready to receive its first guest, and Eustache was moved into the chamber that was to become his permanent home.

Saint-Mars was proud of the new prison chambers he had built ranged along the cliff top that overlooked the sea and the small village of Cannes beyond. He described them as "large, fine and light, and as to their quality, I do not believe that there are any stronger or more secure in Europe."[20] He was certain that his prisoner would not be able to send out or receive messages from near or far, which was something "that could not be found in the places where I had the custody of the late Monsieur Foucquet from the moment he was arrested." Here, Saint-Mars is recalling a time when he served as d'Artagnan's sergeant when the lieutenant-captain of the Musketeers acted as Foucquet's first jailer. Despite apparently tight security, Foucquet had managed to smuggle out the occasional message to friends and members of his family.

Saint-Mars added that, with the appropriate precautions in place, he thought that it would be safe enough to allow prisoners to walk anywhere on the island. With that in mind, he boasted to Louvois of "the value of this place, for when you have some prisoners to place in all security with honest liberty."[21] Saint-Mars was again harking back to the days when he had guarded Foucquet, arguably his most illustrious prisoner, and hinting for another important prisoner, someone equal in rank to Foucquet.

Yet, despite Saint-Mars's blustering overconfidence, news had leaked to the mainland that an important prisoner was being held on the island. He referred to the gossip as he closed his letter: "In all this province people are saying that my prisoner is Monsieur de Beaufort, and others say that he is the son of the late Cromwell." He enclosed a note with his letter outlining the previous year's expenses, adding that he did not write down the details so that he could conceal as much as possible from anyone who might handle and read the note. That letter was dated January 8, 1688, several months after his arrival on Sainte-Marguerite with his prisoner. Eustache is no longer referred to by name; he has even lost his epithet, *La Tour* or *La Tour d'en bas*. Now, he is simply referred to as *mon prisonnier*, "my prisoner."

Eustache lived in great tranquility on Sainte-Marguerite, just as he had done at Pignerol, where he was at peace with God and the king. Meanwhile, Saint-Mars's assurances about the security of the island had not gone unnoticed. Within a short while, he was to receive several more prisoners, even though they were not of a quality he might have expected.

For several years, Louis had been running a systematic campaign of persecution against the Huguenot population of France. Seeing their faith, and their adherence to it, as heretical and schismatic, the king had imposed penalties on the Huguenots with increasing severity in a bid to force them to convert to Catholicism. By 1685 Louis had come to believe that so few Huguenots remained in the kingdom that there was no need to observe the protected status they had been granted by his grandfather, Henri IV. The edict of Nantes, issued in 1598, was an enlightened piece of legislation that had granted freedom of conscience to Huguenots and supported their rights with military and political guarantees.[22] Now Louis rescinded the edict, making Huguenotism illegal. Huguenot ministers were obliged to convert to Catholicism or else leave France; if they defied this imperative, they faced being sent to the galleys. A number of ministers left the kingdom to minister to the French Huguenots who had chosen to settle in England, Holland, Switzerland, and the New World. Some, however, later returned from exile to continue their ministries in secret. Those who were caught were imprisoned in the Bastille, the château de Vincennes, or any one of a number of other strongholds scattered across the kingdom, including the fortress on the Île Sainte-Marguerite. The first of the ministers to arrive at Sainte-Marguerite was Paul Cardel.

Saint-Mars was warned to expect Cardel in a letter dated April 19, 1689. Louvois described him as "a man deserving of death and who could not be treated too severely." He ordered Saint-Mars to take "all necessary precautions so that no one knows that he is in your hands," and he asked to be kept informed of Cardel's behavior by letter every month.[23]

In effect, Louvois was acting beyond his jurisdiction. The Huguenot minister, although imprisoned on Sainte-Marguerite, came under the authority of the marquis de Seignelay, who was secretary of state for the royal house, *la Maison du roi*. There was, therefore, a conflict of interest between the two men. Perhaps this was what lay behind a letter Louvois sent to Saint-Mars the following month. In it, he told Saint-Mars that whenever he had some information to give him regarding Cardel, he must use the precaution of putting his letter into a double envelope, so that no one but Louvois would know what it contained.[24]

These precautions inevitably extended to those who came to look after the prisoners. When Cardel fell ill and needed to be bled, Saint-Mars was unsure of how to proceed and wrote to Louvois for clarification. Louvois in turn, consulted the king before replying that should the prisoner stand in urgent need of bleeding, Saint-Mars could arrange for a surgeon to come to the island to perform the procedure in his presence, "taking all necessary precautions that the surgeon does not know who [the prisoner] is."[25]

Within a few months, Cardel was joined by another minister, Pierre de Salves, who appears in the official correspondence under the name Valsec. In time, more ministers would arrive on the island, and all were lodged in the range of which Saint-Mars was so proud. Eustache occupied the chamber closest to the château in which Saint-Mars had set up home. The ministers were given adjoining chambers, the windows of which featured three layers of strong iron bars. These, however, proved to be no obstacle to the ministers, who communicated with each other by shouting through them.[26]

Despite Louvois's assertion that Cardel could not be treated badly enough, Louis appears to have relented. As he considered the faith of these ministers, he decided that they were wrongheaded rather than wicked, and he felt that they might be persuaded to abjure what he considered to be their heresy. On his orders, Louvois wrote to Saint-Mars to tell him that, should any of the ministers become ill, he was to find an honorable priest to attend them in order that they might be converted before they died.[27]

It was shortly after the arrival of the first Huguenot ministers that two events occurred that would have a profound effect on Saint-Mars's life. One was the death of Mme de Saint-Mars in 1691. She was buried at the monastery on neighboring Saint-Honorat.

The death of his wife was, however, a personal tragedy for Saint-Mars, but the other event would also have an impact on Eustache. This was the death, on July 16, 1691, of the marquis de Louvois, the man with whom Saint-Mars had exchanged letters for some twenty-six years, and who had exercised a great deal of influence over the conditions of Eustache's imprisonment.

The story of Louvois's death, as told by the marquis de Sourches,[28] has it that the minister was working with Louis in his cabinet at Versailles when the king remarked a change in his expression. Louis asked if he was well, upon which Louvois said that he felt ill and asked if, since he had no pressing business, the king would permit him to go home and resume his work the following day. Louis graciously agreed. As Louvois was gathering up his papers, Louis watched him closely and asked if he still felt unwell, to which Louvois replied that he did.

Louvois left the king's cabinet and made his way through the royal apartments and on into the Galerie des glaces supported by one of his gentlemen, Chavigny. As he went, he exchanged a few words with various people and even arranged an interview with a cavalry captain for the next day.

Once inside his own room, he sent for Dionis, the premier surgeon to the dauphin, to bleed him. Louvois declared that he felt a little better, but a moment later, he felt a pain in his left side and asked to be bled on that side. Dionis, who was still bandaging Louvois's right arm, did not have time to fulfil this request, for Louvois just had time to complain of feeling weak before he died.

Several concerned courtiers rushed into Louvois's apartment. It was noticed that the dead minister, who was laid out on his bed, appeared to have a small patch of violet on his cheek. Louis, when given the news of Louvois's death, was visibly touched at the loss. He had worked with Louvois for many years, and now he had lost his trusted minister just as French fortunes at war were not going well.[29]

Louvois was succeeded by his son, Louis Le Tellier, marquis de Barbezieux. Aged twenty-three, Barbezieux was Louvois's third son and the third Le Tellier to inherit the post. His grandfather, Michel Le Tellier, had been something of a bureaucrat, preferring to perform his duties from behind his desk in the comfort of his office. Louvois had taken the opposite approach and often traveled to the front or visited strongholds across the kingdom, often to the annoyance of the generals and intendents who felt he was getting in their way. Just as Louvois had learned his job at his father's side, so had Barbezieux learned from Louvois, and he had been training for the post for the past four years. It would soon become obvious, however, that, while he may have paid attention to those valuable lessons, he was less inclined to apply himself to the task, much to the dismay of the king. Within months of the young man's taking office, Louis began to feel the need to direct the affairs of the ministry for war himself.

That gradual change, however, was yet to come. For now, Saint-Mars awaited a response to a letter he had sent toward the end of July, in which he acknowledged the new minister, pledged his allegiance, and requested instructions on how to proceed. Barbezieux's reply, when it came, was succinct: whenever Saint-Mars had anything to say about the prisoner he had been guarding for twenty years, he should apply the same precautions he had used when writing to the late M. de Louvois.[30]

Here, Barbezieux refers to "the prisoner," whom he does not name. He does note that this prisoner had been in Saint-Mars's custody for twenty years, implying that he was someone who had become a prisoner in 1671. The only one to have entered Pignerol that year was Lauzun, and he had been freed in 1681. It is possible that Barbezieux was merely rounding up his numbers;[31] if so, his letter still allows us to identify which prisoner he meant by a process of elimination.

Of the prisoners Saint-Mars had left behind at Pignerol upon his transfer to Exilles, three remained: Matthioli, imprisoned in 1679; Rousseau, Matthioli's valet who was captured shortly after his master; and Lapierre, the Jacobin, who had been a prisoner since 1674. Dubreuil, imprisoned in 1676, had been released in 1684. Matthioli, Rousseau, and Lapierre had obviously left Saint-Mars's custody and had spent the previous ten years being guarded by Villebois and his successor, La Prade.[32]

Upon his move to Exilles, Saint-Mars had taken two prisoners with him, those he referred to as his two *merles* or the "gentlemen of the Lower Tower." The first was Eustache, described as a valet, who had entered Pignerol in 1669 and had later been allowed to serve Foucquet. The second was La Rivière, who had been hired as a valet to serve Foucquet, who had failed to report a breach of security and was believed to have learned Eustache's secret. For these two offenses, the authorities felt it appropriate to imprison him. A state prisoner, without having been tried and without even a lettre de cachet to authorize his captivity, he had died at Exilles in 1687.

The prisoner referred to by Barbezieux could only have been Eustache, who had been in Saint-Mars's continuous custody since 1669—that is, for twenty-two years. It is a close approximation made by the new young minister who had not been fully briefed about the prisoners in his charge. Barbezieux may not have known who Eustache was or anything about his case.

The Huguenot ministers made Saint-Mars's life, and no doubt that of Eustache, a misery by their constant singing and chanting. "The first of these ministers, who have been sent here, sings psalms all day and night with a loud voice, expressly to make it known who he is," complained the jailer when he wrote to Barbezieux on June 4, 1692. He pointed out that he had ordered Cardel several times to desist on pain of severe punishment, which, he said, he had been forced to administer. He had also been obliged to discipline Salves, who "writes on his pewter vessels and on his linen . . . to make it known that he is detained unjustly for the purity of his faith."[33]

As to Eustache, he continued his lonely existence, staring out of his windows across the blue Mediterranean toward Cannes and the French countryside beyond it. Did he recall the days before his imprisonment? We can only speculate what went through his mind as he looked back over the years, with the stark contrast between freedom and captivity, his reminiscences interrupted by the chanting that drifted into his chamber from his saintly neighbors. What he may not have known was that he was no longer part of the world he had left behind, forgotten by those who directed whatever future he might have. Only Saint-Mars, who looked after his daily needs, seemed now to give any thought to the man who was so quiet and accepting of his fate that his jailer was hard-pressed to find any news about him to report.

In the insulated world in which the prisoners of Pignerol lived, it must have been hard for them to imagine that life continued beyond the thick walls of their prison chambers. Now events were about to break into their solitary existence in the most violent way.

For some time, Victor Amadeus II, duc de Savoie, had looked with envy upon the little town of Pignerol, with its excellent strategic position and impenetrable stronghold. He desired to restore the town and its citadel, lost decades earlier, to his duchy. It was for this reason, with thoughts of regaining this jewel of the Alps as his reward, that he joined the enemies of France in a conflict that would become known to history as the Nine Years' War or, as it is sometimes called, the War of the League of Augsburg.[34] In 1692, Savoie invaded the Dauphine, but his greatest triumph was yet to come.

As dawn broke on the morning of July 29, 1693, the duke's forces marched on Sainte-Brigitte, only a kilometer away from Pignerol. The fortress fell into their hands after a siege lasting four weeks, but the town and the citadel of Pignerol itself held firm as everything from bombs to corpses were sent crashing through its defenses. The corpses were a particularly nasty weapon. Combined with the stifling heat of the Alpine summer, they constituted a primitive but effective form of biological warfare. Inevitably, disease spread among the town's populace and, equally inevitably, the prisoners inside the donjon succumbed to the fevers that raged.

La Prade feared for the safety of his prisoners under his care, whose numbers had increased since Saint-Mars's departure.[35] In November 1682,

Jean Breton, or Le Breton, had been arrested on the orders of Louvois on suspicion of spying. Held at first in a civil jail, Le Breton had been transferred to the donjon a month later, with only bread and water for sustenance. Here he would remain until the following April, when Louis issued an order to the marquis d'Herleville to release him. For reasons unknown, this order was never carried out, and so Le Breton remained at Pignerol, another lost prisoner.

Five years later, in August 1687, one Jean Herse was sent to Pignerol under Louvois's orders. Herse was fifteen years old, an apprentice tailor who had been overheard to say that he would kill the king for payment. For this act of treason, he was imprisoned in the Bastille under a lettre de cachet before being transferred to Pignerol, escorted by the sieur La Coste, an officer of the court police. The young man was violent and difficult to manage; unable to bear his captivity, he attempted suicide in January 1689 and made an unsuccessful escape attempt in May 1692.

Now, in early October 1693, the lives of both Le Breton and Herse, together with their companions in captivity, were threatened by the duc de Savoie's forces, who bombarded Pignerol mercilessly for several days. La Prade, now greatly concerned for the safety of his prisoners, wrote to Barbezieux to ask what options were available to him. The young secretary's reply was not encouraging. If any of them were to die, he told La Prade, they should be buried like the soldiers were. He hastened to add, however, that he did not believe that this would be necessary, as he was persuaded that none of them would die. As it was, both Matthioli and his valet, Rousseau, were ill in bed with fever. La Prade told Barbezieux that he had discovered that the two men had been writing messages inside the linings of their jackets. Barbezieux remained unconcerned. He told La Prade that he should simply burn the messages.[36]

The secretary's belief that the prisoners would not be in any danger naturally proved to have been misplaced. A little more than a fortnight after the latest exchange, he received news that a prisoner had died. Referring to him in his letter as *le plus ancien*, it was clear that Barbezieux did not know the man's name; he wrote to La Prade: "As I do not doubt that you would remember it, I pray you tell me it in cipher."[37] The prisoner described as *le plus ancien* could only have been Lapierre, the Jacobin who had gone insane as a result of the conditions in which he had been kept. The torment of this unfortunate man would come to an end only in death, in December 1693.

As the war progressed, Catinat took the fight to the duc de Savoie and crushed his army outside La Marsaille, or Marsaglia, near Pignerol on October 4, 1693.[38] The siege was lifted, but the threat of hostilities remained ever present. It was clear that some solution had to be found regarding the prisoners. The comte de Tessé, maréchal de France, came up with the ideal solution. This was to evacuate the prisoners from Pignerol and lodge them either at Exilles or on the island of Sainte-Marguerite. With Exilles having been abandoned to the elements, and with newly built, state-of-the-art facilities having been established on Sainte-Marguerite under the capable command of Saint-Mars, the choice was obvious.

The plan was sent to Barbezieux, who passed it on to the king, who approved it. Saint-Mars was duly apprised of the situation; warned that some prisoners were being brought to the island, he was ordered to arrange suitable accommodation for them. There was one problem, however: Barbezieux had no idea how many prisoners were being transferred, but he was sure Saint-Mars would know.[39]

The official correspondence mentions only three prisoners: Matthioli, Le Breton, and Herse. Lapierre, the Jacobin, as has been seen, had died. A fourth man, Rousseau, who was Matthioli's valet, would be transferred alongside his master. As always, the new inmates were to be kept in separate cells and Saint-Mars was to ensure that they could not communicate with anyone, either by word of mouth or in writing.

Despite the danger posed by the presence of foreign troops hiding out along the route between Pignerol and Sainte-Marguerite, Louis and Barbezieux gave orders that the prisoners should make the journey one at a time. The cost of this undertaking, the time it would take, not to mention the risks involved, made this a wholly impractical course of action. The plan was revised and, a few weeks later, on April 7, 1694, the small party of three prisoners and one unfortunate valet set out from Pignerol under the care of M. de Maisonel, captain of the dragoons.

At Briançon, they were handed over to La Prade, who took them the rest of the way. La Prade and his officers were, in turn, escorted by twenty mounted sergeants provided by the comte de Tessé.[40] He had received his orders two weeks earlier, together with instructions on how he was expected to conduct himself on the journey. He assured Barbezieux that he would conduct himself according to his "orders and instructions with the greatest secrecy, entire circumspection, and every possible measure for the security of these prisoners, without having the slightest temptation to the least petty curiosity."[41]

The operation to transfer the four men to their island prison appears to have gone off without a hitch, but it could not have been an easy journey for them. There was the constant fear of attack by the duc de Savoie's troops, and the stress of a long and arduous journey, and at least one of them was still unwell. He arrived on the island in such a weakened state that he died shortly afterward. Saint-Mars informed Barbezieux in a now lost letter of April 29. The secretary's reply was dated two weeks later. In it, he acknowledged the news of the prisoner's death and agreed with Saint-Mars's proposal that the dead man's servant should be put into the vaulted prison, with the usual precaution that the man could not communicate in any way with the outside world.[42] The prisoner who died almost immediately upon his arrival on the island of Sainte-Marguerite could only have been Matthioli because he was the only one of the three prisoners from Pignerol to have had a valet.

In December 1695, Saint-Mars was approaching seventy years of age. Although the climate on Sainte-Marguerite was agreeable, certainly much better than it had been in any of the Alpine fortresses in which he had served for the past thirty years, there were times when ill health prevented his performing his duties as he would have wished. Louis, through Barbezieux, wanted to know what arrangements the jailer had made should he ever be absent from the island or too ill to care for his prisoners. Saint-Mars's reply, dated January 6, 1696, provides some intriguing insights into prison life on Sainte-Marguerite and the routine that had been established there.[43]

Saint-Mars explained that two lieutenants had been assigned to serve the prisoners their meals using the procedure he himself had devised and which they have seen him use many times. The senior of these lieutenants takes the keys of the *ancien prisonnier*, with whom they begin their rounds,[44] opens the three doors that seal the chamber and enters. The prisoner politely hands the lieutenant his dishes and plates, which he has placed neatly one on top of the other. These are then carried through two of the doors and given to one of the sergeants, who takes them to a table two paces off. Here, the second lieutenant examines them carefully, as he does anything that goes in or comes out of the prisoner's chamber. This is to ensure that the prisoner has not written anything on his plates. After everything necessary has been given to the prisoner, the lieutenant searches the chamber, taking particular care to check under the bed and the window bars, and often the prisoner himself. The lieutenant then asks in a very civil manner if the prisoner needs anything. He then shuts the doors and goes away to perform the same procedure with the other prisoners.

The table linen, shirts, and any other linen used by the prisoners is changed twice a week, with every item counted in and out and thoroughly searched. "One can be very much cheated about the linen when it leaves and enters the service of prisoners who are people of consideration," he goes on to explain, "as I have had some who have wished to bribe the laundresses, who have acknowledged to me . . . what had been said to them." In order to get around this problem, Saint-Mars ordered all the linen to be "steeped in water on leaving [the prisoner's] chambers, and when it was clean and half dry, the laundresses came to iron and smooth it in my apartments in the presence of one of my lieutenants." The lieutenant would then lock up the baskets of freshly laundered linen in a chest until they were handed over to the prisoners' servants.

"There is much to be distrusted in candles," Saint-Mars continues. "I have found some that upon being broken or used contained paper instead of wicks. It is also very dangerous for ribbon to leave a prisoner's apartments, as he writes on it as linen without any one being aware of it." Here Saint-Mars is reminiscing of the good old days when he guarded Foucquet and Lauzun, two illustrious prisoners, whose status enhanced his own by association. These men wore handsome suits with laced shirts, which were decorated and tied with silken ribbons. He went on to explain how the late Monsieur Foucquet "made fine and good paper on which I allowed him to write, and afterward I went and took it from a little pocket he had made in the seat of his breeches, which I sent to your late father."

The page is torn at this point, and only the closing paragraph survives: "As a last resort, the prisoners are searched from time to time, both day and night, at hours which are not fixed, when it is often found that they have written on dirty linen that which they alone are able to read, as you will have seen from that which I have had the honor to forward to you. If it is necessary, Monseigneur, that I should do anything else in order to more completely fulfil my duty, I shall glory all my life in obeying you with the same respect and submission . . ." He signed off at that point, assuring Barbezieux that he was his "very humble, very obedient, and very obliged servant."

Barbezieux read out this lengthy letter to Louis. The king listened with his usual attention to detail before expressing his satisfaction with the measures Saint-Mars was implementing. With nothing further to add, Louis merely recommended that the jailer continue to observe them.[45]

From this point onward, the surviving letters become scarce, and those that have survived afford only the occasional glimpse behind the stone walls of the chambers in which Saint-Mars's prisoners passed their long, tedious days.

A letter written on November 17, 1697, from Barbezieux to Saint-Mars appears at first glance to be of little import, but in fact is worthy of consideration. It is written in reply to a note from Saint-Mars, who had forwarded a copy of a letter sent to him by Pontchartrain, successor to the marquis de Seignelay, concerning the prisoners of Sainte-Marguerite. Saint-Mars was disconcerted about this, hence his communication with the secretary.

Barbezieux replied: "You have no other rules of conduct to follow with respect to all those who are confided to your keeping beyond continuing to look to their security, without explaining yourself to any one whatever about what you old prisoner [that is, the ancien prison-nier] has done."[46]

Saint-Mars had been right to be concerned about Pontchartrain's apparent interference. Pontchartrain held several posts in Louis XIV's government. He was controller of finances, secretary of state for the navy and the king's household, as well as minister of state in the *Conseil d'en haut*, or the council of ministers.[47] He was a very important man; in the hierarchy of royal service, he ranked far above Barbezieux, who was only a secretary of state. When he inquired into the prisoners under Saint-Mars's care, it was no surprise that the jailer, who answered only to the king and Barbezieux, should have been annoyed.

As it happens, Pontchartrain's inquiry was not as menacing as Saint-Mars had feared. Louis had ordered him to conduct a survey of the prisoners secretly held in various fortresses throughout the kingdom. He was about to sign the Peace of Ryswick, which would bring to an end the Nine Years' War, and he wanted to identify those prisoners who had been held as spies with a view to releasing them.[48] For the same reason, Barbezieux asked Saint-Mars to furnish him with the names and qualities of the prisoners under his care as well as what he knew about the crimes they had committed. This was so that Louis could better remember who these men were.[49]

While, for some, the promise of freedom had suddenly become a real prospect, for Eustache, as he listened to the continual chanting that drifted into his chamber from his devout companions in captivity, life went on as it had done for the past twenty-nine years. So normal—and predictable—had life as a prisoner become, in fact, that it would be easy for him to imagine that there were no more surprises to come, that he had arrived at the final chapter of his story, where each featureless day blended into the next in a seamless stream that stretched across the weeks, the months, and the years. As it happened, he was wrong. For him, and for his jailer, there was yet one more chapter to come.

ELEVEN
The Bastille

Once again, the fate of both Eustache and Saint-Mars was shaped by a death, this time, it was that of the marquis de Besmaux. François de Monlezun, marquis de Besmaux, had served as captain of the guards under Cardinal Mazarin before being awarded the governorship of the Bastille in 1658. He would maintain this post for almost forty years until his death on December 18, 1697, at the age of eighty-eight.

A successor needed to be found. He had to be a man of integrity, respectable, and of proven ability, someone who had earned the right to govern a château as prestigious as the Bastille. Elie du Fresnoy, who had transferred his services to Barbezieux, put forward the name of his brother-in-law, Bénigne Dauvergne de Saint-Mars, as the most suitable candidate. While there was probably more than a touch of nepotism in this nomination, there was no doubting Saint-Mars's ability and dedication to his work. He had earned his promotion.

With the offer of this new governorship, history seemed to repeat itself for Saint-Mars. Just as he had done upon being offered the post at Exilles, he proved reluctant to accept the promotion to the governorship of the Bastille. At his age, he expected, perhaps even desired, to spend his sunset years in the home he had made for himself on Sainte-Marguerite. His wife, Marie-Antoinette, had died in 1691, and he hoped eventually to be laid to rest alongside her in the peaceful grounds of the monastery on the neighboring island of Saint-Honorat.[1] Yet, he remained open to persuasion should the right circumstances arise—that is to say, if the financial rewards were attractive enough. He wrote to Barbezieux to open a discussion of the terms of the proposal, while his letter has not survived, the secretary's reply makes it clear that Saint-Mars had asked about the revenues he could expect to receive should he take up the proffered governorship.

As Barbezieux explained it,[2] the revenues consisted of 15,168 livres on the estates of the king. In addition, Saint-Mars could expect to receive a further 6,000 livres from the shops that lined the road outside the château. The boats, which depended upon the governor for passage on the Seine, provided yet another source of income. The secretary went on to explain that, out of this money, the late Besmaux had been obliged to pay the sergeants and soldiers who guarded the prisoners. However, he was sure that Saint-Mars, who handled the expenses of his compagnie-franche, would be familiar with the sums involved.

Barbezieux assured Saint-Mars that Louis would not force him to accept the post if he did not want it. Nevertheless, as he reminded the jailer, there was much profit to be made from the allowances the king awarded for the upkeep of the prisoners who would come under his care. In other words, Saint-Mars stood to make a respectable profit by skimming off money allocated by the king for the maintenance of the prisoners. Saint-Mars was certainly familiar with this practice, which had supplemented his income considerably throughout his career, and the news that he would not be prevented from continuing it was another mark in favor of accepting the post.

As a final inducement, Barbezieux ventured to point out that Saint-Mars might find it agreeable to live in Paris, where he would have family and friends nearby. He closed by offering his opinion that Saint-Mars would find it very advantageous to take the governorship and that he would lose nothing should he move to Paris.

It did not go unnoticed by Saint-Mars that Barbezieux's lengthy and persuasive letter had one strange omission: the secretary had failed to make any reference to his ancien prisonnier. This contrasted markedly with the correspondence Saint-Mars had previously exchanged with Louvois. Specifically, Louvois was always insistent that Saint-Mars should take Eustache with him whenever he moved from one prison to another. Now Eustache is not even mentioned.

It is possible that instructions regarding Eustache were given in another letter that has since been lost; however, under Louvois's administration, Eustache had become closely associated with Saint-Mars, the destinies of the two men seemingly intertwined. This was not the case as far as Barbezieux was concerned. The new secretary seemed content to allow Eustache to remain on Sainte-Marguerite under the care of Rosarges, the lieutenant who assisted Saint-Mars in serving him on a regular basis. Saint-Mars was far from content with this and, as a result, took it upon himself to remind Barbezieux that he was the guardian of a long-term prisoner, a man he understood to be important enough to remain under his care. He suggested that this prisoner should accompany him to the Bastille. The question, however, must be asked, to whom was Eustache important?

At Pignerol, Saint-Mars had worked alongside important men, such as d'Estrades and Catinat. Later, when the families and friends of Foucquet and Lauzun were granted permission to visit their loved ones in prison, Saint-Mars found himself in the company of people of quality. Louvois even granted his request to be allowed to host these prestigious guests, and they, Foucquet and Lauzun, together with dignitaries from Pignerol, would dine at his table. In the company of people who came from a higher social class than his own, Saint-Mars could persuade himself that he too had entered the higher reaches of society.

All this came crashing down when he was transferred to Exilles. Those from whom Saint-Mars had borrowed his reflected glory were gone. Foucquet was dead and Lauzun had been released, and their families and friends no longer honored him with their company.

Yet, when Saint-Mars was transferred to the Île Sainte-Marguerite in 1687, Eustache appeared still to be very much a prisoner of consequence. Saint-Mars was ordered to ensure that the lodgings on the island were secure enough to hold him. This required him to journey to Sainte-Marguerite to see what work needed to be carried out in fulfilment of this order. Louvois sent detailed instructions regarding the prisoner's security while Saint-Mars was away from Exilles.

Saint-Mars may not have asked to be appointed jailer and governor of a state prison, but he had quickly settled into his new posting, and it was not long before he found that he could use it to his own advantage. Not only did he dip into the funds sent to him for the upkeep of his prisoners, he became famous, and since he could not go anywhere to spend his wages, he also grew very rich. He very much enjoyed the prestige that came with guarding two of the most renowned and eminent prisoners in France, Foucquet and Lauzun, which enhanced his standing and ego. When Foucquet died in 1680 and Lauzun was released a year later, Saint-Mars lost the two people who had provided the foundation of his own celebrity.

Saint-Mars was almost certainly unaware of Eustache's offense, but it is possible that he believed him to have been an important person. Certainly, Eustache had been described as "only a valet" and a "wretch," and, as he would come to see, the measures for his prisoner's security were not exceptional, but this man had been sent to him because Louis wanted him to be held in the most secure prison he had at his disposal and, of course, Saint-Mars was a most dedicated jailer.

Saint-Mars, seeing that people were showing interest in his prisoners, put out contes jaunes, or fairy tales, to mock those who were eager to find out who it was that was concealed behind the impenetrable walls of the donjon. He may even have been behind the rumor that one of his prisoners, who was thought to have died, was in fact still living. The implication was that it was this prisoner who being was carried to Sainte-Marguerite with his face hidden within a steel mask, as reported in the article attributed to Louis Foucquet. If so, his strategy worked, for shortly after his arrival on the island, people were still talking about the mysterious prisoner in the keeping of M. de Saint-Mars.

By May 8, 1698, Saint-Mars had made up his mind that he would take up the proffered posting. He wrote to Barbezieux requesting clarification regarding the practical matters arising from the transfer. Most important, he wanted to ensure that he could bring his ancien prisonnier with him.

The secretary consulted Louis, but the king was busy with more pressing matters, particularly the suppression of the Quietist movement, a heresy that was spreading among some of the higher-ranking people in the capital and at court. The events occurring in faraway Sainte-Marguerite were of little concern at that moment. Barbezieux's reply was delayed by a month, but when it arrived, it carried welcome news: "I shall tell you now that His Majesty has seen with pleasure that you are determined to come to the Bastille to be governor. You can arrange everything to be ready to leave when I shall write to you, and to bring with you, in all security, your ancien prisonnier."[3]

The following month, Barbezieux wrote once again, his letter dated July 19, 1698: "The king approves of your leaving the Île Sainte-Marguerite to come to the Bastille with your ancien prisonnier, taking your precautions to prevent his being seen or known by anyone. You can write in advance to His Majesty's lieutenant of the château of the Bastille, to have a chamber ready to put this prisoner into upon your arrival."[4] This was very satisfactory to Saint-Mars.

A chamber in the Bastille made a remarkable contrast to the dungeon Eustache had inhabited at Pignerol. There, he was hidden away inside an unpleasant isolated cell sealed behind three locked doors. At Exilles, he had lived in the Tour Grosse, a wonderfully secure structure where he and La Rivière had spent their days and nights detached from the world. Finally, he had occupied a spacious chamber on the island of Sainte-Marguerite, the largest and finest the state-of-the-art fortress had to offer, which was next to the governor's apartments. Now he was once more to move into an ordinary chamber in the Bastille.

Initially built to defend Paris against attack by the English, the Bastille stood at the eastern end of the rue Saint-Antoine in Paris. The first of its huge stones had been laid on April 22, 1307, by the mayor of Paris, Hugues Aubriot.[5] It was a formidable building. Each of its eight towers soared almost one hundred feet into the Parisian sky, and they were joined together by curtain walls of the same height. A moat surrounded the entire structure, which in earlier days had been filled with water from the Seine; more recently, the moat had become a dry ditch.[6]

The château was accessed on the side of the rue Saint-Antoine by a massive gateway, which was decorated with trophies of war, and which led to two courtyards within. During the early part of the 17th century, a small village began to form when enterprising merchants opened up shop outside this gateway. They sold everything from wine to poultry and cheese. There were barbers and cobblers, and others who supplied everyday necessities. As the century wore on, the village grew in size, stretching along the rue Saint-Antoine as far as the convent of the Visitation. The shops attracted people from all over the neighboring area, and although merchants and customers alike were free to come and go as they pleased, they were closely watched by the soldiers based at the château, and anyone thought to be loitering was hastily moved on.[7]

As each new prisoner arrived, they would enter the first of the inner courtyards, where the governor would emerge from his lodgings to receive them. This courtyard also contained the apartments of the governor's staff, which were ranged alongside the armory. The prisoner might look up to see a large clock, which had been installed by d'Argenson, the chief of police. Its face was supported by chained figures as a reminder that, notwithstanding the bustling commerce that went on during the day, this was a place where people were held captive. The reminder was necessary because, for much of its early existence, the Bastille had not been a prison, but a well-appointed château guarding the eastern edge of Paris. It was not until the reign of Charles VI[8] that it was occasionally used to hold prisoners; but even then, it continued to serve as a luxurious lodging for passing dignitaries, while various kings would hold fetes and other court entertainments there.

It was not until the time of Cardinal Richelieu, who had served as first minister to Louis XIII in the first half of the 17th century, that the Bastille began to be used regularly as a royal or state prison. It was now reserved for "those who have committed a crime or misdemeanor not provided for by the common law," or for people who were considered to be "too conspicuous to be punished for a crime at common law on equal terms with the ordinary malefactor, and for whom it would appear inevitable that an exceptional prison should be reserved."[9]

It was also under Richelieu that the administration of the Bastille was first entrusted to someone who might be described as a professional jailer, rather than a member of the aristocracy or a military officer as had previously been the case. The first jailer to hold the governorship was Leclerc du Tremblay, the brother of Père Joseph, Richelieu's éminence grise.

For most of the 17th century, the Bastille would hold little fear for the ordinary citizen of France: the Châtelet was more a source of dread for them. The Bastille, reserved for the aristocracy, was seen to be too good for the peasantry, and those who annoyed the king or who had disgraced their families in some way were sent there to cool their heels. Under Louis XIV, the number of people admitted as prisoners to the Bastille averaged only thirty each year.[10]

Probably because of their status, and the expectation that the nobility would know how to behave and would act honorably even while imprisoned, there was very little in the way of security. As such, even though a prison, the Bastille continued to be a comfortable, even cozy place to be. The chambers within were arranged like any other château, which the prisoner would furnish according to his or her means and tastes.[11]

Prisoners could hear what went on in each other's rooms and talk to each other through the walls of their chambers or through the fireplaces. They were allowed to entertain guests from outside or visit fellow prisoners. Some were permitted to bring their mistresses into their chambers; others were granted permission to leave the château during the day, as long as they returned to their chambers as night fell. Now, in the autumn of 1698, the keys to the Château de la Bastille were to be placed into the hands of Bénigne Dauvergne de Saint-Mars.

Saint-Mars had detailed his plans for the conduct of Eustache to his new prison in a letter to Barbezieux. Dutifully the secretary read this out to the king, who, as the secretary noted, "approves and sees fit that you should leave with him, and as I have sent word in a previous letter, which I have no doubt you will receive presently." He then conveyed Louis's reply to Saint-Mars's request for secure accommodation to be provided along the road to Paris: the king did not think it necessary. Instead, Saint-Mars was told: "It will suffice that you lodge, paying, as conveniently and securely as possible, in places you judge appropriate to stay."[12]

Once again, it is clear that Saint-Mars was the one making suggestions regarding Eustache's security, rather than Louis and Barbezieux, both of whom merely approved or amended Saint-Mars's arrangements. In this case, jailer and prisoner were to stay in ordinary accommodation, for which Saint-Mars was required to pay out of his own pocket. There would be no strongholds or army quarters made available to them, and there was to be no military escort.

Barbezieux's letter was placed into Saint-Mars's hands six days later, and by the beginning of September, he was ready to set out on the long journey northward, passing the governorship of the islands into the care of Jean-François de Johanne, marquis de Saumery.

Saint-Mars left six prisoners on the island: Gabriel Mathurin, who would be released in 1714; Pierre de Salves; Mathieu de Malzac; Jean de Le Breton; Elisée Girault or Gérault; and Jean Gardien-Givry, all of whom would die on the island.[13]

Among those who traveled with Saint-Mars were his nephew, Guillaume de Formanoir de Corbest;[14] the sergeant Jacques Rosarges; and Antoine Ru, a turnkey. There were also two prisoners: Jean Herse, who would be dropped off at the prison of Pierre-Encize at Lyon, and Eustache, who would accompany Saint-Mars to his final destination.

News of the imminent arrival in Paris of Saint-Mars and his party was printed in the August 16 issue of the *Gazette*,[15] but otherwise the event went largely unnoticed. That was until Saint-Mars and his prisoner alighted from his litter on September 18, 1698, at three o'clock in the afternoon. He was met by his new second in command, Etienne Du Junca, the king's lieutenant at the Bastille.[16] As the great gate opened, the cannon on the roof of the château fired a deafening salute to welcome the new governor. As it happened, this tribute should not have taken place, but Du Junca had not received the order to ignore the custom on this occasion, so it went ahead as usual.

As to the custom regarding the reception of a new prisoner, the usual procedure demanded that all the shops that lined the street outside the main gate should be closed and the soldiers of the Bastille should turn their backs or else cover their faces with their hats as the new prisoner passed through the huge gates and disappeared into the gloomy courtyard beyond. However, on this occasion, the loud cannon salute that greeted Saint-Mars defeated any pretense of secrecy or discretion.

Again, under normal circumstances, a new prisoner would be met by the governor, who would emerge from his lodgings in the first courtyard to receive him. The prisoner would then be sent to a temporary chamber, there to wait for a period of time ranging from several hours to a few days until the chamber in which he was to reside was ready for him. Because Saint-Mars and Eustache had arrived together, it is probable that Saint-Mars immediately took over the care of the prisoner even before he had settled into his new lodgings. This much can be inferred from a description of the arrival of Saint-Mars and Eustache left by Du Junca.

Etienne Du Junca, a man in his late fifties and a former adjutant from the Bordeaux region, had been assigned to the Bastille on October 11, 1690, by the king. His main function was to deputize for Besmaux, who had become incapable of fulfilling his duties because of old age. Immediately when he took up his post, Du Junca began to keep two registers: in the first, he recorded the details of all the prisoners who arrived at the Bastille; in the second, he recorded those who left, released either by the king or by death. His entry for Thursday, September 18, 1698, read:

> *M. de Saint-Mars, governor of the château of the Bastille, made his first appearance, coming from his governorship of the Isles of Sainte-Marguerite-Honorat, bringing with him in his litter a prisoner whom he had at Pignerol, who was always masked [and] whose name is never spoken. As soon as he got out of the litter, he put him in the first chamber of the Basinière Tower to wait until night for me to take him, at nine o'clock in the evening, with M. de Rosarges one of the sergeants whom monsieur le governor had brought with him, into the third chamber of the Bertaudière Tower, which I had furnished with everything some days before his arrival, having received the order of monsieur de Saint-Mars.*[17]

Du Junca noted that the prisoner was to be looked after and served by Rosarges and maintained by Saint-Mars.

The Basinière Tower, in which Eustache spent the first few hours at the Bastille, was named after Macé Bertrand, seigneur de la Bazinière, an officer of the treasury who was arrested in 1661 at the same time as Nicolas Foucquet and spent four years as a prisoner in the tower. The tower's first chamber was often, but not always, used as a kind of reception area.

The Bertaudière, or Bretaudière, Tower was named after Berthaud, the mason who had designed it and who had fallen to his death during its construction.[18] In common with the other towers, the Bertaudière had chambers that were below ground and were subject to flooding, as well as very unpleasant *calottes* or vaulted attic chambers. The third chamber, which the prisoner was to occupy, was rather beautiful, comfortable, light, and airy; indeed it was one of the finest in the château, which boasted another three chambers of the same quality. The tower was "double," which meant that it had chambers on either side, separated by a central staircase.[19]

As the clock struck nine, and with the darkness and the chill of the autumn evening lying hard against the stone walls of the château, Du Junca and Rosarges came to collect the prisoner and escort him to his new chamber. Their torches blazed, and the flickering light cast a warm glow in the narrow staircase before the lengthening shadows gathered once again behind them. At last they arrived at the landing of the fourth floor; the large key scraped in the lock of the heavy wooden door. The prisoner stepped inside, the door creaked shut behind him, and the sound of the key turning in the lock echoed into silence.

The doors of history closed upon Eustache. From that moment, there are few references to him, and where he is mentioned, his name is never given. Instead, he is always referred to as l'ancien prisonnier, the old prisoner. However, he was not to remain in the third chamber of the Bertaudière Tower for long. The next time he is heard of is on April 30, 1701, when two men, Maranville and Tirmon, take up residence in the same tower. Of Tirmon nothing is known, although Hopkins describes him as a servant.[20] Du Junca describes Maranville, who is also referred to as Ricarville, as an army officer, "a malcontent who talks too much, a ne'er-do-well, whom I received following the king's orders."[21] The lieutenant placed him with Tirmon in "the second chamber of the Bertaudière Tower with the ancien prisonnier, both well locked in."[22]

This did not mean that Eustache, whom Saint-Mars believed to be in possession of a dangerous secret, suddenly found himself in the company of others. At Pignerol, his companion in the service of Foucquet, La Rivière, had been made a prisoner because he was believed to have learned what Eustache knew. At Exilles, the two men had shared a chamber, but had been kept strictly separate from the third prisoner, Videl. While on Sainte-Marguerite, Eustache was kept apart from the other prisoners, although he could hear them. At the Bastille, he was also accommodated alone, although, once again, he could hear other prisoners nearby.

Given his reluctance to betray any information about himself while in the donjon of Pignerol, it is to be wondered whether or not Eustache availed himself of the chance to speak to any of his new prison companions while in the Bastille. Had he done so, he would have incurred the wrath of Du Junca, who was determined that no prisoner should communicate with a neighbor. He saw any breach of this rule as a great crime, which he punished severely.[23]

One of Saint-Mars's prisoners left a vivid description of the governor as he appeared in this period of his life. Sinister and unflattering, it was written by a man who was imprisoned in the Bastille within a few years of Eustache's arrival. René Auguste Constantin de Renneville entered the Bastille at nine o'clock in the morning of May 16, 1702, and was initially lodged in the second chamber of the Chapel Tower. According to Du Junca, who duly recorded his arrival, Renneville had been employed for a long time abroad in the service of the king and had been falsely accused of spying by the marquis de Torcy.[24] He was arrested at Versailles as he was preparing to leave the country and was taken to the Bastille.[25] Several years later, he wrote a memoir, in which he described Saint-Mars as "a little old man of very meager appearance; his head, hands and whole body was shaking." Renneville went on: "He received us very civilly. He presented his trembling hand, which he put into mine; it was as cold as a block of ice; I said to myself: 'Here is a bad sign, death or his deputy has made an alliance with me.'"[26]

Shortly after his arrival, Saint-Mars had begun to transform the lenient regime he found at the Bastille into a strict system, and the prison gradually took on the sinister character for which it was to become infamous. Du Junca, no doubt on the orders of his superior, had placed double doors on all the chambers, as well as grills on most of the windows in each chamber. This was to deprive the prisoners a view of the streets of Paris. Now, only one window in each chamber was left open, much to the detriment of the well-being of the occupant.[27]

None of this was of any consequence to Eustache, however, for within two years of his having been joined by Maranville and Tirmon in the Bertaudière Tower, he died. Du Junca recorded the passing of the *ancien prisonnier* in his register:

> *Monday 19 November 1703—the prisoner—unknown, always masked with a mask of black velvet, who Monsieur de St Mars governor had brought with him upon coming from the isles St Marguerite whom he had guarded for a long time, the which feeling a little unwell yesterday upon leaving mass, he died today at ten o'clock in the evening without having had a serious illness; it could not have been more slight. M. Giraut our almoner confessed him yesterday is surprised by his death. He did not receive the sacraments, and our almoner exhorted him a moment before he died, and this unknown prisoner kept here for so long, was buried on Tuesday at four o'clock in the afternoon, 20 November in the cemetery of St Paul our parish. On the register of burial he was given a name also unknown; that Monsieur de Rosarges major and Arriel [sic] surgeon who have signed the register.*

In the margin, Du Junca added: "I have since learned that they named him on the register M de Marchiel, [and] that they paid forty livres for the funeral."[28]

The church of Saint-Paul-des-Champs was, as Du Junca wrote, the Bastille's parish church. It was situated on what is today the corner of the rue Saint-Paul and rue Neuve Saint-Pierre. It closed in 1790.[29] Its register was destroyed in a fire set by the Communards in May 1871, but, happily, its contents had already been copied by historians. The section recording the death and burial of the mysterious prisoner read: "On the 19th [November], Marchioly, aged 45 years or thereabouts, died at the Bastille, whose body was buried in the churchyard of St. Paul, his parish, the 20th of the present month, in the presence of M. Reglhe [sic], surgeon major of the Bastille, who signed." The entry was signed by Rosarges and Reilhe.[30]

The ancien prisonnier was dead and buried, and deemed worthy of no further thought. As the darkening chill of the late autumn afternoon descended over the city, the small burial party slowly made its way back toward the Bastille.

TWELVE

Legends of the Iron Mask

The ancien prisonnier was dead. He was remembered only by those who had served him during his thirty-four years as a state prisoner, men who, one by one, followed their captive to the grave. Rosarges was the first to die, in May 1705; Du Junca came next, in September 1706; Saint-Mars in October 1708. The abbé Honoré Giraut had left his post as almoner at the Bastille shortly after Saint-Mars's death; his date of death is not known. Only Antoine Ru, the turnkey, was still living; he would die in January 1713.

With the deaths of these men, Eustache lost his grounding in history; but his story had not yet come to an end. As the sun set over Paris on that November day in 1703, this mysterious man was reborn. He took on a new life, one in which he would eventually find immortality as the Man in the Iron Mask.

The legend began almost unnoticed. Some eight years after the death of the prisoner, on October 10, 1711, Duchesse Elisabeth-Charlotte sat down at her desk and took up her quill. The second wife of Philippe d'Orléans, brother to Louis XIV, the duchesse was a prolific letter writer, and her entertaining and informative correspondence told the story of her life at court and the people who populated it.

On this occasion, as so often, the letter was addressed to her aunt, the Electress Sophia of Hanover. In it, Elisabeth-Charlotte spoke about a mysterious prisoner she had heard about, a man who had "remained long years in the Bastille, and has died there, masked." She went on:

> *At his side he had two musketeers ready to kill him if he took off his mask. He ate and slept masked. No doubt there was some reason for this, for otherwise he was well treated and lodged, and given everything he wished for. He went to communion [mass] masked. He was very devout, and read continually. No one has ever been able to learn who he was.*

The prisoner had clearly excited the duchess's interest, for she made it her business to see what more she could find out about him. Her endeavors were evidently successful, and twelve days later, she wrote once again to her aunt:

> *I have just learnt who the masked man was, who died in the Bastille. His wearing a mask was not due to cruelty. He was an English lord who had been mixed up in the affair of the Duke of Berwick against King William. He died there so that the king might never know what became of him.*[1]

In fact, the prisoner identified by the duchesse d'Orléans was an Englishman named Hunt. He had been implicated in an assassination attempt on William III by the Scotsman George Barclay in 1696.

The information gleaned by Elisabeth-Charlotte is obviously incorrect, but her letters provide evidence that the now mysterious prisoner who had died at the Bastille in November 1703 was still the subject of speculation even eight years after his death. Yet, while some were reduced to speculating about his identity and why he might have been imprisoned, there were those who retained vivid memories of him.

One such person was Renneville, who had been a prisoner at the Bastille at the same time as Eustache. He published a memoir of his experience, *L'Inquisition françoise ou Histoire de la Bastille*, in 1719. In it, he noted that he had entered the Bastille on May 16, 1702, and that, shortly after his arrival, possibly in May 1703,[2] he unexpectedly encountered a mysterious prisoner whose name he was never able to learn.

Renneville recalled being taken into a room by Antoine Ru, only for them to discover that it was already occupied. Ru quickly bundled him into the corridor, and as he accompanied him back to his own chamber, he told the startled Renneville what he knew about his fellow inmate. The man had been a prisoner for thirty-one years, the turnkey explained, and Saint-Mars had brought him to Paris from the Île Sainte-Marguerite when he took up his post as governor of the Bastille. The prisoner had been condemned to perpetual imprisonment when, as a schoolboy of twelve or thirteen years old, he had written two verses against the Jesuits. In time, he had been transferred to the Île Sainte-Marguerite and afterward to the Bastille; during the journey, Saint-Mars had ensured that no one was able to see the mysterious man's face.

Ru told Renneville that the prisoner had left the Bastille two or three months after this encounter, adding that when the officers who had charge of him saw Renneville enter the room, they quickly turned their back toward him, thereby preventing Renneville from seeing the prisoner's face. Nevertheless, Renneville wrote that despite these precautions, he did have time to observe something of the prisoner's appearance. He recalled that he was of average height and well built; his hair, which he wore in a thick black curl, had not yet begun to turn gray.[3]

The basic facts of Ru's story, as they appeared in Renneville's memoir, were corroborated and further embellished by the surgeon at the Bastille, Abraham Reilhe. It is certain, however, that while they appear to have believed what they said, neither man had known the truth about the prisoner, and it is possible that they were told this story by Saint-Mars. As has been seen, Saint-Mars put out what he called contes jaunes, or fairy tales, to mock those curious to learn about the prisoners under his guard.

In 1745, several years after Renneville published his memoir, a book titled *Mémoires secrets pour servir à l'histoire de Perse* was published, a small volume the author of which is unknown. It tells the story of Cha-Abas I, who was the doting father of a young prince named Giafer. The boy's mother was Cha-Abas's beloved mistress, an Indian maiden. One day, Giafer and his half-brother, the heir to the Persian throne, were out playing when Giafer struck the heir. This was a serious offense for which the punishment was death. Cha-Abas was grief-stricken at the thought of handing over his son to be executed, but his ministers proposed a solution. They suggested that the young Giafer should join the army, which was currently on active service on the border of Feldran. After he had been there for a certain length of time, it would be announced that the prince had become ill with plague. This would ensure that he would be kept in isolation, far away from his brothers-in-arms, a sensible precaution designed to ensure that no one else would become infected. After a few days, it would be given out that the young man had died. The whole army would attend the funeral, which would be accompanied by the full honors befitting the young man's royal birth. Giafer would, however, be spirited away under cover of night and taken in great secrecy to the citadel on the island of Ormus, where he would be placed into the care of the governor. This plan was implemented, and the governor of Ormus was alerted to the imminent arrival of the prince. He was given orders from the king not to allow anyone to see the young man. Giafer was allowed to take one servant with him, but the man died during the long journey. In order to prevent his being recognized, the servant's clothes were removed and his face was slashed.

Having arrived on the island of Ormus, Giafer was treated well by the governor, who served him at the table and treated him with the respect due to a man of his status. The governor strictly obeyed his instructions and ensured that no one ever saw the young man's face. If he became ill and required the attentions of a physician, the governor would place a mask over Giafer's face before allowing the physician into the chamber.

One day, Giafer scratched his name onto the back of a plate with the point of a knife and threw it out of the window, where it was discovered by a servant. The man picked it up and took it to the governor, thinking he might receive a reward. In this he was deceived. The governor ordered the servant's immediate execution, and the secret of such great importance was buried with him. Finally, after several years as a captive on Ormus, Giafer was transferred to Ispahan when the governor of the island was promoted for his good and faithful service. At Ispahan, as on Ormus, the precaution of covering Giafer's face with a mask was taken whenever he became ill or made his confession, in order to prevent his face being seen.

As will be obvious, *L'Histoire de Perse* is a thinly veiled satire on the court of Louis XIV. First published in 1745, it was edited more than once, with later editions providing the reader with a key to the characters and locations featured in the tale, a service no doubt provided for those who did not see the connections between these and their historical counterparts. Cha-Abas was Louis XIV, Giafer was the comte de Vermandois, his illegitimate son by Louise de La Vallière. Louise appeared in the story as the Indian maiden. Feldran, where Giafer was sent to join the royal armies, stood in for Flanders, Ormus was the island of Sainte-Marguerite, while the Bastille became Ispahan. The anonymous author, however, included many of the elements that are found in the historical records, such as Saint-Mars serving his prisoner and the precautions taken to ensure the prisoner's face remained hidden; even the story of the dish, which was written on and thrown out of the window, makes an appearance. Saint-Mars, it will be recalled, wrote that one of his Huguenot prisoners, a minister named de Salves, wrote on his pewter dishes and linen. The incident had entered the folk memory of the island and now had taken its place among the emerging legends of the Man in the Iron Mask.

In 1746, a year after the publication of *Mémoires secrets pour servir à l'histoire de Perse*, a book was published under the title *Le masque de fer, ou les avatures admirables du Père et du Fils.* A somewhat unexciting adventure story, it was written by Charles de Fieux, chevalier de Mouhy, who occasionally worked for the police as an informer. While, despite its title, the book has no bearing on the legend of the Man in the Iron Mask as it was developing in the mid-18th century, it is worthy of mention because of information given in the *Advertissement.* Here, de Mouhy states that his story was inspired by historical events. Specifically, he claims that, in the time of Cromwell, a prince of Scotland was sent to the Isles de l'Archipel, or the islands of the Archipelago, with a mask on his face so that he would not be recognized. A second source of inspiration was an event that occurred during the reign of a cruel king of Spain, Don Pedro, who had put one of his sons into a mask because he had disgraced the king with a shameful act. De Mouhy next cites a story from Stockholm, which told of a newly married prince who was jealous of his wife's beauty. The prince gave her a sleeping draft the day after their wedding and, as she slept, enclosed her head in an iron mask like a helmet. When she awoke, the prince told her that the mask was a punishment from Heaven for having inspired love in men other than himself and for her excessive vanity for having boasted about her beauty. De Mouhy goes on to speak of a Turkish emperor who imprisoned his elder brother so that he could seize his throne. Fearing that the guards would be charmed by the sweetness and majesty of the prince and be filled with compassion for him, the emperor made his brother wear a mask of iron. The mask was made so that was impossible for even the most skilled laborer to break it or open it.

Although, as noted, *Le masque de fer, ou les avatures admirables du Père et du Fils* has nothing to do with the legend surrounding the mysterious prisoner, it shows that, by the time of its publication in the mid-18th century, the idea of an iron mask had already taken root in the popular imagination.

The *Histoire de Perse* and, to some extent, the information given in the introduction to *Le masque de fer, ou les avatures admirables du Père et du Fils* can be interpreted as reflecting the mistrust of the general populace toward those who rule over them. Such suspicions can be explored with relative safety in works such as these precisely because they appear under the guise of fiction. This defense, however, could not be applied to the next work. Appearing 1751 and written by Voltaire, *Le Siècle de Louis XIV* is a history of a period seen by its author as one of humanity's "ages of light."[4]

It has been suggested that Voltaire's interest in the legend of the Man in the Iron Mask had been stimulated as early as 1714, when he began attending the salon of Louis-Urbain Lefebvre de Caumartin.[5] He first conceived the idea of writing a history of the age of Louis XIV in 1732, although he anticipated that the work would take a long time to accomplish.

Six years later, in October 1738, Voltaire wrote to a friend, the abbé Jean-Baptiste Du Bos, noting that he had been well informed about the prisoner he called *l'homme au masque de fer*, who had died at the Bastille, claiming that he had spoken to men who had served this person.[6] In fact, Voltaire had himself been imprisoned at the Bastille: in May 1717, April 1718, and again at some point in 1726. It was during these stays that he presumably gathered his information; however, his claim to be privy to firsthand testimony is doubtful at best. As has been seen, every person who had been in personal contact with the ancien prisonnier was dead by the time of Voltaire's first imprisonment. One possible exception was the abbé Giraut, but he had left his post by that time.

Voltaire was correct to believe that his work would take a long time, but he was undaunted by the task and continued his research. By 1751, he was in a position to publish *Le Siècle de Louis XIV*. He dedicated part of one chapter to the prisoner, timing his captivity to the period just after the death of Mazarin and prior to the arrest of Foucquet—that is, the summer of 1661.[7]

It was during this time, Voltaire told his readers, that an event occurred that is "without parallel" and "what is stranger, all historians omit to mention it." He then describes an "unknown prisoner, of height above the ordinary, young, and of extremely handsome and noble figure," who was taken "under great secrecy to the castle on the Island of Sainte-Marguerite, lying in the Mediterranean off Provence." During the journey, the prisoner wore a "mask, the chin-piece of which had steel springs to enable him to eat while still wearing it, and his guards had orders to kill him if he uncovered his face."

The prisoner remained on Sainte-Marguerite until "an officer of the secret service by name Saint-Mars, governor of Pignerol, who was made governor of the Bastille in 1690, went in that year to Sainte-Marguerite, and brought him to the Bastille still wearing his mask." While he was still on the island, the prisoner was visited by the marquis de Louvois, who "remained standing while speaking to him, evidently regarding him with respect."

Upon being taken to the Bastille, the prisoner was "accommodated as well as was possible in that citadel," and nothing he asked for was refused. He had a fondness for fine linen and lace, and was served delicacies by the governor, who rarely sat in his presence. Voltaire notes that an old physician attached to the Bastille would attend the prisoner. The physician declared that he never saw the man's face, "although he had often examined his tongue and the rest of his body." From what he saw of him, the physician, whom Voltaire does not name, was able to see that his patient was "a wonderfully well-made man . . . his skin was rather dark; he charmed by the mere tone of his voice, never complaining about his lot nor giving a hint at his identity." According to Voltaire, the mysterious prisoner died in 1704 and was buried at night in the parish church of Saint-Paul.

"What is doubly astonishing," Voltaire added, "is that when he was sent to the Island of Sainte-Marguerite no man of any consequence in Europe disappeared. Yet, such the prisoner was without a doubt, for during the first few days that he was on the island, the governor himself put the dishes on the table and then withdrew, locking the door after him."

There are several items of interest regarding Voltaire's account. The first thing to note is that he makes several mistakes, namely, his assertion that Saint-Mars had threatened to kill the prisoner if he spoke his name when, in fact, the original order as given to Saint-Mars was that he would be killed if he spoke of anything other than his basic needs. The threat to kill the prisoner if he spoke his name appears in the article attributed to Louis Foucquet and became part of the later legend. Saint-Mars was made governor of the Bastille in 1698, not, in 1690. Moreover, Voltaire is unaware that the prisoner had been in Saint-Mars's charge throughout his prison life, which had begun in 1669. The two men went from Pignerol to Exilles, on to Sainte-Marguerite, and lastly to the Bastille. Louvois did not go to Sainte-Marguerite but to Pignerol, where he inspected the new security arrangements following the failed attempt to rescue Foucquet. The prisoner had died in 1703, not 1704 as asserted by Voltaire, and he was buried at four in the afternoon in November, so the funeral did not take place at night but under the natural darkness of a late autumn afternoon.

On the other hand, Voltaire accurately describes the procedure applied by Saint-Mars as he served the prisoner his meals. He is also correct to say that the prisoner never complained about his lot, an observation that agrees with Saint-Mars's reports that Eustache was at peace with God and the king. Voltaire's description of the mask is elaborate but reminiscent of the steel mask mentioned in the article, attributed to Louis Foucquet, that was passed among the Jansenist priests. He is correct to say that Saint-Mars personally attended his prisoner, although in the Bastille, the work of serving him was largely left to others, particularly Rosarges.

Voltaire's work was revised the following year, with the new edition correcting some of the errors that had appeared in the first, and adding some extra material. Into this new version, Voltaire inserted information about the prisoner playing the guitar and he corrected the date of his death to 1703. He also added this intriguing anecdote:

One day the prisoner wrote something with his knife on a silver plate and threw it out of the window in the direction of a boat lying by the bank almost at the foot of the tower. A fisherman, to whom the boat belonged, picked up the plate and carried it to the governor. In amazement the latter asked him, "Have you read what is written on this plate, and has anyone seen it in your hands?" "I cannot read," replied the fisherman, "I have just found it, and no one else has seen it." The peasant was detained until the governor was convinced that he had not read it and that the plate had not been seen. "Go now," he [Saint-Mars] said to him; "you are a very lucky man not to be able to read."

There is a little inconsistency in this narrative: Voltaire is uncertain as to the identity of the man who discovered the silver plate. Is he a fisherman or a peasant? Undeterred, Voltaire assures his readers that, among those who had firsthand knowledge of this affair, "a very trustworthy one is still alive." He, therefore, attributes this new information to an unnamed, though reliable source.

In the revised edition, Voltaire also adds information involving Michel de Chamillart. As the last secretary of the ministry of war to have jurisdiction over Eustache's imprisonment, Chamillart was the last official "to be acquainted with the strange secret." Chamillart's son-in-law, the second maréchal de la Feuillade, told Voltaire that as his father-in-law lay dying, he "implored him on his knees to tell him the name of this man who had been known simply as *the man in the iron mask*. Chamillart replied that it was a state secret and that he had sworn never to reveal it."[8] As he brings his account to an end, Voltaire notes that there were still many of his contemporaries who could confirm the truth as he had written it; indeed, he knew of no affair "more extraordinary, and at the same time better authenticated."

In fact, Voltaire had constructed his story from several sources.[9] The first of these was Jean Marsolan, surgeon to the duc de Richelieu and the Regent. Marsolan was the son-in-law of Fresquière, a physician who had attended the prisoner in the Bastille. Fresquière had described the prisoner's face to Marsolan, who in turn passed the information on to Voltaire. Despite this connection, however, Voltaire failed to name Fresquière. The second source was Charles de Fournier de Bernaville, who had become governor of the Bastille in 1708 upon the death of Saint-Mars and held the post until 1718. Voltaire was imprisoned at the

Bastille was toward the end of Bernaville's tenure, providing him with the opportunity to gain some insight into the story of the masked prisoner. Voltaire's third source was Louis d'Aubuisson, duc de la Feuillard. The duke was married to Marie-Thérèse Chamillart, daughter of the former secretary of state for war. A hierarchy of sorts can, therefore, be traced in three of Voltaire's sources: Chamillart, Marsolan, and la Feuillade.[10]

In his *Siècle de Louis XIV*, Voltaire had hinted that the Man in the Iron Mask was a man of great importance and described him as tall, young, extremely handsome, and of a noble bearing. In the second edition, he noted that the prisoner had a liking for fine linens and lace and that he played the guitar.[11] Saint-Mars treated him with great respect, Voltaire asserted, and Louvois, a great minister of state, treated the prisoner with deference, even standing in his presence. Although Voltaire made no direct assertions at this point as to the identity of the prisoner, it is clear that he was guiding his readers toward the possibility that this man was very important indeed.

Voltaire's *Siècle de Louis XIV* was criticized by La Beaumelle,[12] who accused the famous writer and philosopher of plagiarizing *Mémoires secrets pour servir à l'histoire de Perse*, in particular, the story of the silver dish and the fisherman. Voltaire replied with the *Supplement to the Siècle de Louis XIV*, published in 1753. In it, he defended himself against the accusation by declaring his surprise that he had found this story in *L'Histoire de Perse* because he had heard it from the marquis d'Argens, with whom he spent some time in Berlin the previous winter. D'Argens's source was one Jean de Riouffe, a former commissioner for war in Cannes. Riouffe claimed that, in his youth, he had seen the prisoner as he was being transferred from the Île Sainte-Marguerite to Paris.[13]

In the *Supplement*, Voltaire also offered more information about Michel Chamillart. He wrote that the secretary for war had become tired of being questioned by la Feuillade and Caumartin about the identity of the mysterious prisoner. In an attempt to satisfy their curiosity, he had revealed that the prisoner was someone "who possessed all the secrets of Monsieur Foucquet."

If Chamillart's words had been reported correctly, he was obviously mistaken. As Saint-Mars had stated in his letter dated April 8, 1680: "Monsieur de Lauzun knows most of the important things that M. Foucquet knew and that the man named La Rivière is not unaware of them." What Lauzun and La Rivière had come to learn and which Foucquet already knew was, of course, Eustache's secret. Be that as it may, Voltaire wondered why such unheard-of precautions had been taken against a confidant of M. Foucquet, a subordinate. "Let it be remembered," he stated, "that no notable man had disappeared at that time. It is therefore clear that this was a prisoner of the greatest importance whose destiny had always been secret."[14]

Another man to write in response to Voltaire's *Siècle de Louis XIV* was a former prisoner at Sainte-Marguerite, Joseph de La Grange-Chancel.[15] He had been sent to Sainte-Marguerite in 1719 for writing the *Philippiques* against the regent, and he noted that the presence of the mysterious prisoner was no longer a state secret by the time. He stated, correctly, that the events spoken of by Voltaire had not taken place a few months after the death of Mazarin in 1661, but eight years later in 1669. The governor of the island in 1719 was Charles de La Motte-Guérin, who had once served under Saint-Mars as king's lieutenant. He had told La Grange-Chancel that the prisoner was, in fact, the duc de Beaufort, who was said to have been killed at the siege of Candia, and whose body had never been found. This, it will be recalled, corresponds with the gossip reported by Saint-Mars when he first took up his post as governor of the Île Sainte-Marguerite. Despite his precautions, the local people had learned of the presence of a mysterious and, presumably, important prisoner, whom they speculated must have been the duc de Beaufort or the son of the late Cromwell.

La Grange-Chancel noted that Saint-Mars was said to have held the prisoner in high regard, personally serving his meals on a silver service every day and providing him with fine clothes. Whenever the prisoner was ill or needed a surgeon, he was obliged, on pain of death, to wear his iron mask, and when alone, he would amuse himself by pulling stray hairs out of his beard with a pair of highly polished tweezers. La Grange-Chancel claimed to have seen these tweezers in the hands of the sieur de Formanoir, Saint-Mars's nephew and lieutenant of the compagnie-franche. Several people had told La Grange-Chancel that, when Saint-Mars was preparing to take up his post at the Bastille, taking his prisoners with him, the man wearing the iron mask was heard to ask, "Does the King want my life?" "No, my Prince," replied Saint-Mars, "your life is safe; you have only to let yourself be led."

La Grange-Chancel also mentions a man named Dubuisson, who, having been a prisoner at the Bastille for several years, was taken to Sainte-Marguerite where he was lodged with a group of other prisoners. Their chamber was directly above that of the mysterious prisoner, and by means of the chimney flue, they were able to speak to him. When they asked him why he persisted in refusing to tell them his name and the adventures that had led him to the island prison, he replied that such a confession would cost him not only his own life, but that of those to whom he revealed his secret. If this is true, it is reminiscent of the unsuccessful attempt made by Foucquet's valets to talk to Eustache. In this instance, the prisoner warned of the mortal danger in revealing his identity and his story to both himself and to his companions in captivity.

Interest in the legend of the Man in the Iron Mask continued to spread far and wide, and among those who took it upon themselves to investigate the story was Germain-François Poullain de Saint-Foix, a man of letters.[16] The first theory to come under his scrutiny was that which was set out in the *L'Histoire de Perse*, which identified the face behind the iron mask as that of the comte de Vermandois. This was instantly dismissed by Saint-Foix because, as he pointed out, none of the contemporary memoirs had recorded such a story about the young comte as it had been set out in that anonymous work. Moreover, the comte had been only sixteen years old at the time the incident was supposed to have occurred, while the dauphin was twenty-two, married, and with a son, the duc de Bourgogne. Saint-Foix found it inconceivable that Louis XIV would treat a beloved son, even a natural one, with such severity, and even if the king had felt obliged to demand satisfaction on behalf of the dauphin, he would not have punished the boy in secret for so public a crime, but would instead have sought a more visible form of reparation.

Saint-Foix next turned his attention to the theory that the Man in the Iron Mask was the duc de Beaufort, a theory noted by Saint-Mars and supported by La Grange-Chancel. Once again, the theory was refuted because Louis XIV, "adored by his subjects, respected by his neighbors, enjoying a glorious peace after conquests," would not have had anything to fear from the duc de Beaufort. There was nothing to justify his sending the duke to prison and hiding his whereabouts. Moreover, all those who had spoken of the prisoner agreed that he was young and of a noble bearing, characteristics that, according to Saint-Foix, could not be applied to Beaufort. As though this were not proof enough, Saint-Foix offers anecdotal evidence from the marquis de Saint André Montbrun, who had been a commander on Candia at the time of the siege. Montbrun stated that Beaufort had been killed at the siege, after which his head was removed and carried through the streets of Constantinople on a pike on the orders of the grand vizier.

At the time Saint-Foix's work was published, the official records had not yet been made public but were still stored in the archives belonging to the appropriate ministries. The precise date of the Man in the Iron Mask's imprisonment was not available to researchers. Nevertheless, Voltaire thought that the prisoner had been put away in 1661, while La Grange-Chancel gave 1669. The *Histoire de Perse*, on the other hand, set the date at 1683. None of these dates were correct according to Saint-Foix, who concluded that the Man in the Iron Mask had been imprisoned in 1685 and that he was James, duke of Monmouth, the son of Charles II of England and his mistress Lucy Walter.

Saint-Foix justified his theory by explaining that, following the death of his father and the subsequent accession of James II, the young duke had led an unsuccessful rebellion against his uncle and was captured and imprisoned in the Tower of London. He was condemned to be beheaded on July 15, 1685, but his place was taken by an officer who resembled him and who had also been condemned to death. The officer stepped onto the scaffold in order that the prince might escape.

Saint-Foix appeals to several pieces of evidence to support his theory. In one, a lady who had known the prince persuaded those who were watching over the coffin to open it. Upon seeing the corpse's right arm, she cried, "Ah, it is not him!" Another piece of evidence came in the form of a book, *Amours de Charles II & de Jacques II Rois d'Angleterre*, in which it is stated that on the night following Monmouth's supposed execution, King James accompanied by three men removed the duke from the Tower and covered his face with a hood before the king and the duke drove off in a carriage, with the three men following on behind. This anecdote reminded Saint-Foix of a story told to him by a certain abbé Tournemine that stated that the king's confessor, Father Sanders, had assured the duchess of Portsmouth that Monmouth had not been executed.

Saint-Foix was convinced that Monmouth had been spirited away to France in order to distance him from those who continued to nurture hopes that he would one day return as a messianic figure and save his supporters. The duke ended up in the Bastille, where he came to the attention of one Nelaton, an English surgeon, who recalled an incident that occurred when he was serving as chief assistant to the surgeon at the Porte Saint-Antoine. Upon being summoned to the Bastille to bleed a sick prisoner, the governor took him into one of the chambers, where "he had a man who complained of a lot of headaches." This man's face was covered with a towel, which was knotted at the neck. Nelaton was unable to see the patient's face, but he could tell "by his accent that this man was English."

Saint-Foix's theory caught the attention of Guillaume-Louis Formanoir de Palteau. The son of Guillaume Formanoir de Corbest, Palteau was the great nephew of Saint-Mars, and he had been interested in the mysterious prisoner for some time. He shared what he knew of him in a letter to Elie Fréron, editor of *L'Année litteraire*.[17] He noted that the prisoner was known only as *La Tour* during the time he had been held on Sainte-Marguerite and at the Bastille. Palteau said that the governor and the officers had great regard for this man, to whom they gave everything that could be given to a prisoner. La Tour was allowed to walk outside as long as he wore his mask, but, wrote Palteau, it had not been until the publication of Voltaire's *Siècle de Louis XIV* that he heard it said that the mask was made of iron and was fitted with springs. He added that the prisoner was required to wear the mask only when he went out to take the air or when he was obliged to appear before some stranger. This contradicts the information unearthed by the duchesse d'Orléans, who thought that the prisoner was obliged to wear the mask at all times.

Palteau spoke of the sieur de Blainvilliers, Saint-Mars's cousin and an officer in the compagnie-franche, who had often told Palteau of his curiosity to know more about La Tour. Blainvilliers had tried to satisfy this curiosity by dressing in the uniform and carrying the arms of a sentinel stationed in the gallery beneath the windows of the prisoner's chamber on Sainte-Marguerite. The officer watched him throughout the night and managed to get a good look at him. He noted that the prisoner was not wearing his mask, his face was white, he was tall and well made, his lower leg was a little swollen, and his hair was white, even though he was still in his prime. The prisoner had spent the entire night pacing in his chamber. Blainvilliers added that the prisoner was always dressed in brown, that he was given fine linen and books, and that Saint-Mars and his officers would remain standing before him uncovered until he told them to put their hats on and sit down. They would often keep him company and eat with him. Palteau continued:

In 1698, M. de Saint-Mars passed from the governorship of the isles of Sainte-Marguerite to that of the Bastille. On his way to take up his post, he stayed with his prisoner on his estate at Palteau. The masked man arrived in a litter which preceded that of M. de Saint-Mars; they were accompanied by several men on horseback. The peasants went to meet their lord.

M. de Saint-Mars ate with his prisoner, who had his back to the windows of the dining-room, which looked out onto the courtyard. The *peasants whom I have questioned could not see whether he ate with his mask on, but they observed very well that M. de Saint-Mars, who sat at the table opposite him, had two pistols at the side of his plate. They were served by only one valet de chambre, who carried the plates from an ante-room, carefully closing the dining-room door behind him.*

When the prisoner crossed the courtyard he always had his black mask over his face. The peasants remarked that they could see his teeth and lips, that he was tall and had white hair. M. de Saint-Mars slept on a bed that had been put up for him next to that of the masked man.

That Saint-Mars was said to have had two pistols at either side of his plate in readiness to shoot the prisoner is reminiscent of the duchesse d'Orléans's account, in which two musketeers were on hand to fire on his if he tried to remove his mask.

Blainvilliers also told Palteau that when the prisoner died, the year of which Palteau gave as 1704, he was secretly buried in the cemetery at Saint-Paul and that they placed chemicals in the coffin to consume the corpse. Palteau had not heard that the prisoner spoke with a foreign accent, thereby refuting Saint-Foix's assertion that he might have been the English duke of Monmouth.

In 1769, an important development was made in the study of the Man in the Iron Mask when Père Henri Griffet published some extracts from Etienne Du Junca's registers.[18] A respected historian and scholar, Griffet taught at the Jesuit school Louis-le-Grand in Paris, preached at court, and had served as a chaplain at the Bastille between 1745 and 1764. The extracts, which included the entry in which the death and burial of the mysterious prisoner was announced, were printed in the book *Traité des différentes sortes de preuves qui servent à établir la vérité de l'Histoire* and annotated by Griffet:

The memory of the masked prisoner was still preserved among the officers, soldiers, and servants of the Bastille, when M. de Launay, who has long been the governor, came to occupy a place on the staff of the garrison.[19] *Those who had seen him with his mask, when he crossed the courtyards on his way to mass, said that after his death the order was given to burn everything he had used, such as linen, clothes, cushions, counterpanes, &c.: and that the very walls of the room he had occupied had to be scraped and whitewashed again, and that all the tiles of the flooring were taken up and replaced by others, because they were so afraid that he had found the means to conceal some notes or some mark, the discovery of which would have revealed his name.*

Père Griffet speculates that these measures had to be related in some way to the incident of the plate on which the prisoner had engraved his name and which had been found by a fisherman and carried to Saint-Mars. The pewter vessels upon which Pierre de Salves scratched had become a part of the legend of the Man in the Iron Mask, with the engraving now being attributed to the mysterious prisoner.

Griffet speculated that the destruction of the items used by the prisoner, as well as all traces of his existence, were designed to preserve the secret of his identity, a conclusion that contrasts with Louvois's requirement that the secret of how the prisoner was previously employed must be guarded.[20] He also reported a story, which he attributed to Launay, that concerned Monsieur d'Argenson, lieutenant of the police, who had the task of periodically inspecting the Bastille. He was aware that there was still talk among the staff of the mysterious prisoner, and one day he asked the officers what was being said. They told him the various conjectures, to which he replied that "we will never know that."

The year following the first edition of Père Griffet's book saw the publication of a letter written to the editors of the *Journal encyclopédique* by Baron de Heiss, a former captain of the Alsace regiment. He explained that, since the publication of Voltaire's *Siècle de Louis XIV*, his curiosity about the Man in the Iron Mask had been piqued, and he had taken it upon himself to try to discover who the prisoner might have been.[21] He admitted that his research had so far been unsuccessful, but, by a happy accident, he had come across a section of an article titled "Mantoue" in a book, *Histoire abrégé de l'Europe pour le mois d'Août 1689.*

From what he read, Heiss deduced that the secretary of the duke of Mantua could have been the Man in the Iron Mask, who had been transferred from Pignerol to Sainte-Marguerite and from there to the Bastille in 1690 [*sic*], when Saint-Mars took over as governor. He noted that he found this hypothesis all the more believable because, as Voltaire had said, no prince or any person of note in Europe had disappeared.

The secretary Heiss spoke of was, of course, Matthioli. Although a nobleman, Matthioli was largely unknown beyond the borders of his own country, and to those who arrested him, interrogated him, and held him at Pignerol, he was merely another prisoner to be guarded. He, therefore, could be seen to fit the criterion of being a person of no note. Heiss's hypothesis resonated with many researchers at the time, and Matthioli would be accepted as the Man in the Iron Mask for many years to come.

In 1770, Voltaire returned to the subject of the Man in the Iron Mask in *Questions sur l'encyclopédie*, a work that contained articles on a variety of subjects. Some of these had been reedited and modified from a previous work, the *Dictionnaire philosophique*, which had been published six years earlier. The new work followed the same format as the earlier one and included an article titled "Anecdote on the Man in the Iron Mask."[22] In it, the theories that the unknown prisoner might have been Beaufort, Vermandois, or Monmouth were dismissed. While Voltaire did not name his favored candidate, he did offer some details that complemented his earlier research and dropped hints that might lead a perceptive reader to a certain conclusion. Specifically, he noted that if the prisoner had not been allowed to cross the court of the Bastille or to see his physician unless he was wearing his mask, it must have been out of fear that someone would have "recognized in his face some too striking resemblance." There was really only one person in France at the time whose face would be instantly recognizable, and that was the king's. As to the prisoner's age, a few days before he died he had said to the apothecary at the Bastille that he thought he was about sixty years old. Voltaire's source was Jean Marsolan, who had also assisted him when he was researching the *Siècle de Louis XIV.* Since the prisoner died in 1703, he would have been born in or close to 1643.

The following year, 1771, Voltaire republished *Questions sur l'encyclopédie* and whatever doubt there might have been regarding the true identity of the Man in the Iron Mask was removed. The revised edition contained a note purportedly written by the publisher but which some think may have been written by Voltaire himself.[23] It stated that the "Iron Mask was without doubt a brother, and an older brother, of Louis XIV." This assertion challenges the claim in the first edition, which states that the prisoner thought he was about sixty at the time of his death; for to be older than Louis XIV, he would of necessity have been born prior to 1638. Nevertheless, the editor's note appealed to Anne of Austria's "taste for fine linen with which M. de Voltaire has supported his case." It goes on to say that it was "in reading the memoirs of the times, which reported that anecdote on the subject of the queen, which recalled the same taste of the Iron Mask, I no longer doubted that he was her son; which all other circumstances had already persuaded me." The anecdote in question refers to the legendary origins of Louis XIV:

> *It is known that Louis XIII had long ceased to live with the queen, that the birth of Louis XIV was due only to a happy accident; an accident which obliged the king to sleep in the same bed with the queen. Here is, then, what I believe happened. The queen had come to imagine that it was her fault that no heir had been born to Louis XIII. The birth of the Mask undeceived her. The cardinal [Richelieu], whom she had taken into her confidence, knew how to take advantage of this secret; he believed he could turn this event to his own profit and that of the state. Persuaded by this example that the queen could give the king children, he arranged it so that the king and the queen would be obliged to share a bed. But the queen and the cardinal, both aware of the need to hide the existence of the Iron Mask from Louis XIII, had the child brought up in secret. This secret was kept from Louis XIV*

until after the death of Cardinal Mazarin. But this monarch, learning that he had a brother and an older brother whom his mother could not disown, who, moreover, perhaps bore marked features which announced his origin; reflecting that this child born in wedlock could not, without great disadvantage and a terrible scandal, be declared illegitimate after the death of Louis XIII, Louis XIV could not have used a more wise and more just means than that which he employed to assure his own peace and the calm of his state, a means which spared him from committing a cruel act which politics would have held as necessary to a monarch less conscientious and less magnanimous than Louis XIV.

This, then, was the opinion attributed to Voltaire in the introduction of *Questions sur l'encyclopédie*: gone was the ambiguity that had been present in the first edition; now it was affirmed that the mysterious prisoner had been Louis XIV's elder brother.

The implications of this were that Louis had not been the rightful king because his older brother was still living. He had, nevertheless, been unaware of the existence of this brother until after the death of his first minister, Cardinal Mazarin, in 1661. The king, who was twenty-two years old at the time, could not deny his older brother, nor could he declare him illegitimate because the resulting scandal would have caused great harm to the monarchy. Moreover, the possibility that the brother bore a strong resemblance to the king meant that he could not simply be put away; there had to be some other means of keeping his identity a secret. As such, Louis devised the strategy of imprisoning his brother and making him wear a mask of iron so that his face would always be concealed.

In suggesting that the Man in the Iron Mask was an older brother of Louis XIV, Voltaire appears to have been influenced by Père Griffet, who wrote a legendary account of Louis XIV's conception based on earlier accounts by the marquis de Montglat, an officer in the army of Navarre and grand master of the king's guard, and Mme de Motteville, lady-in-waiting to Queen Anne of Austria.[24] However, Voltaire fails to explain why the elder brother should have been a problem. He would simply have become king upon the death of his father, while the younger son, Louis, would have assumed the role played by his own younger brother, Philippe duc d'Orléans.

While Voltaire had been a prisoner at the Bastille, he naturally had had no access to the records that were stored there; instead, he had to rely on the reminiscences of those who had encountered the prisoner. This was not the case with Henri Godillon-Chevalier, who served as major of the Bastille from 1749 until his death on February 21, 1787. Third in command after the governor and the king's lieutenant, Chevalier managed the internal administration of the Bastille and was charged by M. de Malesherbes[25] to make a study of its archives. Like Père Griffet before him, Chevalier came across Du Junca's registers, including the entries concerning the death and burial of the mysterious prisoner. He summarized these and added his own observations:[26] "This is the famous masked man whom no one has ever known," he wrote. "He was treated with great distinction by the governor, and was seen only by M. de Rosarges, major of the said château, who had sole charge of him; he was not ill except for a few hours, and died rather suddenly: interred at St Paul's on Tuesday November 20, 1703, at four o'clock, under the name of Marchiergues [*sic*]." He went on to add that the prisoner "was buried in a new sheet and generally everything that was found in his room was burnt, such as his bed, including the mattress, tables, chairs, and other items, [which were] reduced to dust and ashes and thrown into the privies." Other items used by the prisoner were similarly destroyed. "This prisoner was lodged in the third chamber of the Bertaudière Tower, which chamber was scraped back to the stone and whitewashed. The doors and windows were burned with the rest."

Three years after the publication of Chevalier's book, Jean-Pierre Papon, a librarian at the Collège de l'Oratoire at Marseille, was traveling through Provence. He was gathering stories and anecdotes about the area for a book, *Voyage littéraire de Provence*, which he would publish in 1780.

His journey inevitably took him to the Îles de Lérins, where he researched the story of the "famous prisoner with the Iron Mask, whose name we will perhaps never know."[27] He learned that there were only a few people who had access to the prisoner, one of whom was his jailer, Saint-Mars, whose name here is incorrectly given as Saint-Marc.

In one of the stories Papon heard, Saint-Mars was talking to the prisoner one day, standing just outside the room as he did so in order that he might see if anyone approached who should not be there. As it happened, the son of one of his friends appeared unexpectedly in the corridor, causing Saint-Mars hurriedly to close the door before the young man could see who was inside. Disconcerted, the jailer asked the youth if he had heard anything, and the boy assured him that he had not. Even so, Saint-Mars sent the boy away that same day with a letter to the father saying that the adventure had almost cost his son dearly and that he was sending the boy home for fear of anything else happening.

Papon then heard of another alleged incident, this time involving a fisherman who had found a silver plate. He had taken it to Saint-Mars, who told him that he was fortunate that he could not read. Papon did not elaborate upon this story, but it is clear that it was inspired by the antics of the Huguenot minister, Pierre de Salves, who used to write his name on his pewter vessels and linen.[28] Papon related this story on the strength of Voltaire, who, he says, had not imagined it, but he added that the oldest people at the fort assured him that they had never heard of it.

Intrigued by these stories, Papon visited the chamber said to have been occupied by the masked prisoner. It was lit by one north-facing window, which was set into a very thick wall and closed behind three sets of iron bars, each placed at equal distance from the other. The window looked out onto the sea. He found an officer of the compagnie-franche in the citadel, a man of seventy-nine, whose father had also served in the regiment. This man recalled a story his father had told him about a barber who one day had seen something white floating in the water below the prisoner's window. The barber had fished out the item to discover that it was a shirt of fine white linen, carelessly folded, and which was covered with writing. He took it to Saint-Mars, who, having unfolded it and read a few lines of the writing, asked the barber if he had not had the curiosity to read what was written on it. The barber protested several times that he was unable to read; however, two days later, he was found dead in his bed. This was the story the officer had heard from his father, and which was also known to the almoner who had served at the same time.

Papon goes on to explain that at one stage a search had been made for a woman to serve the prisoner, and a lady from the village of Mougins applied, thinking that such a job would allow her to make her children's fortune. When she was told that she would no longer be able to see her children, or even to maintain contact with anyone outside the prison, she refused to be shut in with the prisoner. Papon added that two sentinels were placed at either side of the fortress on the sea side, and that they had orders to fire on any boats that approached within a certain distance of the island.

Papon's account shows now classic hallmarks of the legend in the making. Historical facts, such as Saint-Mars's assertion that he could not find valets for his prisoners because they did not wish to be imprisoned themselves, and de Salves writing on his plates and shirts and throwing them out of the window, have become associated with stories of the mysterious prisoner. That the shirts have now become fine white linen suggest the influence of Voltaire and the connection between the prisoner and the royal family.

While the story that the Man in the Iron Mask was an older brother of Louis XIV is most associated with Voltaire, the city of Chartres was home to a different version of the legend. This time, the mysterious prisoner was said to have been the son of Anne of Austria and a lover, possibly George Villiers, duke of Buckingham. The handsome English duke had famously flirted with the queen during a visit to France in 1625.

The story can be traced to Genevieve-Antoinette du Bois de Saint-Quentin, who was the mistress of Barbezieux, secretary of state for war. Barbezieux died in 1701, leaving his mistress with enough money to allow her to live comfortably for the rest of her life. Mademoiselle de

Saint-Quentin withdrew from court and retired to Chartres, where she would remain until her death. It was here that she began to circulate the story that Anne of Austria had secretly given birth to a child by a lover, adding that she had been given this information by Barbezieux. The story persisted in Chartres, where it was heard by Jean-Benjamin de La Borde, first valet de chambre to Louis XV. He later included it in his book, *Histoire de l'Homme au masque de fer, tirée du Siècle de Louis XIV par Voltaire*, which he published in London in 1783.

Mlle de Saint-Quentin's story was also known to the historian Charpentier, who wrote about the prisoner in his book, *La Bastille dévoilée*.[29] He noted that Louis XIV and Louvois were the first trustees of the Iron Mask's secret. Upon Louvois's death, the secret passed to his son, Barbezieux, whose successor, Chamillart, inherited it in his turn. Chamillart, however, refused to tell his son-in-law, la Feuillade, who the mysterious man was, although he did hint at what the secret might have been about.

According to Charpentier, the second duc d'Orléans became privy to the secret upon becoming regent, and that he may even have learned it from Louis XIV as the latter lay on his deathbed. Charpentier accepted Mlle de Saint-Quentin's account that the prisoner was Anne of Austria's illegitimate son by the duke of Buckingham, and that there was a "perfect resemblance" between him and his younger half-brother, Louis XIV, which is why the prisoner was put into the mask.

Charpentier also comments on the stories of the extraordinary measures that were taken following the death of the prisoner. To the accounts of Griffet and Chevalier he adds others by Saint-Foix and Linguet, all making similar claims regarding the destruction of the chamber, linen, and other items used by the prisoner. These accounts were confirmed by M. le chevalier de Saint-Sauveur, whose father had been governor of the château de Vincennes at the same time that Saint-Mars was at the Bastille. Saint-Sauveur's father had paid a visit to Saint-Mars and personally witnessed these precautions, which were taken to ensure that the secret of the Man in the Iron Mask was buried with him.

Like others before him, the philologist and writer Louis Dutens was curious to find out anything he could about the Man in the Iron Mask.[30] He recalled that the duc de Choiseul, Louis XV's foreign minister, had frequently heard the king say that he knew who the Iron Mask was. The duke's interest was naturally piqued, and he would occasionally pluck up the courage to question the king directly about the man's identity. The king, however, would never divulge any information except to say that the conjectures that had so far been made were all untrue. Undeterred, Choiseul urged the king's mistress Madame de Pompadour to press her royal lover on the subject only for her to be told that the prisoner had been a minister of an Italian prince.

Dutens researched the Italian prince and his ministers and discovered Matthioli, who had first been proposed as the Iron Mask in 1770. He contacted the marquis de Castellane, a former governor of the island of Sainte-Marguerite, who was also researching the story of the famous prisoner. He had come across a memoir written by one Claude Souchon.

A man of seventy-nine years of age, Souchon was the son of Jacques Souchon, who had served as a cadet in Castellane's compagnie-franche. Claude claimed to have been privy to Saint-Mars's secrets and had often heard his father and the sieur Favre, Saint-Mars's almoner, speaking about the prisoner who had been kept with such care and mystery on the island, and who was referred to as the Iron Mask. Souchon had deduced that the prisoner had been an imperial envoy of the court of Turin who had been abducted by the French, made to write to his secretary ordering him to send his papers to Louvois, and who had died on Sainte-Marguerite nine years after his arrest. Souchon denied many of the assertions made by Voltaire, including the story of the fisherman and the silver dish and that the Iron Mask had been taken to the Bastille by Saint-Mars. He did, however, know that the person who had served the prisoner had died on Sainte-Marguerite. This is obviously Rousseau, Matthioli's valet, who died on the island and was buried on Saint-Honorat.

Dutens's account suggests that Claude Souchon was aware of several aspects of the prisoner's story, although he did know the man's name and he was mistaken about when Matthioli died. Matthioli was captured and imprisoned in 1679 and died in 1694, a period of fifteen years, not the nine stated by Souchon. It is probable that Matthioli's death on Sainte-Marguerite was remembered by the officers who had staffed the prison at the time. Matthioli had been a prominent figure who had been abducted in a daring and illegal operation. After fifteen years as a prisoner, only one of which had been under the care of Saint-Mars, he had arrived on Sainte-Marguerite, only to die very shortly afterward. His story was exciting and his rank made it all the more memorable, but his imprisonment had not been a secret for very long; indeed, the only secrecy attached to his story related to the circumstances surrounding his abduction, not the fact of his captivity. That Souchon disagreed with Voltaire over the Iron Mask's going to the Bastille is consistent with his own belief that the prisoner died on Sainte-Marguerite.

Despite this, however, Dutens continued to believe that the Iron Mask had been Matthioli. For proof, he appealed to Du Junca's registers, extracts of which had been published by Griffet twenty years earlier.[31] Du Junca, it will be remembered, wrote that the prisoner had been buried under the name of Marchioly. This confirmed Dutens in his belief.

Louis XV did indeed show a genuine interest in the subject of the Man in the Iron Mask. He and another of his valets de chambre, Jean-Benjamin de La Borde, would often discuss the prisoner. The king, however, would never reveal what he knew. One day, La Borde discovered a letter written by Charlotte d'Orléans to her lover, the maréchal de Richelieu. Charlotte, who was known as Mademoiselle de Valois, was the third daughter of the regent, Philippe. In his turn, Philippe was thought to have imparted the truth of the mysterious prisoner to Louis XV shortly before his death in 1723. The letter came to the attention of Friedrich Melchior, baron de Grimm, a German journalist living and working in France, and was printed in *Correspondance littéraire*, a collection of letters he had exchanged with Diderot, complete with anecdotes.[32] According to Mademoiselle de Valois:

While the queen, Anne of Austria, was pregnant, two shepherds arrived at the court and demanded to speak to the king. They revealed to him that they had been warned in a revelation that the queen was pregnant with two dauphins, whose birth would presage a civil war which would throw the whole kingdom into turmoil. The king immediately wrote of this to Cardinal Richelieu, his first minister, who replied that the king should not be alarmed, but to send the two shepherds to him and he would send them to the asylum of Saint-Lazare.

In due course, the queen gave birth to a son while the king was at dinner. The birth of the boy who would grow up to be Louis XIV was witnessed by all whose presence was demanded by royal protocol. Four hours later, however, Madame Perronet, the queen's midwife, was obliged to find the king to tell him that the queen's labor pains had begun again. He sent someone to look for the chancellor and together they went to the queen's bedroom in time to see her give birth to a second son, this one being more beautiful and more vigorous than the first. The birth was certified in an official record signed by the king, Mme Perronet, the doctor and a nobleman of the court, who later became the governor of the Iron Mask, and was imprisoned at the same time.

The king drew up a formal oath to be said by all those who had witnessed the birth of the second child. They were never to reveal this important secret unless the dauphin died, and they were forbidden to speak of it even among themselves. The child was then given to Mme Perronet, who was told to say that he had been entrusted to her care by a lady of the court.

When the child reached the age to pass into the care of men, that is, about seven years old, he was given into the care of the court nobleman who had been present at his birth. He went with his new pupil to Dijon, from where he corresponded with the queen, Cardinal Mazarin, who had taken over as first minister upon the death of Richelieu, and the king, now Louis XIV. Despite living in retreat, he remained a faithful courtier and showed the young prince all the respect due to a young man who could one day become his master. Such deference puzzled the young prince, who regarded the courtier as a father; he would question his governor about his birth and his status, but he found the nobleman's answers unsatisfactory. One day, the prince asked his governor for a portrait of the king, only to be passed off with platitudes, a strategy used by the nobleman each time the young prince tried to discover the mystery of his origins.

Now, the handsome young prince was no stranger to love. His first sighs were addressed to a chambermaid at the house, and he begged her to procure for him a portrait of the king. She refused at first, having been ordered, along with the other servants, not to give the prince anything unless their master was present. The prince, however, was insistent, and he eventually persuaded the chambermaid to obtain the requested portrait for him. As soon as he looked at the portrait, he was struck by his own resemblance to the king. He spoke to his governor again, asking questions about his origins in a manner more pressing and assured. He again asked to be shown a portrait of the king, but the governor tried to elude him. The prince answered: "You deceive me, here is a portrait of the king and a letter addressed to you reveals a mystery that you wanted to hide from me, in vain, for a long time. I am the king's brother, and I want to go to court immediately to enjoy my state." As an aside, the governor declared on his deathbed that he could never be sure how the young prince had gotten hold of the letter that he showed him; he said only that he was unaware that he had opened a casket in which he kept all the letters from the king, the queen, and Cardinal Mazarin. The governor shut away the prince and immediately sent a courier to Saint-Jean-de-Luz, where the court was staying to negotiate the peace of the Pyrenees and the king's marriage. The king sent an order to remove the prince and his governor, who were taken firstly to the Îles Sainte-Marguerite, and then to the Bastille, followed by the governor of the îles Sainte-Marguerite.

La Borde, who for a long time had been close to Louis XV, astonished the king with his extraordinary interest in the story of the Man in the Iron Mask. The king sympathized and would always say of the prisoner: "I pity him, but his detention harmed no one but himself and it prevented great misfortune; you cannot know." La Borde went on to tell of how Louis XV would recall that he had been very curious to know about the prisoner since he was a child, but had been told that he had to wait until he reached his majority before he could learn anything. When the fateful day finally dawned, he asked once again to be told the secret of the Man in the Iron Mask. The courtiers assembled at the door of his chamber waiting for him to emerge so they could interrogate him about what he had learned, but all he would say to them was that "You cannot know it."

The reign of Louis XV eventually gave way to that of his grandson, who ascended the throne as Louis XVI. Upon his succession, the new king spent time in several of the royal estates before settling at Versailles. Here, as Madame de Campan, lady-in-waiting to Marie-Antoinette, explains, Louis immersed himself in the study of his grandfather's papers.[33] He had promised the queen that he would tell her whatever he might discover about the history of the Man in the Iron Mask. This prisoner, he thought, "had become so inexhaustible a source of conjecture only in consequence of the interest which the pen of a celebrated writer had excited respecting the detention of a prisoner of State, who was merely a man of whimsical tastes and habits."

Having completed his research, the disappointed Louis informed Marie-Antoinette that he had not found anything among his predecessor's papers to shed light on the existence of the mysterious prisoner. Undaunted, the royal couple turned to Monsieur de Maurepas, "whose age made him contemporary with the epoch during which the story must have been known to the ministers." Maurepas, who was Louis XVI's chief adviser, said that the prisoner was a man "of dangerous character, in consequence of his disposition for intrigue." He went on to explain that he had been the subject of the duke of Mantua who had been enticed to the frontier where he was arrested. Held at first at Pignerol, he was moved to the Bastille when the governor of Pignerol was transferred there. "It was for fear the prisoner should profit by the experience of a new governor that he was sent with the Governor of Pignerol to the Bastille," he explained.

Mme de Campan further elaborated on "the man on whom people have been pleased to fix an iron mask." She appealed to the authority of a certain unnamed author, who had scoured the archives of the foreign office and laid the true story before the public, but the people "would not acknowledge the authenticity of his account." Instead, they relied upon the authority of Voltaire, and now the general belief was that the masked prisoner had been a natural or a twin brother of Louis XIV.

"The story of this mask," speculated Mme de Campan, "perhaps had its origin in the old custom, among both men and women in Italy, of wearing a velvet mask when they exposed themselves to the sun." As such, it was possible "that the Italian captive may have sometimes shown himself upon the terrace of his prison with his face thus covered." Campan then turned her attention to the silver plate that the prisoner was said to have thrown from his window: "It is known that such a circumstance did happen," she affirmed, "but it happened at Valzin, in the time of Cardinal Richelieu." As a result, the anecdote "has been mixed up with the inventions respecting the Piedmontese prisoner."

By the time Mme de Campan's memoir was published, the Revolution had taken place and her mistress, Marie-Antoinette, was dead. The events that had rocked France and swept away the ancien régime nevertheless led to a happy outcome for historians and researchers: the state papers and archives, which had long been the jealously guarded property of officialdom, were made available for the first time.

Eager scholars flocked to see what might be revealed about the mysterious prisoner who had lived and died within an iron mask. A special commission was established with Charpentier as its chairman, whose task was to sift through the dusty and yellowing records and note those that contained any information about the prisoner. As it turned out, nothing new was found. The Bastille's archives could add nothing more to what was already known, much of which had already been published several years earlier by Griffet.

Disappointed researchers turned their attention to the ministry for war to see what secrets its archives might reveal. These were meticulously researched and classified by Bishop Jean-Baptiste Massieu, who, between 1797 and 1815, worked his way through some eight hundred volumes of documents. Among these precious papers they found the correspondence that was exchanged between the ministry for war and Bénigne Dauvergne de Saint-Mars.

Under Louis XIV, official correspondence was handled according to a carefully set out procedure.[34] When a minister wanted to send a letter, he would write down what he had to say in a Minute. A clerk would use this to produce the letter, which was then sent to the intended recipient. The Minute was kept in the files of the ministry, which eventually formed an archive of correspondence for that ministry. This seemingly straightforward procedure did not mean, however, that the documents were kept in any kind of order. The clerks were kept busy and had little time to organize these papers into a classified collection.

The documents relating to the prisoners of Pignerol, Exilles, and the Île Sainte-Marguerite began in 1664 with Saint-Mars's appointment as jailer to Nicholas Foucquet at Pignerol. They came to an end in 1698 upon his transfer to the Bastille. Some of these documents were printed by Pierre Roux-Fazillac, whose *Recherches historiques et critiques sur l'homme au masque de fer* was published in 1800. Joseph Delort published a selection of letters in 1825 in *Histoire de l'homme au masque de fer*; four years later, he published the correspondence in its entirety in the first volume of *Histoire de la Détention des Philosophes et des Gens de Lettres à la Bastille et à Vincennes, précédée de celle de Foucquet, de Pellisson et de Lauzun, avec tous les documents authentiques et inédits*. Marius Topin printed a selection of letters, including some new discoveries, in *L'Homme au masque de fer* in 1869 as did Théodore Iung in his 1872 work, *La Verite sur le Masque de Fer (Les Empoisonneurs), d'après des documents inedits*. Iung's beautiful book also contains floor plans of the various prisons in which the Man in the

Iron Mask was held. Finally, the *Archives de la Bastille* was published in sixteen volumes between 1866 and 1884. The first three volumes, edited by François Ravaisson, contain the relevant documents under the heading "Fouquet." A. S. Barnes published a collection of original documents in his *The Man of the Mask* in 1912.

The content of some of this correspondence was taken from surviving letters, but in other cases the editors had to rely on the Minutes because letters would often be destroyed, end up in private collections, or simply go astray. Sometimes, the content of missing letters can successfully be reconstructed from matters addressed in the replies.

As extensive as this material was, however, scholars quickly encountered a major impediment: Eustache's name had been omitted from the Minute from which the order for his arrest had been taken, although it had been written into the letter sent to Saint-Mars in July 1669 and the lettre de cachet that was sent to Vauroy several days later. This omission would have an impact on researchers because it cast doubt upon the name that appeared in the letters, and it came to be accepted that the name written on the letter sent to Saint-Mars, Eustache Dauger, must have been false. The sole purpose of this, it came to be believed, was to disguise the prisoner's true identity.

As a result, historians continued to look for anyone whose story they thought best fit the circumstances of the mysterious prisoner.[35] He had to be an important person, imprisoned under conditions of unprecedented secrecy as an annoyance to the king or a threat to France. A prince of the royal house was favored by some; others went further, suggesting that he must have been a brother of Louis XIV or even his twin, a suggestion that captured the imagination of writers such as Alexandre Dumas and Victor Hugo. Louis XIV himself was proposed as a candidate by baron de Gleichen, with the king imprisoned and masked by his elder brother, who took his throne and his name. Matthioli, who had betrayed Louis XIV, was for many the true face behind the iron mask, while Nicolas Foucquet's name was put forward at the time of the Revolution, the ultimate victim of royal tyranny.[36] On one occasion the Jacobin monk was proposed, as was the playwright and actor Molière.[37] In 1899, historian Maurice Boutry[38] explored various possibilities: a son of Christina of Sweden and her lover Monaldeschi; a son of Louis XIV and Henriette d'Angleterre; a son of Henriette d'Angleterre and the comte de Guiche; a child born to Marie-Louise d'Orléans, the result of an adulterous affair; a natural child of Marie-Anne de Neubourg, second wife of Charles II of Spain; or even a son born to Marie-Thérèse of Austria and her black page. Boutry eventually settled on Matthioli. A valet known as Martin was proposed by Andrew Lang. James Stuart de la Cloche, an illegitimate son of Charles II of England, was put forward by Edith F. Carey. Monsignor A. S. Barnes proposed the abbé Giuseppe Prignani, who had swindled the English royal court out of a lot of money; Dr. Franz Scheichl's choice was Jacques Bretel de Grémonville, a Maltese diplomat. More tragically, Frantz Funck-Brentano suggested that the prisoner wore the mask not out of cruelty or punishment, but to hide the disfiguring effects of a cancroid on his face.[39] In time, more faces would be found behind the mask, including Claude Imbert, who had served Mazarin as a valet-cum-secretary and whose candidacy was explored by Sonnino, and d'Artagnan, the famous musketeer, who was proposed by Macdonald.

By this time, however, the iron mask had already been lifted and the true face of the man within had been revealed. In 1890, the lawyer and historian Jules Lair published a two-volume biography of Nicolas Foucquet. Out of necessity, he wrote about Foucquet's life as a prisoner at Pignerol and the people he encountered there. One of these was a man who had been imprisoned under conditions of great secrecy and held in dreadful surroundings before being allowed to serve Foucquet as his valet. Lair identified the prisoner as Eustache Dauger, but the mystery did not stop there.

THIRTEEN

The Man in the Iron Mask

Who was this person and why had he been arrested? He was French, Catholic, a valet by profession. Everything leads us to believe that he was really called Eustache Dauger. He had been employed for a certain task, which has never been specified. Presumably, he was one of those men who were charged with shady missions, carrying off money or people, perhaps even worse, and whose silence, once the deed is accomplished, is ensured by death or imprisonment.[1]

J ules Lair revealed the mysterious prisoner to be a valet called Eustache Dauger in his two-volume biography of Nicolas Foucquet, which was published in 1890. Although he provided an overview of scholarly speculation about the various proposed identities of the Man in the Iron Mask in an appendix to the second volume, Lair did not investigate the mystery any further: his book was about Foucquet, not the masked prisoner, and he had already shown this person to have been the man sent to join Foucquet as a prisoner at Pignerol and, later, to serve him as a valet.

While, as we have seen, even after Lair's revelation some historians continued to search for men who may have been the Iron Mask, others accepted Lair's conclusions or subsequently came to agree with him as a result of their own research. For them, the search shifted from looking for a suitable candidate to trying to find a man who fit a particular set of criteria. Eustache had to be French and a Catholic; he had to have been arrested at Calais and to have disappeared in July 1669.

One historian, Maurice Duvivier, set about the task of tracking down Eustache and discovered him to have been a man named Eustache Dauger de Cavoye. His book, *Le Masque de fer*, was published in 1932.

The family d'Oger or Dauger originated in Picardie. François Dauger de Cavoye was captain of Cardinal Richelieu's musketeers, a regiment every bit as proud as the king's musketeers with whom they would compete for military glory. In an interesting coincidence, François's father had acquired the epithet of *Bras-de-fer*, or Iron Arm.[2] On September 16, 1625, François married Marie de Lort de Sérignan, a woman famous for her beauty, who served as lady of honor to Anne of Austria, the mother of Louis XIV.

Unusually, the Cavoye marriage was a love match, and, in a period with a high child-mortality rate, the couple were blessed with eleven surviving children: Henriette, Pierre, Constance, Marie, Charles, Eustache, Armand, Louis, Anne, and two other children whose place in the order of birth is not known, Jacques and Charlotte. Three of their sons sometimes went by other names: Pierre was also known as Gaspard, Charles was Hector, and Eustache was called Jacques, despite having a brother with that name. By all accounts, the Cavoyes were a model family, but there was one black sheep: Eustache.

Eustache Dauger de Cavoye was born on August 30, 1637, in Paris and was baptized at the church of Saint-Eustache on February 18 the following year.[3] Like his brothers, he followed his father into a military career and joined the French Guards, but he soon drifted into a life of depravity that brought shame on his family.

At Easter 1659, Eustache and his field commander, the comte de Guiche, were invited to a party at the château de Roissy.[4] The guests were all in their early twenties except for one, Roger de Bussy-Rabutin, who was twice their age. All, however, were out for a good time. The party began on Good Friday, a day of strict religious observance, fasting, abstinence, and the contemplation of Christ's Passion. The group, however, interpreted these obligations in their own way. While they observed the fast, they made up for the deprivation by drinking throughout the day. When it came to their evening meal, they accepted that they were required to eat fish and not meat, so they took a piglet to the chapel and baptized it "carp" before slaughtering and eating it. They indulged in fun and games, drinking and homosexual sex, which continued until Easter Sunday, when the party broke up and the revelers went their separate ways.

News of the party quickly spread, and all who heard about it were scandalized. The king ordered an inquiry, and those who had taken part were sent from court. Eustache's punishment is not known, but his outraged family was not forced to share it. Mazarin assured Madame de Cavoye that her reputation would remain untarnished, and Anne of Austria invited her to Louis's wedding the following year.

Eustache, despite being labeled "Cavoye de Roissy" as a result of the scandal, managed to put any shame he felt behind him and became a lieutenant in 1662. Three years later, however, he became involved in another scandal when, stationed at Saint-Germain, he got into an argument with a drunken page and ran the boy through with his sword. Louis was furious that such a thing could occur in a place sanctified by his presence and refused to allow Eustache to appear before him.

It was at about this time that Madame de Cavoye died suddenly. She had, however, already endured enough of her son's antics and had made arrangements for her disappointment with him to be felt in a way that would injure him the most. Her eldest sons having died in battle, she had drawn up her will on May 6, 1664, and, making use of a clause in her marriage contract that allowed her, under the custom of Picardie, she disinherited both Eustache and Armand in favor of their younger brother, Louis. Eustache would receive 1,000 livres a year, while Armand would have 2,000. Armand meant to contest this, but he was killed in 1667 before he could do so. As for Eustache, he came to an arrangement with Louis, in which he received an extra 1,000 livres a year in exchange for some small properties he had inherited several years earlier when he became titular head of the family.

At this point Duvivier loses sight of Eustache Dauger de Cavoye. Indeed, Eustache disappears entirely from the historical record in May 1668. As Duvivier scoured the archives in an attempt to pick up his trail, he discovered a man named Auger, a surgeon operating in the Parisian underworld. Auger was involved in the infamous Affair of the Poisons, working alongside the abbé Guibourg. Duvivier saw that, on one occasion, Auger and the abbé were said to have participated in a black mass held at the Palais-Royal.

According to one of their accomplices, Lesage, the black mass had been said for Henriette, duchesse d'Orléans, and its purpose had been to bring about the death of her husband, Philippe.[5] It was said that Henriette hated Philippe because he preferred his male favorites over her, particularly the chevalier de Lorraine, who ruled Philippe's house. The mass itself, therefore, had to have taken place prior to March 1668, which was when Lesage was imprisoned in the Bastille and two months before Eustache disappeared from history. Duvivier quickly realized that Auger and Eustache Dauger had to be one and the same man. Now here he was working satanic rituals for the highest in the land.

Duvivier claims that Louvois arranged for Eustache de Cavoye, aka Auger, to be arrested in July 1669 and sent off to Pignerol, far away from the court. However, even in this grim fortress, Eustache failed to learn from his harsh imprisonment. Rather than mend his ways, he brought down an even worse fate upon himself by poisoning Nicolas Foucquet. This provided the solution to Louvois's enigmatic reference to "drugs" in his letter to Saint-Mars of July 10, 1680. Further, Duvivier speculates that

Eustache had probably killed Foucquet on behalf of Colbert, but instead of being released as his reward, he was shut away for the rest of his life.

Duvivier provides a fascinating theory as he seeks to identify who Eustache really was and to explain the truth behind his story. He has found a man with a very similar name. In that period, there were almost always several variant spellings of most names, so this accounted for the inconsistencies in the spelling of Eustache's name: Dauger, d'Auger, Auger. Duvivier also provides a motive for Eustache's extended imprisonment: that he murdered Foucquet, and even the timing is accurate. There is one vital element that Duvivier's theory fails to address, however, which is the need to hide Eustache's face within an iron mask.

This point is answered by Rupert Furneaux in his book *The Man behind the Mask: The Real Story of the "Ancient Prisoner,"* which was published in 1954. Furneaux discovered a striking resemblance between Eustache's younger brother, Louis, and Louis XIV. There was only one explanation for this: Marie de Sérignan, the mother of Eustache and Louis de Cavoye, had been the mistress of Louis XIII, and he had been the father of these two boys.

Furneaux's theory is interesting, but it does not take into account how Louis XIII, a sullen man with a deep distrust of women in general, could have been inclined to father two sons out of wedlock. The two relationships he did have with women other than his queen had been close but were entirely platonic.

It would take a further twenty years before another historian approached the subject of Eustache de Cavoye. In 1974, Marie-Madeleine Mast published *Le Masque de fer: Une solution révolutionnaire.* She agreed with Furneaux that Louis de Cavoye and Louis XIV looked very much alike, but she rejected his conclusion. Her revolutionary solution was that the two men did not share the same father, but the same mother. Mast argues that Cardinal Richelieu was concerned about Louis XIII's infertility and the dire consequences for France if he did not produce an heir to the throne. Richelieu ordered the captain of his musketeers, François de Cavoye, to do something about it.

François de Cavoye was a handsome, virile man who had fathered eleven children, including six strapping sons. It was he, according to Mast, who fathered the child born to Anne of Austria on September 5, 1638, not Louis XIII. This explained the resemblance between Louis de Cavoye and Louis XIV, but it also explained why Eustache was arrested. Having become head of the family upon the deaths of his elder brothers, he had become privy to the family papers and discovered the secret of his royal origins. He then began to talk about what he had discovered and had to be silenced, his features forever hidden behind a mask of iron.

Each of these theories, fascinating and convincing though they might be, have serious flaws. Emile Laloy[6] correctly asserts that no gentleman, no matter how low he might have fallen, would have stooped to making a living as a surgeon. In 17th-century France, a surgeon performed several tasks: among others, as a barber, a peddler in folk remedies, and an apothecary. There is a discrepancy of time, too: the surgeon, Auger, was still at large in 1676, seven years after Duvivier supposed him to have entered Pignerol. As to the resemblance between Louis de Cavoye and Louis XIV, even if it were true, there is nothing to say that it would have been shared by Eustache de Cavoye. Moreover, as Noone points out,[7] Louis XIV's courtiers made it their business to try to look like the king, copying his clothes and even trying to match their wigs to his.

As it is, each of the theories that make Eustache Dauger de Cavoye the Man in the Iron Mask fall in the face of the historical record. More damning still is that, at the time Duvivier, Furneaux, and Mast place him inside Pignerol, the real Eustache Dauger was languishing in Saint-Lazare. This institution, originally a hospital for lepers, had, by the second quarter of the 17th century, been used to confine people who had become a liability to their families. Eustache de Cavoye had been held there since January 1668, when his brother, Louis, obtained an order for his arrest for nonpayment of a debt.

Eustache sent several letters to his sister, Henriette, to explain how he had ended up in Saint-Lazare. Ten years later, he was still there, and, on January 23, 1678, he wrote again to Henriette begging her to help secure his release. He reproached his brother for having put him away and for keeping him there all these years. Louis de Cavoye had been the architect of Eustache's misery. Eustache would never be freed. He died from the effects of alcoholism at Saint-Lazare in about 1680. A fellow inmate, Brienne, wrote an elegy for his friend, and he was the only one to have mourned his passing.[8] Eustache Dauger de Cavoye was not the Man in the Iron Mask.

The true identity of the Man in the Iron Mask is no longer a mystery. His prison career can be followed in original sources, particularly the letters that were exchanged between the marquis de Louvois and Bénigne Dauvergne de Saint-Mars, and the occasional communication sent by Louis XIV.

The prisoner has been referred to throughout this book as Eustache. As it is written on the original letter de cachet, his name is given as Eustache, but what appears to be his surname is disputed, with some scholars reading it as Dauger, with a *u*, and others as Danger, with an *n*. In the letter in which he warned Saint-Mars to prepare for the arrival of a new prisoner, Louvois gave the prisoner's name as Eustache d'Auger, and this, or more usually the variant Dauger, is the name by which this mysterious man has been best known ever since.

However, Eustache's name would have several variations in the official correspondence as time went on: Eustache *Danger* (February 15, 1679), *Dangers* (September 13, 1679), *d'Angers* (April 8, 1680), or even simply 'the man Eustache (December 23, 1678; January 20, 1680; July 10, 1680). In his paper presented at a colloquium at Pignerol in 1987, historian Bernard Caire convincingly demonstrated that the prisoner's name was Danger, Dangers, or d'Angers.[9] Variants of this name occur most frequently in the correspondence, and it could be that it refers to the prisoner's place of birth or the town with which he is most associated, implying that Eustache was actually a surname.[10] This is by no means implausible, since serving men were usually known and addressed by their surnames, such as La Forêt, Champagne, and La Rivière, all of whom had served Foucquet, or Matthioli's valet, Rousseau.

It can be accepted, then, that the prisoner's real name was Eustache. Louis XIV, as we have seen, signed the letter de cachet authorizing the arrest of a man of that name. That the name was not written into the minutes from which the three letters sent to Vauroy, Saint-Mars, and the marquis de Piennes respectively were prepared is sometimes interpreted as evidence of a cover-up. However, had Eustache been arrested under a false name, such a precaution would not have been necessary, as Petitfils points out.[11]

In due course, Eustache would lose his name altogether and would be referred to as one of the *messieurs de la Tour d'en bas* or as one of Saint-Mars's *merles*. Later still, he would be known as the ancien prisonnier or as Saint-Mars liked to call him, *mon prisonnier*.

As to Eustache's age, the burial register of the Bastille states that he was forty-five years old or thereabouts at the time of his death. This would mean that he entered Pignerol at about the age of eleven. Clearly, his exact age could not be known, but was this register entry part of an attempt at a cover-up, or was it simply a mistake? Had Eustache indeed entered Pignerol at the age of eleven, it would come close to the story told to Renneville, which had it that the prisoner had entered Pignerol as a schoolboy of twelve or thirteen years of age for having written two verses against the Jesuits. This almost certainly originated with Saint-Mars, who was known to spread such stories in an attempt to confound and mock the inquisitive.

By contrast, the apothecary at the Bastille who spoke to Eustache a few days before he died reported that Eustache had told him that he thought he was about sixty years old. This would have made him twenty-six years old at the time of his arrest. This is all the more believable, for had he been imprisoned as a child, he would have been about seventeen when he was placed with Foucquet; while this is not impossible, he would have been very young to hold such responsibility.

In his discussion of the story of the Man in the Iron Mask, Rupert Furneaux speaks of the special interest taken by Louvois and Louis in the welfare and security of this one particular prisoner.[12] Similarly,

Voltaire wonders why this man should be subjected to such unheard-of precautions. In answer, it should be noted that the security precautions that were applied to Eustache were not entirely unheard of, nor were they unique to him. Indeed, such measures would be employed for most of the prisoners sent to Saint-Mars at Pignerol.

As he escorted Eustache to Pignerol, Captain Vauroy received no special order to hide his prisoner's face or to otherwise conceal his identity. Eustache was not heavily guarded on his lengthy journey through France, across the Alps, and into Northern Italy. He was escorted instead by Vauroy and a small group of men using regular roads and stopping at post-houses each night. This is in marked contrast to the journeys made by Foucquet and Lauzun, both of whom were escorted by a large company of musketeers under the command of d'Artagnan, who was required to find, often with difficulty, secure lodgings for his prisoners.

As he received Eustache at Pignerol, Saint-Mars, obeying orders, imprisoned him alone in a temporary cell until the one in which he was to be lodged was ready to receive him. Eustache, once transferred into his isolated cell, was shut away behind three sets of doors, where Saint-Mars could ensure that no one would hear whatever he might have to say. Saint-Mars was told to restrict his visits to the prisoner to one each day, during which he was to bring him whatever food he needed for that day. He was also authorized to kill the prisoner if he spoke of anything other than his needs.

These apparently excessive precautions were imposed in order to ensure that no one beyond the impenetrable walls of his cell could hear Eustache should he attempt to give away any information about what he had done prior to his imprisonment. This was clearly an important consideration, but the necessity for such precautions could also have stemmed from Eustache's social status. He was not nobility, so he would have no valet to keep an eye on him. Once again, this contrasts with the security used for Foucquet and Lauzun; they were served by valets, who spied on their master and each other. As seen in the case of La Rivière, the consequences of not doing so were serious.

One noteworthy feature regarding Eustache's security is that, during the time he was serving as Foucquet's valet, he was allowed to mix with people who came into his master's prison apartment. Louvois even left it to Saint-Mars to arrange with Foucquet "as you judge appropriate, regarding the security of the person named Eustache Danger, recommending you above all, to see to it that he speaks to no one in private."[13] Eustache could associate with Foucquet's guests, but he was not allowed to speak to anyone privately.

When the security arrangements for each of the prisoners of Pignerol are compared, we note that the apparently excessive precautions surrounding Eustache were the norm. Saint-Mars was ordered to hold Butticari under "good and sure guard" and cut off from all communication. Lapierre was to be treated in the same manner as Eustache, subject to harsh and unpleasant conditions. Lapierre, Louvois assured Saint-Mars, could not be treated badly enough. Later, when Matthioli arrived, Saint-Mars was ordered to guard him "in a manner, that not only he may not have communication with any one, but that also he may have cause to repent of his bad conduct; and that it may not be discovered that you have a new prisoner."[14] Moreover, unlike Eustache, Matthioli was hidden behind a further layer of security: a false prison name, Lestang. This was not in itself necessarily significant, since prisoners were sometimes assigned false names, and it was not unheard of for these names, and the prisoners who bore them, to be forgotten. While Matthioli appears to have been treated "very kindly in all that regards cleanliness and food,"[15] he was also allowed to have his own valet in prison with him. This was probably because of his noble birth as well as his former status as a diplomat in the service of the duke of Mantua. His valet, Rousseau, was imprisoned because he was privy to his master's secrets. As with all the prisoners of Pignerol, however, vigorous efforts were made to prevent Matthioli having communication with anyone.

Such measures continued on the Île Sainte-Marguerite. The protestant minister Cardel was described by Louvois as "a man deserving of death and who could not be treated too severely."[16] Saint-Mars was required to take "all necessary precautions so that no one knows that he is in your hands." Saint-Mars was also ordered to send Louvois monthly updates about Cardel's behavior, although requests for such information concerning the prisoners appears to have been standard. When Cardel became ill and needed to be bled, Saint-Mars was told that he could arrange for a surgeon to come to the island to perform the procedure in his presence, "taking all necessary precautions that the surgeon does not know who [the prisoner] is."[17]

When more new arrivals came to Sainte-Marguerite, they were to be kept in separate cells and Saint-Mars had to ensure that they could not communicate, whether by word of mouth or in writing. Later, when Matthioli died shortly after his arrival on the island, Louvois ordered Saint-Mars to put his servant, Rousseau, into the vaulted prison with the usual precaution that the man could not communicate in any way with the outside world.[18] If Eustache's treatment seemed unusual in the earliest days of his imprisonment, it came to be standard practice shortly afterward. In each case, Saint-Mars accepted without question his orders regarding the security of those in his charge, suggesting that he thought it to be the normal procedure to be taken with state prisoners.

The salient point of Eustache's story and the foundation of the legend that grew up about him is the mask he was apparently forced to wear. Accounts disagree regarding the material of which it was made, whether steel, iron, or black velvet.

The mask captured the imagination of the second duchesse d'Orléans, whose letter implies that the prisoner was masked at all times: "He ate and slept masked," she stated, adding that the two musketeers were on hand to shoot him if he ever tried to remove it.

By contrast, when he came to write his memoir of his time as a prisoner at the Bastille, Renneville made no mention that the mysterious man he had encountered wore a mask. However, what he had taken to be black hair without a hint of gray could have been a mask or hood of black velvet, while what he had interpreted as a ponytail could have been the knot tied back of the man's head.

Much later, as he wrote a history of Louis XIV's reign, Voltaire referred to the prisoner as "the man in the iron mask," but there is no evidence to support any assertion that the mask was made of this material. Indeed, Voltaire himself described it as "a mask, the chin-piece of which had steel springs to enable [the prisoner] to eat while wearing it." Of course, a mask made of velvet would surely not have required such modification.

Palteau noted that he first heard that the mask was made of iron from Voltaire's account. He mentions the mask four times in his letter: "the masked man arrived"; "ate with his mask on"; "black mask over his face"; "that of the masked man." Perhaps he did indeed capture the accurate recollections of the peasants of Palteau, who were struck by the sight of this curious figure. However, the mask they described was said to have covered the upper portion of the wearer's face, which suggests that it was a loo mask. These were masks of black velvet, most usually worn by ladies to protect their delicate complexions from the sun, that covered the area around the eyes and the upper cheeks but not the mouth. Mme de Campan also spoke of a velvet mask, comparing it to those worn by Italian men and women.

The mask enhances the mystery that surrounds the prisoner and adds an element of horror to any narrative of his incarceration, but where did it originate? There is a historical precedent, a story linking a mask and the Bastille. According to Gatien Courtilz de Sandras, the marquis de Besmaux, who was Saint-Mars's predecessor as governor of the Bastille, was so jealous of his wife's beauty that he bought her "one of the biggest masks in Paris with a large face-cloth, and obliged her always to wear it upon her face."[19] Elsewhere, we have seen that the chevalier de Mouhy mentions shocking accounts of people being made to wear iron masks in the introduction to his romance. Masks, and particularly those made of iron, had already entered the realm of the public imagination.

In Eustache's case, the situation was different. As has been seen, Captain Vauroy received no instructions to cover his prisoner's face or to otherwise conceal his identity. Once in prison, there was no reason to hide Eustache's face because no one at Pignerol nor any of the other prisons in which he was held knew who he was. Any physicians who tended him or priests who took his confessions could look upon his face: here, the only concern was that he should not have an opportunity to tell whatever secret he might have been keeping. Similarly, when Eustache was allowed to walk on the citadel walls with Foucquet, he was not required to cover his face. Later, when he encountered Foucquet's wife and family, and other guests, there was no mention of his being made to wear a mask. It would certainly have been noted and commented upon had he had done so.

In the letter attributed to Louis Foucquet that was written during the prisoner's own lifetime, the man being transported to Sainte-Marguerite was said to have been wearing a mask made of steel. This, as far as is known, is the first reference to the now secret prisoner having been made to wear a mask of any description. There is only one other contemporary reference to a mask, and it comes from Etienne Du Junca, who stated that the prisoner who arrived at the Bastille in September 1698 was always masked. Five years after this, when he recorded the prisoner's death, Du Junca noted again that the prisoner was always masked, adding that the mask was made not of steel, but of black velvet.

While a prisoner in the Bastille, and contrary to Du Junca's assertions, Eustache was required to wear the mask only when he could be seen by others, not when he was in his cell, where he was seen only by Saint-Mars and Rosarges. The mask was important because it covered Eustache's face and concealed his identity, but it also attracted attention to him. This was a deliberate ploy by Saint-Mars and part of his effort to make people believe that his prisoner was a man of consequence. By extension, Saint-Mars would share in Eustache's prestige and bask in the full light of his fame as he had done with Foucquet, Lauzun, and, to some extent, Matthioli. The mask was one element in a story that grew in the telling, a terrifying legend to capture the imagination today as it had done in the prisoner's own time.

Aside from the mask, the greatest mystery surrounding Eustache is the reason for his imprisonment. What could this man have done to deserve being sent to prison for the rest of his life? In the letter he sent to Saint-Mars, Louis stated that he was "dissatisfied with the behavior" of Eustache. This does not reveal very much; but, of course, the king was not obliged to explain his reasons to anyone.

In order to understand Eustache's story, it is necessary to place it in its correct historical context. The prisoner who would come to be known as the Man in the Iron Mask was arrested at Calais in July 1669. He was French and, therefore, one of Louis XIV's subjects. Had he not been, his seizure would have ignited the threat of a diplomatic incident, as would later occur in the case of Matthioli. That masses were said for him and priests took his confession shows that he was Catholic. This much can easily be gleaned from the extant documents. His occupation and how he might have been employed prior to his imprisonment is not so straightforward, but it is crucial if his story is to be understood.

That Eustache was allowed a book of prayers has inspired some historians to believe that he might have been a priest, thinking that only members of the clergy would be allowed to read prayer books. However, other prisoners were allowed books of prayers, which would be used by them and their valets,[20] while Foucquet was given a Bible.

Louvois describes Eustache as "only a valet," thereby revealing both his occupation and his social status. Ambelain[21] argues that had Eustache been a servant from the lower social classes, Louvois would more likely have referred to him as a *laquais*, or lackey. He did not; he specifically described him as a valet. Ambelain goes on to explain that while a valet would usually occupy a slightly more elevated position in the hierarchy of the serving class, he was still a servant, and this accounts for the cheap furniture he was given. By the time of his transfer to Sainte-Marguerite from Exilles, his bed, table linen, and furniture was so old and worn out that Saint-Mars thought "it was not worth the trouble of bringing it here; they sold for only thirteen écus."[22] Eustache, therefore, while not highborn himself, he might best be described as a gentleman's gentleman. Ambelain is keen to point out, however, that for a gentleman to act as a valet was not necessarily to dishonor him, for much depended upon whom he worked for.

Similarly, Duvivier, who believed Eustache to have been a gentleman, was concerned that someone of his rank should be reduced to working as a valet.[23] He argued that Louvois's reference to him as being "only a valet" was an act of spite typical of the minister. This insult was deepened when Eustache was sent to serve Foucquet. This, he argued, was no doubt mitigated by the fact that Foucquet had two servants, with Eustache acting as a secretary or companion, while La Rivière performed the menial tasks. Both Amberlain and Duvivier, however, ignore the strong traditions that underpinned French society at the time. As Petitfils[24] argues, French society in the 17th century was organized along class lines and to put a nobleman into service would never have been tolerated, no matter what his crime might have been. Had a noble officer been forced into work below his rank, the same could easily have applied to Matthioli or Lauzun had the circumstances demanded it. This did not, and never would have, happened.

As it was, a valet might be employed in the service of a king, a prince, a member of the aristocracy or a minister, perhaps as a valet de chambre or similar position. Often, a valet would serve his master in secret and often dangerous missions, as Rousseau, Matthioli's servant had done. Herein lies the secret of Eustache's crime, his secret and his fate.

At the time of Eustache's arrest, in July 1669, Louis XIV was busily making preparations for a war against the Dutch. It was a long-standing ambition, the aim of which was to acquire the Spanish Netherlands and Franche-Comté, which would expand the borders of France and ensure the greater security of his kingdom. He had already made an attempt to gain these territories two years previously, claiming them in right of his Spanish queen, Marie-Thérèse of Austria,[25] as compensation for the nonpayment of the balance of her dowry. In that campaign, which came to be known as the War of Devolution, Louis had made important gains, but he had been obliged to relinquish much of the captured territory under the terms of the Treaty of Aix-la-Chapelle, signed on May 2, 1668.

Louis, however, remained determined to fulfil his original objective. He knew that his best plan was to go to war against the Dutch, whom he despised because of their republicanism, their Protestantism, and their scurrilous propaganda campaigns against him. Once he had defeated this enemy, he would be free to mount a fresh assault on the Spanish Low Countries and Franche-Comté, but in order to ensure success he needed the support of England. He was aware that Charles II had recently entered into a treaty of alliance with Holland, but Louis was confident that he could persuade his English cousin to break this treaty, transfer his allegiance to France, and support Louis in a war against his former allies.

For his part, Charles had long desired a close coalition between England and France. He saw himself and Louis as natural allies standing united against the Dutch and the Spanish. It was true that he had sided with these two powers against France in a pact known as the Triple Alliance, but he claimed to have done so in order to redress the balance of power in Europe and to curtail Louis's worrying seizure of territories along his borders and holding them hostage while he sought favorable terms from Spain. Charles's membership of the Triple Alliance had forced Louis to make peace with Spain.

While Charles had several reasons for wanting to ally with Louis, his primary and most secret aim was to secure Louis's support in readiness for his proposed public announcement of his commitment to Roman Catholicism. He and his beloved sister, Henriette, who was married to Louis's brother, the duc d'Orléans, had for some time been working toward Charles's conversion and for a closer alliance between England and France.

January 25, 1669 (old style),[26] was a significant date for Charles, for it marked the feast of the conversion of St Paul. Charles chose this day to hold a meeting at the Whitehall lodgings of his brother, the duke of York. Besides the king and his brother, three other men were present: Lord Arlington, Lord Arundell, and Sir Thomas Clifford. Charles notified them of his intention to convert to Roman Catholicism and to have the support of Louis XIV. He asked those gathered for "their advice about the ways and methods fittest to be taken for the settling of the Catholic religion in his kingdoms and to consider of the time most proper to declare himself."[27]

Charles's projected aim was that he and Louis should join forces to form an "offensive and defensive league toward one and all."[28] Louis would then provide Charles with a significant sum of money while placing troops and ships at the disposal of the English king, should they be required. In exchange for Louis's support, Charles would lend military assistance to Louis in his forthcoming Dutch War. The negotiations, conducted under the utmost secrecy between Charles and Henriette, would ultimately lead to the Treaty of Dover.

A few days prior to his secret meeting at Whitehall, Charles decided he ought to send Henriette a cipher "by the first safe occasion, and you shall then know the way I thinke most proper to proceede in the whole matter." He added, "I will say no more by the post upon this business, for you know tis not very sure."[29]

Charles sent the cipher with a letter dated January 20, 1669 (old style): "I send you heere a cipher which is very easy and secure, the first side is in single cipher, and written within such names I could thinke of necessary to our purpose."[30]

As secure as Charles considered his cipher to be, he and Henriette took still more precautions. They employed trusted servants to carry their secret correspondence, men who often remained anonymous even to the recipient. On December 27, 1668, for example, Charles sent a message to his sister "by a safe way, and you know how much secrecy is necessary for the carrying on of the business, and I assure you that nobody does nor shall know any thing of it here but my self and that one person more till it be fit to be public, which will not be until all matters are agreed on."[31]

The identity of this "one person more" is not disclosed, and it is clear that not all the messengers that sailed the English Channel were known to both parties. Indeed, it was not unusual for one messenger to pass on correspondence to another, so that there was a relay of letters passing back and forth. In another letter to Henriette, Charles notes that he had received her letter by "the Italian whose name and capasity you do not know, and he delivered your letter to me in a passage where it was so darke as I do not know his face againe if I see him."[32]

The negotiations between Charles and Henriette were so secret that even Ralph Montagu, the English representative in Paris, did not know that they were taking place at all.[33] He was, however, aware that some sort of intrigue was going on, for he mentioned that the French court, like its English counterpart, was "full of cabals and stories." As he wrote to Lord Arlington, "great consultations" were taking place with Louis's minister, Colbert, the maréchal Turenne, Henriette, and Ruvigny, and that "couriers are some time dispatched into England, which perhaps you do not know, but if you would give order to the post-master at Dover, you would easily find it out."[34]

In fact, the negotiations referred to by Montagu were to do with the proposed military support Charles expected from France. Colbert, for instance, would have been involved by necessity because he was the minister for the navy, while Turenne was one of France's greatest military men.

As to Charles's intentions to convert to Catholicism, the "great secret" was known to very few people, most of whom were in France. These were Louis XIV, Henriette, Turenne, the comte de Saint-Albans, the abbé Walter Montagu, and Lionne. Toward the middle of April 1669, two more people were admitted into the secret negotiations: Michel Le Tellier, minister of state for war, and his son, the marquis de Louvois, who worked under his father at the same ministry. Eustache could have been in the service of any one of these people, carrying the secret correspondence between his master or mistress to be passed to the recipient directly or through another courier. Had this been the case, it would go some way to explaining the angry tone to Louvois's letter, in which Eustache is referred to as a "wretch" and "only a valet." Had Le Tellier or Louvois felt that Eustache had somehow betrayed them or committed some transgression while in their service, this would account for the anger and Louvois's desire to keep Eustache under seclusion in unpleasant circumstances.

In July 1669, with the negotiation with Charles well underway, Louis suddenly and inexplicably fell out with Henriette. This was an unexpected development since the two had previously been very close, and it did not go unnoticed. On July 23, Henriette withdrew from Saint-Germain to go to Saint-Cloud to prepare for the birth of her child.[35] Three days later, on July 26, Ralph Montagu wrote in her defense to Lord Arlington:

> *She is the most that can be beloved in this country by everybody but the King and her husband. She has too great a spirit I believe ever to complain, or to let the King her brother know of it, but I tell your Lordship of it, that you may take all the occasions wherein the King can, of putting his Majesty upon supporting her, both as his sister, and as a sister that deserves it from him by her real concern in everything that relates either to his honor or interest.[36]*

Some weeks after this, Henriette wrote to Lord Arlington about some "suspicions" she had, which were:

> *founded on reasons of which I informed the King some time ago by a Page of the Backstairs to the Queen. He may have told you of them, and I gave some credence to them, because at the same time I had perceived a coldness in the feelings of the King of France for me, which made me think that, fearing that I might discover that he was not acting in good faith, he wished to remove me from the business [of the negotiations], for fear that I might warn the King my brother of it, as assuredly I should have done.[37]*

What had caused this coldness is not known. Hartmann thought it stemmed from Louis's belief that Henriette was favoring Charles's interests over those of France.[38]

Henriette's biographer, Jacqueline Duchêne, believed that Henriette, a former lover of Louis's, was jealous of Madame de Montespan, who was expecting the king's child.[39] While either of these suggestions is plausible, Petitfils had suggested a third, which is that Louis's coldness toward Henriette originated with some indiscretion on the part of one of her servants, which threatened to compromise relations between Louis and Charles.[40] Had Eustache been that servant, it would explain his arrest and subsequent imprisonment without trial in July 1669. Petitfils points out that Louvois, having announced Eustache's imminent arrival at Pignerol to Saint-Mars on July 19, waited until July 23, the date Henriette left Saint-Germain, to set a trap for Eustache with a view to having him arrested at Calais.

It was during the summer of 1669, then, under a heady atmosphere of secrecy and intrigue, as diplomats, couriers, spies, and servants crossed from France to England and back again, when Louis was soliciting Charles II's cooperation and Charles was seeking Louis's support, that Louis took the time to authorize the arrest and incarceration of someone who had displeased him. This was affected by means of a letter de cachet, which allowed the prisoner to be held at the king's pleasure without having to go through the judicial process.

Eustache was taken to Pignerol, a secure prison on the very frontier of France. His identity was not hidden; instead, Eustache was subject to stringent security measures in order to ensure that he could not tell of what he knew. In time, he was allowed to serve one prisoner, Foucquet, but on no account was he allowed to have contact with another, Lauzun.

Later, he was transferred to another strong fortress, accompanied by a valet who had learned Eustache's secret and who had failed in his duty to alert the authorities of a breach in the prison security. Now both men lost their names and were hidden away from a world that had forgotten them. In these terrible conditions, his companion died, leaving Eustache entirely alone.

A change in Eustache's imprisonment occurred following the death of Louvois on July 16, 1691. At this point, he fell deeper into obscurity and was no longer the focus of ministerial attention. Even Louvois's son and successor, Barbezieux, was unaware of who Eustache was or why he had been sent to prison. If the theory that Eustache was somehow connected with the negotiations that would lead to the signing of Treaty of Dover in 1670 is correct, then many of the main players were dead by the time of Louvois's death. Henriette had died many years previously in 1670; Charles II in 1685. Charles's successor, James II, was overthrown in 1688, and whatever hopes he might have harbored of regaining his throne were shattered at the Battle of the Boyne in 1690. Eustache's secret was no longer important, and neither was he, except to Saint-Mars.

As the jailer of two of the most important men in France, Saint-Mars had found fame, glory, and wealth. Even after the death of one distinguished prisoner and the release of the second, Saint-Mars was able to continue his privileged life by allowing people to think that he still had a man of substance in his charge, and Barbezieux was in no position to contradict him. Eventually, Saint-Mars reached the high point of his career when he was offered the governorship of the Bastille. It was a fitting end to an illustrious career, and he accepted the post, taking his apparently important prisoner with him.

By this time, the prisoner had long been a man without a name, even without a face, and it was as a man of mystery that he arrived at the Bastille in 1698. Although this prison was used for aristocrats and exceptional people, Eustache was neither. He went to the Bastille by virtue of his being Saint-Mars's prisoner. Here, he disappeared from the view of history until his death five years later, when he was buried under a false name, one that would suggest to anyone who saw the burial register that he was Matthioli. Even in his grave, Eustache still had his uses. Foucquet was known to be long dead and Lauzun still had several years to live; that left Matthioli as the only prisoner of consequence with whose name Saint-Mars was associated. As such, Eustache was buried under a name that closely resembled his, a final twist to the mystery that he had become.

Many people continue to believe that the Man in the Iron Mask must have been a famous person, perhaps even a member of the royal family. A favorite explanation is that he was a brother, even a twin, of Louis XIV, and this is the reason why his face had to be covered.

Nevertheless, while there are many aspects of the prisoner's life that will forever remain a mystery, there are still some conclusions that can be drawn. He was not a well-known figure at court, and his disappearance was not noted nor remarked upon in contemporary letters or memoirs. Eustache was a young man, a valet who lived an anonymous existence on the edge of the court, never being part of it but perhaps serving someone who was.

Who that person might have been is open to speculation. It could have been Henriette, duchesse d'Orléans, with Eustache being involved as a messenger in the secret and sensitive negotiations that she was holding with her brother, Charles II. On the other hand, there is circumstantial evidence to suggest that Eustache might have served Louvois in some capacity and that he was angered when he thought his valet had somehow betrayed him. While it is true that he abused most of the prisoners he sent to Saint-Mars and subjected almost all of them to harsh prison conditions, he appears to have taken a particular interest in Eustache. For example, there is the letter in which he wanted to know how Eustache might have gotten hold of the drugs Saint-Mars had found in his possession. Elsewhere, Louvois asks Saint-Mars for a list of the prisoners under his care and what he knew of the reasons for their imprisonment. As to Eustache and his companion, they were simply to be referred to as "the two prisoners in the lower part of the tower"; Saint-Mars was told he "need only designate them by this name without adding anything else." Prisoners could, and did, become lost in the prison system. Louvois might have forgotten the names and the crimes of those prisoners who came under his jurisdiction, but he never forgot Eustache or why he had been arrested. Upon the death of Louvois, Eustache was no longer of importance to anyone other than Saint-Mars, who used him for his own profit and to boost his own grandeur. Whatever the truth, and we may never know, Voltaire was more right than he realized when he said that, upon the arrest of Eustache, "no man of any consequence in Europe disappeared."

BIBLIOGRAPHY

Amato, Claude. *L'Homme au masque de fer: La solution à une énigme dédalienne*. Nice: Editions Bénévent, 2003.

Ambelain, Robert. *La Chapelle des damnés: La véritable Affaires des poisons, 1650–1703*. Paris: Éditions Robert Laffont, 1983.

Annales des Alpes. Recueil périodique des Archives des Hautes-Alpes, III année. Gap: Archives Départementales, 1899.

Anonymous. *Mémoires secrets pour servir à l'histoire de Perse*. Amsterdam, 1746.

Arrèse, Pierre-Jacques. *Le Masque de fer: L'énigme enfin résolue*. Paris: Robert Laffont, 1969.

Azema, Xavier. *Un prélat janseniste: Louis Foucquet évêque et comte d'Agde (1656–1702)*. Paris: Librairie philosophique J. Vrin, 1963.

Barnes, Arthur Stapleton. *The Man of the Mask: A Study in the Byways of History*. London: Smith, Elder & Co., 1912.

Bournon, Fernand. *La Bastille: Histoire générale de Paris*. Paris: Imprimerie nationale, 1893.

Boutry, Maurice. "Une mystification diplomatique," in *Revue des études historiques* (1899), pp. 167–178.

Bussy-Rabutin, Roger de Rabutin, comte de. *Lettres de Messire Roger de Rabutin, comte de Bussy*. Paris: Chez Florentin Delaulne, 1721.

Bussy-Rabutin, Roger de Rabutin, comte de. *Histoire Amoureuses des Gaules, suivie de La France Galante*. Paris: Garnier Frères, 1868.

Bussy-Rabutin, Roger de Rabutin, comte de. *Correspondance de Roger de Rabutin comte de Bussy avec sa famille et ses amis 1666–1695*. Paris: Charpentier, 1859.

Caire, Bernard. "Eustache et son secret," in *Il y a trois siècles le masque de fer*. Cannes: Office Municipal de l'Action Culturelle et de la Comunication de la Ville de Cannes, 1989.

Campan, Jeannne, Louise Henriette de. *Memoirs of Madame de Campan on Marie Antoinette and her Court*. Boston: J. B. Millet Company, 1909, volume 1.

Carey, Edith F. *The Channel Islands*. London: A. & C. Black, 1904.

Caylus, Madame de. *Les Souvenirs de Madame de Caylus*. Paris: Chez Ant. Aug. Renouard, 1806.

Challes, Robert. *Mémoires de Robert Challes, écrivain du Roi*, publiés par A. Augustin-Thierry. Paris: Librairie Plon, 1931.

Charpentier. *La Bastille dévoilée, ou Recueil de pièces authentiques pour servir à son histoire*, neuvième livraison. Paris: Chez Desenne, 1790.

Chatelain, Urbain-Victor. *Le Surintendant Nicolas Foucquet, protecteur des lettres, des arts et des sciences*. Genève: Slatkine Reprints, 1971.

Chéruel, Adolphe, ed. *Mémoires sur la vie publique et privée de Fouquet, surintendant de finances, d'après ses lettres et des pièces inédite, conservées à la Bibliothèque impériale*. Paris: Charpentier, 1862.

Courtilz de Sandras. *Memoires de M.L.C.D.R. (Le Comte de Rochefort)*. Cologne: Chez P. Marteau, 1687.

Courtilz de Sandras, Gatien. *Memoirs of Monsieur d'Artagnan*, translated by Ralph Nevill. Boston: Little, Brown and Company, 1903, volume III.

Curran, M. Beryl, ed. *The Despatches of William Perwich, agent in Paris 1669–1677*. London: Offices of the Royal Historical Society, 1908.

Delort, Joseph. *Histoire de la Détention des Philosophes et des Gens de Lettres à la Bastille et à Vincennes, précédée de celle de Foucquet, de Pellisson et de*

Lauzun, avec tous les documents authentiques et inédits. Paris: Firmin Didot Père et fils, 1829.

Delort, Joseph. *Histoire de l'homme au masque de fer.* Paris: Chez Delaforest, libraire, 1825.

Dessert, Daniel. *Fouquet.* Paris: Fayard, 1987.

Dijol, Pierre-Marie. "L'Homme au Masque de Fer." Cannes: Office Municipal de l'Action Culturelle et de la Comunication de la Ville de Cannes, 1989.

Duchêne, Jacqueline. *Henriette d'Angleterre, duchesse d'Orléans.* Paris: Librairie Arthème Fayard, 1995.

Du Junca, Etienne. *Registres des entrées et des sorties de la Bastille, écrits par Du Junca, lieutenant du roi de la Bastille,* manuscript written 1690–1705, two volumes.

Dutens, Louis. *Correspondance interceptée.* London: s.n., 1789.

Dutens, Louis. *Mémoires d'un voyageur qui se repose; contenant des anecdotes historiques, politiques et littéraires, relatives à plusieurs des principaux personnages du siècle.* Paris: Bossange, Masson et Besson, 1806.

Duvivier, Maurice. *Le Masque de fer.* Paris: Librairie Armand Colin, 1932.

Ellis, George Agar. *The True History of the State Prisoner commonly called The Iron Mask.* London: John Murray, 1826.

Formanoir de Palteau, Guillaume-Louis. "Lettre du 19 juin 1768," *l'Année littéraire,* tome IV, pp. 351–354.

Fraser, Antonia. *King Charles II.* London: Weidenfeld and Nicolson, 1979.

Funck-Brentano, Frantz. *Legends of the Bastille,* translated by George Maidment. London: Downey & Co. Limited, 1899.

Funck-Brentano, Frantz. *Le Masque de fer.* Paris: Flammarion, 1933.

Furneaux, Rupert. *The Man behind the Mask: The Real Story of the "Ancient Prisoner."* London: Cassell & Company, 1954.

Gazette. Théophraste Renaudot, contributor. Paris: Bureau d'adresse, 1631–1761.

Gourville, Jean-Hérauld, sieur de. *Mémoires*. Paris: Librairie Renouard, 1894.

Grand Larousse de la langue française, en sept volumes. Paris: Larousse, 1989.

Griffet, Henri. *Histoire de La Vie de Louis XIII, Roi de France et de Navarre*. Paris: Chez Saillant, Libraire, 1758.

Griffet, Henri. *Traité des différentes sortes de preuves qui servent à établir la vérité de l'Histoire*. Liège: J.-F. Bassompierre, publisher, 1770.

Grimm, Friedrich Melchior, baron de. *Correspondance littéraire*, nouvelle édition, tome quatorzième 1788–1789. Paris: Chez Furne et Ladrange, 1831.

Hartmann, Cyril Hughes. *Charles II and Madame*. London: William Heinemann Ltd., 1934.

Heiss, baron de. "Lettre au sujet de l'homme au masque de fer." *Journal encyclopédique*. 15 août 1770, tome VI.

Hilton, Lisa. *The Real Queen of France: Athénaïs & Louis XIV*. London: Abacus, 2003.

Hopkins, Tighe. *The Man in the Iron Mask*. London: Hurst and Blackett, Limited, 1901.

Huguet, Adrien. *Le Marquis de Cavoye: Un grand maréchal des logis de la maison du Roi*. Paris: Édouard Champion. 1920.

Iung, Théodore. *La Verite sur le Masque de Fer (Les Empoisoneurs), d'après des documents inédits*. Paris: Henri Plon, 1873.

La Fare, marquis de. *Mémoires et Réflexions sur les principaux événements du règne de Louis XIV* in Michaud et Poujoulat, series 3, volume 30. Lyon; Paris: Guyot Frères, 1854.

La Grange-Chancel, Joseph. "Lettre à Fréron," *L'Année littéraire*. 1759, tome III.

Lair, Jules. *Nicolas Fouquet*. Paris: Librairie Plon, 1890.

Laloy, Emile. *Enigmes du Grand Siècle: Le Masque de fer, Jacques de La Cloche, l'abbé Prignani, Roux de Marsilly*. Paris: Librairie H. Le Soudier, 1912.

Lang, Andrew. *The Valet's Tragedy and Other Stories*. London: Longmans, Green and Co., 1903.

Lioret, G. *Le Surintendant Foucquet et ses compagnons d'infortune au Château de Moret*. Moret-sur-Loing: Librairie E. Sauvé, 1897.

Loisleur, Jules. *Trois Enigmes Historiques. La Saint-Barthélemy; L'Affaire des Poisons et Madame de Montespan; le Masque de Fer Devant la Critique Moderne*. Paris: E. Plon et Cie, 1882.

Louis XIV. *Œuvres de Louis XIV*. Paris: Chez Treuttel et Würtz, 1806.

Macdonald, Roger. *The Man in the Iron Mask*. London: Constable, 2005; London: Constable, 2008.

Mast, M. M. *Le Masque de fer: Une solution révolutionnaire*. Paris: Tchou, 1974.

Mongrédien, Georges. "Le problème de Masque de fer," in *Pinerolo: La Maschera di Ferro e il suo tempo*. Pinerolo: L'Artistica Savigliano, 1976.

Montoya, Alicia C. *Medievalist Enlightenment: From Charles Perrault to Jean-Jacques Rousseau*. Cambridge: DS Brewer, 2013.

Montpensier, Anne-Marie-Louise d'Orléans. *Mémoires de Mlle de Montpensier: Petite-fille de Henri IV*, edited by A. Chéruel. Paris: Bibliothèque-Charpentier, 1858.

Montpensier, Anne-Marie-Louise d'Orléans. *Memoires of Mademoiselle de Montpensier, granddaughter of Henri IV and niece of Queen Henrietta-Maria*. London: H. Colburn, 1848.

Mouhy, Charles de Fieux. *Le Masque de fer, ou les avantures admirables du père et du fils*. The Hague: Chez Pierre de Hondt, 1750.

Noone, John. *The Man behind the Iron Mask*. Stroud: Sutton Publishing, 1994.

Ormesson, Olivier Lefèvre d'. *Journal*. Paris Imprimerie Impériale, 1860.

Pagnol, Marcel. *Le Secret du masque de fer*. Paris: Editions de Fallois, 1998.

Papon, Jean-Pierre. *Voyage littéraire en Provence*. Paris: Chez Barrois l'âiné, 1780.

Patin, Gui. *Lettres*. Paris: Chez J.-B. Baillière, 1846.

Pélissier, L.-G. "Un voyage en felouque de Saint-Tropez à Gènes," *Revue des études historiques*. 1907.

Petitfils, Jean-Christian. *Fouquet*. Paris: Perrin, 1999.

Petitfils, Jean-Christian. *Le Masque de fer: Entre histoire et légende*. Paris: Perrin, 2003.

Pitts, Vincent J. *Embezzlement and High Treason in Louis XIV's France. The Trial of Nicolas Fouquet*. Baltimore: Johns Hopkins University Press, 2015.

Ravaisson, François. *Archives de la Bastille*, volumes I, II, III, VII. Paris: Durand, 1866.

Renneville, Constantin de. *L'Inquisition Françoise, ou L'Histoire de la Bastille*. Amsterdam: Chez Etienne Roger, 1715.

Roux-Fazillac, Pierre. *Recherches historiques et critiques sur l'homme au masque de fer*. Paris: L'imprimerie de Valade, an IX [1800].

Sainte-Beuve, Charles-Augustin. *Causeries du lundi*, second edition. Paris: Garnier frères, 1852.

Saint-Foix, Germain François Poillain de. "Lettre de M. de Saint-Foix au sujet de l'Homme au masque de fer." *l'Année littéraire*, 1768, tome IV.

Saint-Foix, Germain François Poillain de. "Lettre de M. de Saint-Foix à l'auteur des ces Feuilles sur l'Homme au Masque de Fer." *l'Année littéraire*, 1768, tome V.

Saint-Simon, Louis de Rouvroy. *Mémoires complètes et authentiques de duc de Saint-Simon*, ed. A Chéruel and A. Régnier, fils. Paris: Librairie Hachette et Cie, 1873–1886.

Saint-Simon, Louis de Rouvroy. *Mémoires complètes et authentiques de duc de Saint-Simon . . . collationnés sur le manuscrit original par M. Chéruel*, edited by M. Sainte-Beuve. Paris: Librairie de L. Hachette et Cie, 1858.

Saint-Simon, Louis de Rouvroy. *Memoirs of the duc de Saint-Simon on the times of the regency*, translated and edited by Katharine Prescott Wormeley. Boston: Hardy, Pratt & Company, 1902.

Sandars, Mary F. *Lauzun: Courtier and Adventurer. The Life of a Friend of Louis XIV*. New York: Brentano's, 1909.

Savine, Albert. *La Vie á la Bastille: Souvenirs d'un prisonnier*. Paris: Louis-Michaud, 1908.

Scheichl, Franz. *Der Malteserritter und general-leutnant Jakob Bretel von Grémonville, der Gesandte Ludwigs der Vierzehnten am Wiener Hofe von 1664 bis 1673, der Mann mit der schwarzen Maske.* 1914.

Sévigné, Marie de Rabutin-Chantal. *Recueil des Lettres.* Paris: Chez Rollin, 1754.

Sévigné, Marie de Rabutin-Chantal. *Lettres de Mme de Sévigné, de sa famille et de ses amis.* Paris: J. J. Blaise, 1818.

Somerset, Anne. *The Affair of the Poisons: Murder, Infanticide & Satanism at the Court of Louis XIV.* London: Weidenfeld & Nicolson, 2003.

Sonnino, Paul. *The Search for the Man in the Iron Mask: A Historical Detective Story.* Lanham, Md.: Rowman & Littlefield, 2016.

Sourches, marquis de. *Mémoires du marquis de Sourches sur le règne de Louis XIV.* Paris: Librairie Hachette et Cie, 1884.

Thompson, Harry. *The Man in the Iron Mask: An Historical Detective Investigation,* revised and updated edition. London: New English Library, 1990.

Topin, Marius. *The Man with the Iron Mask,* translated and edited by Henry Vizetelly. London: Smith, Elder and Co., 1870.

Voltaire. *The Age of Louis XIV.* London: J. M. Dent & Sons Ltd; New York: E. P. Dutton & Co. Inc., 1935.

Voltaire. *Dictionnaire philosophique.* Paris: Imprimerie de Crosse et Gaultier-Laguionie, 1838.

Voltaire. *Les Œuvres complètes de Voltaire,* t. 13C, *Siècle de Louis XIV, chapitres 25–30* ed. Venturino. Oxford: The Voltaire Foundation, 2016.

Voltaire. *Questions sur l'encyclopédie par les amateurs.* Geneva: s.n., 1770–1771.

Voltaire. *Supplément au Siècle de Louis XIV.* Dresden: Chez George Conrad Walther, 1753.

Wade, Isa O. *Intellectual Development of Voltaire.* Princeton, N.J.: Princeton University Press, 2015.

Wilkinson, Josephine. *Louis XIV: The Power and the Glory.* New York: Pegasus Books Ltd., 2019.

ENDNOTES

CHAPTER ONE: "ONLY A VALET"

1   Maurice Duvivier, *Le Masque de fer* (Paris: Librairie Armand
    Colin, 1932), 113; Joseph Delort, *Histoire de la Détention des
    Philosophes et des Gens de Lettres à la Bastille et à Vincennes, précédée
    de celle de Foucquet, de Pellisson et de Lauzun, avec tous les documents
    authentiques et inédits* (Paris: Firmin Didot Père et fils, 1829),
    volume I, 155–156.

2   To hold the survivance meant that Louvois would inherit the
    office in the event of his father's death or retirement.

3   Antoine de Brouilly, marquis de Piennes, was the governor-general
    of Pignerol.

4   Jean-Christian Petitfils, *Le Masque de fer: Entre histoire et légende*
    (Paris: Perrin, 2003), 111; John Noone, *The Man behind the Iron
    Mask* (Stroud: Sutton Publishing, 1994), 151.

5   Ibid.

6   Pignerol is the French name for the town which, in Italian, is
    called Pinerolo. It is thought that it takes its name from the pine
    forests that surround it.

7   Counter-gardes are *V*-shaped fortifications placed on the exterior faces of bastions and demi-lunes to offer further protection from the enemy.

8   For the details of Saint-Mars's early life, see Petitfils, *Masque*, 76; Noone, 257–258. Les Mesnuls is situated in the Yvelines to the southwest of Paris.

9   Delort (1829), volume I, 87.

10 Théodore Iung, *La Verite sur le Masque de Fer (Les Empoisoneurs), d'après des documents inédits* (Paris: Henri Plon, 1873), 149.

11 One of Saint-Mars's nephews, Guillaume Formanoir de Corbest, would inherit the château de Palteau from his uncle, and it was his son, born in 1712, who provided the information about the Man in the Iron Mask's visit to Voltaire in 1763 and Fréron in 1768. See below, pp.193–194, 223.

12 Many of Louvois's letters to Saint-Mars were collected and printed by Arthur Stapleton Barnes, *The Man of the Mask: A Study in the Byways of History* (London: Smith, Elder & Co., 1912); Delort, Ravaisson, Pierre Roux-Fazillac, *Recherches historiques et critiques sur l'homme au masque de fer* (Paris: L'imprimerie de Valade, an IX [1800]); and Marius Topin, *The Man with the Iron Mask*, translated and edited by Henry Vizetelly (London: Smith, Elder and Co., 1870). Much of Saint-Mars's correspondence has been lost, but its content can be reconstructed from Louvois's replies.

13 Roux-Fazillac, 105. The original document was destroyed by fire during the Paris Commune.

CHAPTER TWO: NICOLAS FOUCQUET

1   For the summation of charges against Foucquet and the verdict of Olivier Lefèvre d'Ormesson, whose opinion carried the day, see Vincent J. Pitts, *Embezzlement and High Treason in Louis XIV's France. The Trial of Nicolas Fouquet.* (Baltimore, Md: Johns Hopkins University Press, 2015), 141–147, 157.

2   Antonia Fraser, *King Charles II* (London: Weidenfeld and Nicolson, 1979), 203.

3   Jean-Christian Petitfils, *Fouquet* (Paris: Perrin, 1999), 329. Foucquet chose La Bastide de La Croix, a man fluent in English, as his negotiator. Edward Hyde was created earl of Clarendon in April 1661.

4   Cited in Jules Lair, *Nicolas Fouquet* (Paris: Librairie Plon, 1890), volume II, 407.

5   Foucquet had married twice, the first time to Louise Fourché, who left him a widower with a small daughter in 1641. Ten years later, he married Marie-Madeleine de Castile, by whom he had five children, the eldest of whom had died. Foucquet's youngest child, another son, was born some three months before his arrest.

6   Marie de Rabutin-Chantal Sévigné, *Lettres de Mme de Sévigné, de sa famille et de ses amis* (Paris: J. J. Blaise, 1818), volume 1, 477. Madame de Sévigné states that Foucquet was escorted by fifty musketeers, but official accounts state one hundred. See François Ravaisson, *Archives de la Bastille* (Paris: Durand, 1866), volume II, 392.

7   It is not certain in what capacity La Forêt served Foucquet. In some sources he is described as an equerry; in others he is a valet de chambre.

8   Sévigné (1818), volume I, 480.

9   Ibid., 481.

10 *Annales des Alpes. Recueil périodique des Archives des Hautes-Alpes*, III année (Gap: Archives Départementales, 1899), 54–55.

11 Sévigné (1818), volume I, 482. Foucquet and d'Artagnan were of a similar age. While d'Artagnan's exact date of birth is unknown, he is generally believed to have been born c. 1610–1615. Foucquet was baptized on January 27, 1615, the probable day of his birth.

12 Sévigné (1818), volume I, 482.

13 Ravaisson, volume II, 397.

14 Louis XIV. *Œuvres de Louis XIV* (Paris: Chez Treuttel et Würtz, 1806), 371–372.

15 Delort (1829), volume I, 90.

16 Ibid., 93–94.

17 When news of Foucquet's miraculous escape reached Paris, his friends rejoiced. It was universally agreed that God must have rejected the verdict of the court and released the prisoner: "very often those who appear criminal before men are not criminals before God" (Charles-Augustin Sainte-Beuve, *Causeries du lundi*, second edition [Paris: Garnier frères, 1852], volume 5, 247). Olivier d'Ormesson, the lawyer who had sacrificed his own career to defend Foucquet, felt entirely vindicated (Olivier Lefèvre d'Ormesson, *Journal* [Paris Imprimerie impériale, 1860], volume II, 372). Inspired by Madame de Sévigné and Mademoiselle de Scudéry, the poet Ménage pleaded with Louis to complete God's work and release the former superintendent: "In your turn, oh Louis, image of the Divinity, imitate the supreme God and pardon this unfortunate man" (cited in Lair, volume 2, 427). Alas, Louis remained unmoved.

18 Delort (1829), volume I, 104.

19 Ibid., 105.

20 Ibid., 95. Today, la Pérouse is known by its Italian name, Perosa Argentina. The ruins of the fortress, which was called "the bastion," lie just beyond the town in a place called the Bec Dauphin.

21 Georges Mongrédien, "Le problème de Masque de fer," in *Pinerolo: La Maschera di Ferro e il suo tempo* (Pinerolo: L'Artistica Savigliano, 1976), 214.

22 Delort (1829), volume I, 157.

23 Ibid.; Petitfils, *Fouquet*, 463, note 12.

24 See below, p. 132.

25 Delort (1829), volume I, 157.

26 Ibid., 158.

27 Ibid., 91.

28 A full transcript of the *Projet de Saint-Mandé* can be found in
    Daniel Dessert, *Fouquet* (Paris: Fayard, 1987), 354–362, and Lair,
    volume I, 411–416.

29 Foucquet's assertion that he did not share his plan with anyone was
    not true, if his friend and colleague Jean Hérauld de Gourville is
    to be believed. In his *Mémoires* (Paris: Librairie Renouard, 1894),
    volume I, 171–173, he describes how Foucquet took him into his
    study at Saint-Mandé and showed him the document. Gourville
    said he thought the plan was foolish and advised Foucquet to burn
    it. Foucquet agreed and called for a candle, but just then someone
    entered the study and Foucquet hastily stashed the document
    behind a mirror and forgot about it. A year or so later, following
    Foucquet's arrest, it was discovered when Colbert's men made a
    search of the house.

30 Delort (1829), volume I, 160–162.

31 Ibid., 159, 161–162.

32 Ibid., 163.

33 Ibid., 167–168.

34 Ibid., 157.

35 Ibid., 167–168.

36 Ibid., 169.

37 Iung, 153.

38 Rissan will stay in post until September 1680, when illness will
    force him to take a long break. He will be temporarily replaced by
    Saint-Mars, who receives an extra 6,000 livres in wages. Jacques
    de Villebois will succeed Rissan in February 1682 (Delort [1829]),
    171–172; Petitfils, *Masque*, 36, 48, 51.

CHAPTER THREE: THE COMTE DE LAUZUN

1 Ravaisson, volume III, 99.

2 Ibid.

3 Ibid.

4   Delort (1829), volume I, 174.

5   Lauzun was born in 1633, and so was aged thirty-eight when he entered Pignerol.

6   Delort (1829), volume I, 176–178. Louvois's letter is dated November 26, the day after Lauzun's arrest.

7   Ravaisson, volume III, 105.

8   Ravaisson, volume III, 104. Although in his letter Saint-Mars stated that Lauzun's apartment was above Foucquet's, it will be seen that this is a mistake. He was actually lodged in the apartment below Foucquet's.

9   Ravaisson, volume III, 105.

10 Mary F. Sandars, *Lauzun: Courtier and Adventurer. The Life of a Friend of Louis XIV* (New York: Brentano's, 1909), volume 2, 361–362; Ravaisson, volume III, 104.

11 Ravaisson, volume III, 108.

12 Ibid.

13 Lauzun was given to fits of melancholy (Sandars, volume 1, 111). Sévigné (1818, volume 2, 290) speaks of the "continual rages of Lauzun."

14 Sandars, volume 1, 111–112.

15 Ibid., 125–126; Louis de Rouvroy Saint-Simon, *Mémoires complètes et authentiques de duc de Saint-Simon*, ed. A Chéruel and A. Régnier, fils (Paris: Librairie Hachette et Cie, 1873–1886), volume XIX, 175.

16 Saint-Simon (Chéruel), volume XIX, 176.

17 Roger de Rabutin Bussy-Rabutin, *Histoire Amoureuses des Gaules, suivie de La France Galante* (Paris: Garnier Frères, 1868), volume II, 64.

18 Ravaisson, volume II, 451; Saint-Simon (Chéruel), volume XIX, 174. Some months after his release from the Bastille, Lauzun took further revenge on the princesse de Monaco. As she sat on the floor with her ladies watching a game, Lauzun came up to her, planted the heel of his shoe firmly on her hand, pirouetted, and calmly walked away (Saint-Simon [Chéruel], volume XIX, 175–176).

19 Armand-Charles de La Porte, duc de La Meilleraye, duc de Mazarin (1632–1713), was the husband of the late Cardinal Mazarin's favorite niece, Hortense.

20 The story of Lauzun's expected appointment as grand master of the artillery and his antics with Mme de Montespan is recounted in Saint-Simon (Chéruel), volume XIX, 172–173; see also Sandars, volume 1, 176–184.

21 Sandars, volume 1, 286–287.

22 Sandars, volume 2, 310; Louis's letter is also reproduced in Anne-Marie-Louise d'Orléans Montpensier, *Mémoires de Mlle de Montpensier: Petite-fille de Henri IV*, edited by A. Chéruel (Paris: Bibliothèque-Charpentier, 1858), volume IV, 624–627.

23 Sandars, volume 2, 311.

24 Ibid., 312.

25 Ibid., volume 1, 298–299.

26 Ibid., volume 2, 312–313.

27 Ibid., 313.

28 Ibid.

29 Marquis de La Fare, *Mémoires et Réflexions sur les principaux événements du règne de Louis XIV* in Michaud et Poujoulat, Series 3, volume 30 (Lyon; Paris: Guyot Frères, 1854), 270.

30 Sandars, volume 2, 323.

31 The marquis de Guitry was master of the royal wardrobe.

32 The future marquise de Maintenon, Mme Scarron would go on to become Louis's morganatic second wife following the death of Queen Marie-Thérèse.

33 La Fare, 271.

34 Montpensier (Chéruel), volume IV, 320.

35 Known as le Petit d'Artagnan, he was not d'Artagnan's nephew, as suggested by Sandars, but his cousin. With the mission accomplished, Pierre d'Artagnan would be sent to on ahead to Paris, where he would relate the details of the journey to Mademoiselle, who later included them in her *Mémoires*.

36 For Lauzun's journey, see Montpensier (Chéruel) volume IV, 313–324; Sandars, volume II, 350–355.

37 Montpensier (*Mémoires*), volume III, 73.

38 Ravaisson, volume III, 114.

39 Delort (1829), volume I, 181.

40 Ravaisson, volume III, 113.

41 Ibid., 117.

42 Ibid., 117–118.

43 Ibid., 106–107.

44 Ibid., 118.

45 Ibid., 120.

46 Delort (1829), volume I, 186.

47 Sévigné (1818), volume II, 369.

48 Ravaisson, volume III, 134.

49 Ibid., 134, 136.

50 Ibid., 134.

51 Sandars, 375.

52 Petitfils, *Masque*, 104 note; Ravaisson, volume III, 131. Louis Foucquet mentions a suicide in his letter, see Xavier Azema, *Un prélat janseniste: Louis Foucquet évêque et comte d'Agde (1656–1702)* (Paris: Librairie philosophique J. Vrin, 1963), 150; Petitfils, *Masque*, 103–104, 190.

53 Delort (1829), volume I, 191.

54 Ravaisson, volume III, 136.

55 Delort (1829), volume I, 195–196; Ravaisson, volume III, 137. Although she would eventually engage a businessman to help her, she still had to defer to her husband for certain matters. Mme Foucquet had received her reply by January 10, 1673, several weeks after it had been sent (Ravaisson, volume III, 141).

56 Delort (1829), volume I, 195, 196–197.

57 Ibid., 191–193, 197, 199. Plassot was given 20 crowns out of charity as he returned to the world (Sandars, *Lauzun*, volume 2, 378).

58 Delort (1829), volume I, 200.

59 Quoted in Sandars, volume 2, 382; see also Ravaisson, volume III, 147.

60 Quoted in Sandars, volume 2, 383.

61 Delort (1829), volume I, 207.

CHAPTER FOUR: THE FATEFUL ENCOUNTER

1   Ravaisson, volume III, 121.

2   Iung, 199–200.

3   Ravaisson, volume III, 141. Saint-Mars became the chevalier de Saint-Mars. Pierre-Marie Dijol, "L'Homme au Masque de Fer" (Cannes: Office Municipal de l'Action Culturelle et de la Comunication de la Ville de Cannes, 1989), 62.

4   Iung, 217.

5   Ibid., 219. The order for Butticari's release was dated August 11, 1675.

6   Topin, 195. Letter dated May 6, 1673.

7   Unpublished letter, March 17, 1673, Topin, 195–196.

8   Petitfils, *Masque*, 260.

9   Sandars, volume 2, 384–385.

10 Sandars, volume 2, 386.

11 Ravaisson, volume III, 151; order dates February 11, 1673.

12 Notwithstanding Louvois's promise that no more would be said, several attempts were made to force Lauzun to resign, all of which he refused. In the end, the post was awarded to Luxembourg without the formality of the resignation of its previous incumbent. Lauzun would eventually sign a formal letter of resignation, but as Louvois told him, it was four years too late and so of no use. See Sanders, volume 2, 387.

13 Ravaisson, volume III, 142–143.

14 Delort (1829), volume I, 218. Foucquet had also sent a *compliment* to Louvois, a polite note of greeting, but Louvois did not wish to receive it, thinking that Foucquet might take advantage of any

friendship that might develop between them. Louvois sent it back to Saint-Mars, saying he could either return it to Foucquet or burn it in front of him (Delort [1829], volume I, 217).

15 Ravaisson, volume III, 175.

16 Ibid., 176.

17 Ibid., 177.

18 Petitfils, *Masque*, 44–45. Saint-Mars lost track of which prisoner was which, and he referred to Castanieri as Lapierre (see Ravaisson, III, 171, 173). They were, however, two different people.

19 Rupert Furneaux, *The Man behind the Mask: The Real Story of the "Ancient Prisoner"* (London: Cassell & Company, 1954). 72. Furneaux confuses Lapierre with Dubreuil, who will enter Pignerol as a prisoner in 1676.

20 Delort (1829), volume I, 229.

21 Dessert, *Fouquet*, 365–368; Chéruel, *Fouquet*, volume II, 452–460; Lair, *Foucquet*, volume II, 447–451.

22 Delort (1829), volume I, 233.

23 Ibid.

24 Sandars, volume 1, 176.

25 Delort (1829), volume I, 234.

26 Louis de Rouvroy Saint-Simon, *Memoirs of the duc de Saint-Simon on the times of the regency*, translated and edited by Katharine Prescott Wormeley (Boston: Hardy, Pratt & Company, 1902), volume 1, 106.

27 Delort (1829), volume I, 230–232; Bussy-Rabutin, volume II, 91; Sandars, volume II, 388–389.

28 Courtilz de Sandras, *Memoires de M.L.C.D.R. (Le Comte de Rochefort)* (Cologne: Chez P. Marteau, 1687), 221–222; Saint-Simon (Wormeley), volume 1, 106–107.

29 Petitfils, *Masque*, 47.

30 Courtilz de Sandras published his *Mémoire de M.L.C.D.R.* in 1687, with other editions following. It is, therefore, an earlier

source than Saint-Simon's. While neither author is entirely trustworthy, the question must be asked, why would Courtilz de Sandras mention Eustache, even if not by name, if he had not been present at the encounter between Foucquet and Lauzun? He clearly had no idea of the significance of this revelation, but what was his source? It can be speculated, but not more, that he was given this information by Lauzun or someone whom Lauzun had told and who then passed on the information to Courtilz de Sandras.

31 Montpensier (Chéruel), volume IV, 379–380, 401; Ravaisson, volume III, 182, 184–185; Sandars, volume 2, 394–397.

32 Delort (1829), volume I, 242.

33 Ravaisson, volume III, 186–187.

34 Delort (1829), volume I, 246.

35 Delort (1829), volume I, 248.

36 Delort (1829), volume I, 242–243. Even before this, a telescope Lauzun had somehow managed to get hold of had been confiscated (Sandars, volume 2, 393).

37 Petitfils, *Masque*, 43–44.

38 Ravaisson, volume III, 188.

39 Ibid., 189.

40 Ibid., 189.

41 Ibid., 190.

42 Noone, 163.

43 Ravaisson, volume III, 191.

44 Delort (1829), volume I, 247–248.

45 Ibid., 250.

46 Ibid., 252.

47 Ibid., 254–255.

CHAPTER FIVE: MYSTERY

1 Barail was a former lieutenant at the Bastille. A great friend and confidant to Lauzun, he frequently assisted him in his intrigues.

Rollinde acted as a secretary to Mademoiselle de Montpensier. In 1673, he would serve the king in the same capacity.

2   Montpensier (Chéruel), volume IV, 387–388; Sandars, volume 2, 401.

3   Delort (1829), volume I, 260–264.

4   Isarn wrote an account of the proceedings, which can be read in Ravaisson, volume III, 197–204.

5   A third death occurred a few months after this when, in May 1678, Mme de Monaco, Lauzun's old flame, died. As Sanders says in her biography (volume 2, 413), Lauzun was probably not made aware of this at the time.

6   Delort (1829), volume I, 265–267.

7   Ibid., 271–272.

8   Foucquet was also to be allowed to receive copies of the *Mercure Galant*, an illustrated magazine dedicated to fashion, the arts, etiquette, society news, gossip, and, perhaps most importantly, life at the court, all of which Foucquet would have taken part in were he not in prison (Delort [1829], volume I, 270). Foucquet was also to be allowed to hear news of promotions at court and the king's progress in the Dutch War: see, for example, Ravaisson, volume III, 205–206.

9   Paul Sonnino, *The Search for the Man in the Iron Mask: A Historical Detective Story* (Lanham, Md.: Rowman & Littlefield, 2016), 148–149.

10 Sévigné (1754), volume IV, 79–80; Lair, volume II, 457–458.

11 Delort (1829), volume I, 279.

12 Ravaisson, volume III, 208.

13 Petitfils, *Masque*, 124; Bernard Caire, "Eustache et son secret," in *Il y a trois siècles le masque de fer* (Cannes: Office Municipal de l'Action Culturelle et de la Comunication de la Ville de Cannes, 1989), 46–47. Caire suggests that Foucquet may have been forced, or volunteered, to swear an oath not to disclose Eustache's secret. There is nothing, however, to support this suggestion.

14 Petitfils, *Masque*, 124.

15 Pagnol, 29.

16 Petitfils, *Masque*, 153.

17 This *Mémoire* is printed in Delort (1829), volume I, 280–285.

18 Ravaisson, volume III, 209.

19 Delort (1829), volume I, 286–288.

20 Ibid., 290.

21 Delort (1829), volume I, 292. Curiously, although the order to remove the screens had been issued in March, the windows were still covered in April. Saint-Mars was told he could open the screens during the day provided security could be assured.

CHAPTER SIX: MATTHIOLI

1 Casale is known today as Casale Monferrato.

2 Isabella Clara was the daughter of Archduke Leopold of Austria and Claude de Médicis.

3 George Agar Ellis, *The True History of the State Prisoner Commonly Called The Iron Mask* (London: John Murray, 1826), 90. Casale was also coveted by the Spanish for the same reason it appealed to Louis.

4 Ibid., 91.

5 Matthioli married Camilla Piatesi, widow of Alessandro Paleotti, January 13, 1661. The couple had two sons.

6 Ellis, 91.

7 Charles II of Spain.

8 Ellis, 92–93.

9 Ibid., 94.

10 Ibid., 97.

11 Ibid.

12 Ibid., 101–102.

13 Ibid., 116–117.

14 Ibid., 117.

15 Ibid., 123–124.

16 Ibid., 148–149.

17 Ibid., 189.

18 Ibid., 23; Petitfils, *Masque*, 86.

19 Ellis, 23–24.

20 Ibid., 246; Delort (1825), 209.

21 Ellis, 221; Delort (1825), 189.

22 Ellis, 251.

23 Indeed, as it transpired, Matthioli had also spoken to President Turki, the duchesse de Savoie's minister, who was known to act in the interests of Spain, and who had later paid Matthioli for his valuable information (Ellis, 32, 261–262, 281, 297–298; Delort (1825), 221, 225, 237, 249–250, 252–253).

24 Topin, 267.

25 Ellis, 227.

26 Ibid. 29; Delort (1825) , 195.

27 Ellis, 343–335; Roux-Fazillac, 19–20.

28 Ellis, 35–36; Delort (1825), 35.

29 Ellis, 271.

30 Ibid., 248–249.

31 This secrecy contradicts the assertion that all Europe knew what happened to Matthioli. However, as will be seen, the secrecy had nothing to do with Matthioli's arrest, but the manner of it.

32 Furneaux, 83–84.

33 Ellis, 37–40; Roux-Fazillac, 27–28.

34 Ellis, 250–251; Delort (1825), 212–213; Roux-Fazillac, 62–63.

35 Ellis, 251; Delort (1825), 214; Roux-Fazillac, 64.

36 Ellis, 251–252; Delort (1825), 213–214; Roux-Fazillac, 63–64.

37 Ellis, 253; Delort (1825), 215; Roux-Fazillac, 66.

38 Ellis, 255; Delort (1825), 216; Roux-Fazillac, 66.

39 Ellis, 267–268; Delort (1825), 225–226; Roux-Fazillac, 76–77.

40 Ellis, 255–256; Delort (1825), 217; Roux-Fazillac, 67.

41 Ellis, 275; Delort (1825), 232–233.

42 Ellis, 298; Delort (1825), 246.

43 Ellis, 302–303; Delort (1825), 254.

44 Ellis, 309; Delort (1825), 259.

45 Ellis, 310–311.

46 Ellis, 311–312

CHAPTER SEVEN: STAT SPES

1 G. Lioret, *Le Surintendant Foucquet et ses compagnons d'infortune au Château de Moret* (Moret-sur-Loing: Librairie E. Sauvé, 1897), 25.

2 Delort (1829), volume I, 294. Foucquet was by this time aware that plans were being made to allow his wife and children to visit him at Pignerol. See the letter dated April 23, 1679, in Ravaisson, volume III, 211.

3 Delort (1829), 295–296. Foucquet had been made aware of the impending visit even before Saint-Mars had been told of it, see Ravaisson, volume III, 211.

4 Delort (1829), volume I, 297.

5 Ravaisson, volume III, 211; Delort (1829), volume I, 297–298, 299.

6 Life imprisonment meant that the prisoner was judicially dead, hence the vicomte's holding his father's title.

7 Saint-Simon (Wormeley, volume 1, 107). Saint-Simon added that he "never knew what it was that displeased Lauzun, but he came out of Pignerol Foucquet's enemy, and then did all the harm he could to him, and after his death to his family."

8 Delort (1829), volume I, 306.

9 Ibid., 314–315.

10 Ibid., 296.

11 Ibid., 295.

12 Ibid., 296–297.

13 Montpensier (Chéruel), volume IV, 401.

14 As it happened, Le Nôtre would begin work on Louvois's estate at Meudon at about this time, a project that would last for several years.

15 Delort (1829), volume I, 311.

16 Ravaisson, volume III, 211–212.

17 Ibid., 212–213.

18 Delort (1829), volume I, 303.

19 Ibid., 305.

20 Ibid.

21 Delort (1829), volume I, 310.

22 Ibid., 312–313.

23 Delort (1829), volume I, 300; Ravaisson, volume III, 212. Where Foucquet's youngest son, Louis, was at this point, is not known. Since he is not mentioned again in the correspondence, it is probable that he also accompanied his mother.

24 Delort (1829), volume I, 309.

25 Ibid.

26 Ibid., 310.

27 Ibid., 300–301.

28 Ibid., 302.

29 Ibid., 305–307.

30 Ibid., 316.

31 Ibid., 303.

32 Ibid.

33 Ibid., 312.

34 Ibid., 316–317.

35 Ibid., 306.

36 Ibid., 313–314.

37 Saint-Simon (1858), volume XX, 48–49.

38 Montpensier (Chéruel), volume IV, 401.

39 Delort (1829), volume I, 307.

40 Ibid., 308, 310. Of course, security remained of paramount concern, and when Lauzun asked for a new servant to help him to care for the horses, this was denied, probably for reasons of security. Instead, he was obliged to make use of one of Saint-Mars's grooms or an officer of the compagnie-franche whenever he wanted help to look after the horses.

CHAPTER EIGHT: LA TOUR D'EN BAS

1   Petitfils, *Masque*, 129.

2   Caire, 47; Petitfils, *Masque*, 129.

3   Sévigné (1818), volume VI, 217. Mme de Sévigné's letter is dated April 3, 1680.

4   Ravaisson, volume III, 213; see also Delort (1829), volume I, 321.

5   Delort (1829), volume I, 317–320. Louvois's letter is dated April 8, 1680.

6   Noone, 255.

7   Delort (1829), volume I, 321–322.

8   Ibid., 323–324.

9   Ibid., 326.

10 Foucquet's translation of Psalm 118 is accompanied by annotations explaining his choice of words, various repetitions and paraphrases (Urbain-Victor Chatelain, *Le Surintendant Nicolas Foucquet, protecteur des lettres, des arts et des sciences* [Genève: Slatkine Reprints, 1971], 544).

11 Delort (1829), volume I, 318.

12 Ibid., 323.

13 Ibid., 325.

14 Ibid., 326.

15 See also Furneaux, 161, who wonders if Foucquet had written information about Eustache that was previously unknown to Louis and Louvois.

16 This letter appears in many studies of the Iron Mask. The original is printed in Delort (1825), volume I, 261–262; Ellis, 312–313; and others, and it is reproduced in facsimile in Duvivier, 251.

17 The theory that Foucquet had been poisoned originates with Maurice Duvivier and is continued by Marcel Pagnol.

18 Bussy-Rabutin, *Lettres*, volume IV, 83.

19 *Gazette*, Théophraste Renaudot, contributor (Paris: Bureau d'adresse, 1631–1761), 1680, 168.

20 Sévigné (1818), volume VI, 221.

21 Ibid., volume I, 481.

22 Gui Patin, *Lettres* volume III (Paris: Chez J.-B. Baillière, 1846), 505.

23 Delort (1829), volume I, 271.

24 Ravaisson, volume III, 165.

25 Bussy-Rabutin, *Lettres*, volume IV, 83.

26 Lair, *Foucquet*, volume II, 446.

27 Bussy-Rabutin, *Correspondance*, volume V, 80.

28 Ibid., 84.

29 Lair, *Fouquet*, volume I, 457.

30 Duvivier, 260–274; cf. Pagnol, 197–196, 201–202.

31 Duvivier, 119–120; Petitfils, *Masque*, 167–168.

32 Ravaisson, volume III, 175.

33 Pagnol, 196–197; Ravaisson, volume III, 165.

34 Ravaisson, volume III, 118.

35 Petitfils, *Fouquet*, 504.

36 Caire, 47.

37 Foucquet's remains were returned to Paris the following year. He was interred in the family vault of the convent of the Dames de Sainte-Marie, on the rue Saint-Antoine in Paris, on March 28, 1681. His mother had died shortly before, and mother and son were buried together. The nuns of the convent, five of whom were Foucquet's sisters, registered a memorial listing Foucquet's achievements (reproduced in Ravaisson, volume III, 213–214).

38 *Grand Larousse de la langue française, tome deuxième: CIR-ERY*, 1385.

39 Ravaisson, volume III, 157–158. Foucquet was a skilled apothecary, an art he learned from his mother, Marie de Maupeou. She had collected the recipes for her remedies into a book, but she had always refused to publish it. Following her death, her son, the bishop of Agde, printed and published her book. She worked hard assisting the poor and the sick under the auspices of Vincent de Paul.

40 Ravaisson, volume III, 212.

CHAPTER NINE: EXILLES

1 Delort (1829), volume I, 327.

2 Lisa Hilton, *The Real Queen of France: Athénaïs & Louis XIV* (London: Abacus, 2003), 284.

3 Anne-Marie-Louise d'Orléans Montpensier, *Memoires of Mademoiselle de Montpensier, granddaughter of Henri IV and niece of Queen Henrietta-Maria* (London: H. Colburn, 1848), 187.

4 Ibid., volume III, 187.

5 Ibid., 194–195.

6 Ibid., 200.

7 Ibid., 200–201.

8 Delort (1829), volume I, 327–328.

9 Ibid., 330.

10 Hilton, 287.

11 The comte de Lauzun has no further part to play in this narrative. He returned briefly to court, where he had an interview with the king, another with Louvois and a third with Colbert. He did see Mademoiselle again on several occasions, but it was clear that their love story was destined never to have a happy ending. Lauzun was permitted to withdraw to his estates, but he would win back royal favor in the service of King James II of England. He eventually married, at the age of sixty-three, the sister-in-law of the duc de Saint-Simon, a young lady only fourteen years of age.

12 Ellis, 313; Delort (1825), 262; Jules Loiseleur, *Trois énigmes historiques. La Saint-Barthélemy, l'affaire des Poisons et Mme de Montespan, le Masque de fer devant la critique moderne* (Paris: Plon, 1883), 241.

13 Saint-Mars's letter is printed in Ellis, 314–315.

14 Ellis, 316–317; Delort (1825), 264–265.

15 Ellis, 315–317; Delort (1825), 264–265.

16 Ellis, 318; Delort (1825), 266.

17 Ellis, 317–18; Delort (1825), 165–166.

18 Ellis, 318–319; Delort (1825), 266–267.

19 Ellis, 319–320; Delort (1825), 267.

20 Although dating no earlier than the medieval period, the Tour Grosse was also known as the Tour César; see Petitfils, *Masque de fer*, 61.

21 Ellis, 320–322; Delort (1825), 268–269.

22 Ellis, 321; Delort (1825), 269.

23 Ellis, 323; Delort (1825), 270.

24 Ellis, 324; Delort (1825), 271.

25 Ellis, 324; Delort (1825), 271.

26 Ravaisson, volume III, 214.

27 Ellis, 323–324; Delort (1825), 270.

28 Ellis, 325–326; Delort (1825), 271–272.

29 Ellis, 326; Delort (1825), 272.

30 Ellis, 327–328; Delort (1825), 273–274; Roux-Fazillac, 110.

31 Ellis, 328–329; Delort (1825), 274–275.

32 Ellis, 330–331; Delort (1825), 276–277.

33 Ellis, 61.

34 Barnes, 281.

35 See Petitfils, *Masque de fer*, 61.

36 The fortress known to Saint-Mars was demolished in the early 19th century following Napoleon's conquest of Italy. The building now standing on the site dates from 1818–1829.

37 Ellis, 333; Barnes, 281.

38 Barnes, 281.

39 Barnes, 282.

40 Ellis, 334–336; Roux-Fazillac, 111–113.

41 Barnes, 283.

42 Petitfils, *Masque de fer*, 57.

43 Ellis, 333–334.

44 Barnes, 283.

45 Ibid.

46 Petitfils, *Masque de fer*, 54.

47 Ravaisson, volume III, 218; Barnes, 289.

48 Barnes, 284.

49 Ibid.

50 Ibid., 284–285.

51 Ibid., 285.

52 See above, p. 23.

53 Furneaux, 98, suggests that Eustache would not have been allowed to write a will, as it would have revealed his whereabouts and his fate—but the same applies to La Rivière.

54 Ellis, 336; Roux-Fazillac, 113; Delort (1825), 281.

55 Ibid.

56 Barnes, 285.

57 Iung, 405. Videl can be ruled out as the prisoner who died because he is mentioned in the royal treasury accounts after Saint-Mars's departure from Exilles; see Petitfils, *Masque de fer*, 61.

CHAPTER TEN: THE ÎLE SAINTE-MARGUERITE

1 Iung, 405.

2 Ibid.

3 Ibid.

4 Ellis, 387–388; Iung, 405–406; Roux-Fazillac, 114–115; Barnes, 286.

5 Barnes, 287.

6 The fishing village of Cannes was situated in the area now known as the Pointe Croisette.

7 Petitfils, *Masque de fer*, 63.

8 Ibid.

9 Iung, 170.

10 Barnes, 287.

11 Ellis, 339; Delort (1825), 283–288; Roux-Fazillac, 115.

12 Iung, 408.

13 The prisons and the governor's residence built by Saint-Mars are now a maritime museum, the Musée de la Mer.

14 Ellis, 340; Barnes, 288; Delort (1825), 284; Roux-Fazillac, 116.

15 Ibid.

16 L.-G. Pélissier, "Un voyage en felouque de Saint-Tropez à Gènes," *Revue des études historiques* (1907), 232–233. The article also mentions a man who committed suicide at Pignerol. This probably refers to Jean Herse, who attempted suicide but survived.

17 This gazette was the forerunner of the *Nouvelles ecclésiastiques*, which began to appear as a printed newssheet in the 18th century.

18 Azema, 150.

19 Barnes, 288.

20 Ibid., 289.

21 Ibid.

22 Josephine Wilkinson, *Louis XIV: The Power and the Glory* (New York: Pegasus Books Ltd., 2019), 232–235.

23 Ravaisson, volume IX, 168–169.

24 Ibid., 170.

25 Ibid., 171.

26 Petitfils, *Masque de fer*, 70.

27 Ravaisson, volume IX, 177.

28 Marquis de Sourches, *Mémoires du marquis de Sourches sur le règne de Louis XIV*, volume III (Paris: Librairie Hachette et Cie, 1884), 436.

29 Louis was currently engaged in the Nine Years' War, or the War of the League of Augsburg.

30 Petitfils, *Masque de fer*, 68; Furneaux, 106.

31 See Petitfils, *Masque de fer*, 69.

32 Major de Villebois died at Pignerol on April 20, 1692. He was succeeded on May 18 by Jean de La Prade, musketeer and lieutenant of Saint-Mars's compagnie-franche.

33 Barnes, 290; Ellis, 341–342; Delort (1825), 285; Roux-Fazillac, 117.

34 Petitfils, *Masque de fer*, 73–74.

35 Ibid., 71.

36 Barnes, 290.

37 Ibid., 290–291.

38 In accordance with his secret treaty with Louis XIV, the duc de Savoie, Victor Amadeus II, agreed to the return of Pignerol to the Savoie. The treaty was signed on June 29, 1696. The following month, on September 19, the demolition of the donjon and fortifications of Pignerol began.

39 Petitfils, *Masque de fer*, 75.

40 Barnes, 292.

41 Topin, 340.

42 Barnes, 293.

43 Barnes, 293–294; Topin, 342–344, note 24.

44 Eustache is served first because he is Saint-Mars's longest-serving prisoner, but he is also regarded as the most important.

45 Barnes, 295.

46 Topin, 61.

47 Petitfils, *Masque de fer*, 162.

48 Ibid., 162. The Peace of Ryswick was established in two treaties: one between France, Spain, and the maritime powers on September 20; the second between France, the emperor, and the empire on October 30.

49 Petitfils, *Masque de fer*, 162 note.

CHAPTER ELEVEN: THE BASTILLE

1 Of Saint-Mars's two sons, Antoine Bénigne died on July 29, 1693, at the battle of Neerwinden, at the age of twenty-one. André Antoine was still alive at this point. He would die on November 15, 1703, of wounds sustained in the battle of Spire at the age of twenty-four.

2 Petitfils, *Masque de fer*, 163–164.

3 Iung, 419. Barbezieux's letter is dated June 15, 1698.

4 Ibid., 419.

5 Frantz Funck-Brentano, *Legends of the Bastille*, translated by George Maidment (London: Downey & Co. Limited, 1899), 58.

6   This description of the Bastille is taken from Funck-Brentano, *Bastille*, 60–62.

7   Ibid., 61–62.

8   Charles VI reigned 1380–1422.

9   Funck-Brentano, 63–64, quoting Bournon.

10 Ibid., 79.

11 Ibid., 86.

12 Iung, 420.

13 See Petitfils, *Masque*, 261–264.

14 Formanoir de Corbest would inherit the château de Palteau from his uncle, and it was his son, born in 1712, who provided the information about the Man in the Iron Mask's visit to Voltaire in 1763 and Fréron in 1768. See below, pp. 193–194, 223.

15 *Gazette*, 1698, 396.

16 The title of king's lieutenant at the Bastille indicated an administrative post and should not be confused with the more general use of the title, which referred to the governor of a town, a city, or a province.

17 Etienne Du Junca, *Registres des entrées et des sorties de la Bastille, écrits par Du Junca, lieutenant du roi de la Bastille,* manuscript written 1690–1705, two volumes; volume I, 37v. Documents relating to the arrest of prisoners were not kept, but were destroyed as soon as the prisoner was safely inside his or her chamber; see Funck-Brentano, 70.

18 Petitfils, *Masque*, 23, notes.

19 Constantin de Renneville, *L'Inquisition Françoise, ou L'Histoire de la Bastille* (Amsterdam: Chez Etienne Roger, 1715), tome I, 111.

20 Hopkins, 338. Hopkins states that in December 1701, Tirmon was transferred to the Bicêtre prison "half-prison, half-madhouse." He went insane after two years and died in 1709.

21 Du Junca, volume 1, 60r; Ravaisson, volume x, 369.

22 Ravaisson (volume X, 369, note 3) agrees that the ancien prisonnier must have been Eustache, but suggests that Du Junca meant that

Maranville and Tirmon were put into the same tower as him, but not in the same chamber.

23 Du Junca had himself once been reproached for talking too much with the prisoners, behavior of which Louis did not approve.

24 Jean-Baptiste Colbert, marquis de Torcy (1665–1746), secretary of state for foreign affairs.

25 Du Junca, volume 1, 71v; Ravaisson, volume x, 423 and note.

26 Renneville, 32–33.

27 Ibid., 78–79.

28 Du Junca, volume 2, 80v. Rosarges was not a major but a sergeant, and the surgeon's name was Reilhe.

29 The church of Saint-Paul-des-Champs is not to be confused with the church Saint-Paul-Saint-Louis in the rue Sainte-Antoine.

30 Funck-Brentano, 117.

CHAPTER TWELVE: LEGENDS OF THE IRON MASK

1 The letters, dated October 10 and 22, 1711, are printed in Funck-Brentano, *Bastille*, 125.

2 Renneville (tome I, xlvii) thought he had seen the mysterious prisoner in 1705, but this was clearly impossible if the man he had seen was indeed Eustache.

3 Renneville, xlvii–l. There were three turnkeys at the Bastille: Antoine Ru, or Larue, Boutonnière, and Bourgouin (Albert Savine, *La Vie á la Bastille: Souvenirs d'un prisonnier* [Paris: Louis-Michaud, 1908), 51], all of whom worked under the supervision of L'Ecuyer, the chief turnkey. They were not confined to any particular tower, but performed their duties wherever and whenever they were required. They were obliged to be gentle and polite with the prisoners, and were forbidden to accept gifts from them.

4 Alicia C. Montoya, *Medievalist Enlightenment: From Charles Perrault to Jean-Jacques Rousseau* (Cambridge, UK: DS Brewer, 2013), 47. Voltaire identified four stages of light in all. The first was that of Alexander and Pericles; the second was the age of

Caesar and Augustus; the third was the Italian Renaissance. That of Louis XIV was the fourth.

5   *OCV*, vol. 13C, 165.

6   Petitfils, *Masque de fer*, 210.

7   Voltaire, *The Age of Louis XIV* (London: J. M. Dent & Sons Ltd; New York: E. P. Dutton & Co. Inc., 1935), 260–262.

8   Chamillart died in 1721.

9   Voltaire, *Supplément*, 24–25; *OCV*, vol. 13C, 165.

10 La Feuillade was related to Lauzun, who had also encountered the mysterious prisoner while at Pignerol. At that point, however, the prisoner had been put to work in the service of Foucquet. There is nothing to suggest that, after his release, Lauzun equated Foucquet's valet with the masked prisoner, if indeed he and la Feuillade had ever discussed him.

11 The prisoner's apparent love of linen and lace may have come from the memory of Mme Le Bret, mother of the governor of Provence, who would obtain such items for Mme de Saint-Mars. See Furneaux, 29.

12 Laurent Angliviel de La Beaumelle was a Protestant writer and contemporary of Voltaire.

13 Voltaire, *Supplément*, 24; *OCV*, vol. 13C, 165.

14 Voltaire, *Supplément*, 25.

15 Joseph La Grange-Chancel, "Lettre à Fréron," *L'Année littéraire*, 1759, tome III, 188–195.

16 Germain François Poillain de Saint-Foix, "Lettre de M. de Saint-Foix au sujet de l'Homme au masque de fer," *L'Année littéraire*, 1768, tome IV, 73–85. Saint-Foix wrote about his findings in a letter to Elie-Catherine Fréron, editor of *L'Année littéraire*, who in turn summarized the theories that had so far come to Saint-Foix's attention.

17 Guillaume Louis Formanoir de Palteau, "Lettre du 19 juin 1768," *L'Année littéraire*, tome IV, 351–354.

18   Henri Griffet, *Histoire de La Vie de Louis XIII, Roi de France et de Navarre* (Paris: Chez Saillant, Libraire, 1758), 295–300.

19 René Jourdin de Launay had been on the staff at the Bastille since 1710 and became governor in 1718. His son, Bernard-René Jourdan de Launay, was governor at the time of the storming of the Bastille in 1789 and was murdered by the crowd.

20 Ravaisson, volume III, 208; see above, pp. 79, 80–81.

21 Baron de Heiss, "Lettre au sujet de l'homme au masque de fer," *Journal encyclopédique*, 15 août 1770, tome VI, 132–133.

22 Voltaire, *Questions sur l'encyclopédie*, tome 1, 251–254.

23 Voltaire, *Dictionnaire philosophique*, 78–79; *OCV*, volume 38 (II), 301–303.

24 Griffet, tome 3, 374–376; Wilkinson, 7–8.

25 Chrétien Guillaume de Lamoignon de Malesherbes was president of the Cour des aides and director of the royal library.

26 Funck-Brentano, 122.

27 Jean-Pierre Papon, *Voyage littéraire en Provence* (Paris: Chez Barrois l'âiné, 1780), 246–249.

28 See above, pp. 155, 182, 195, 200.

29 Charpentier, *La Bastille dévoilée, ou Recueil de pièces authentiques pour servir à son histoire*, neuvième livraison (Paris: Chez Desenne, 1790), 36–37, 95–96, 141, 122–170.

30 Louis Dutens, *Correspondance interceptée* (London: s.n., 1789), 26–32; *Mémoires d'un voyageur qui se repose; contenant des anecdotes historiques, politiques et littéraires, relatives à plusieurs des principaux personnages du siècle* (Paris: Bossange, Masson et Besson, 1806), 204–210.

31 Dutens, *Correspondance*, 33–34.

32 Friedrich Melchior Grimm, *Correspondance littéraire*, nouvelle édition, tome quatorzième 1788–1789 (Paris: Chez Furne et Ladrange, 1831), tome IV, 419–423.

33 Jeanne Louise Henriette de Campan, *Memoirs of Madame de Campan on Marie Antoinette and her Court* (Boston: J. B. Millet Company, 1909), volume 1, 171–172.

34 Furneaux, 42.

35 There have been a great many books published over the past decades in which the various candidates have been discussed. Usually, the author presents the candidates in the order in which they were imprisoned and offers the reasons why he could not have been the Man in the Iron Mask before offering their solution in the final chapters. The most recent books of this type, in English and in French respectively, are *The Man in the Iron Mask* by John Noone and *Le Masque de fer* by Jean-Christian Petitfils. Both are well worth reading.

36 The theory that Foucquet was the Man in the Iron Mask first appeared in newssheets that were published following the fall of the Bastille. It later found support with writers such as Paul Lacroix and Pierre-Jacques Arrese.

37 The Jacobin monk was the candidate of Domenico Carutti. Molière was proposed by Marcel Diamant-Berger despite the fact that the playwright's death was well attested.

38 Boutry explored these theories in an article, "Une mystification diplomatique," before settling on Matthioli.

39 Funck-Brentano, *Le Masque de fer*, 22.

CHAPTER THIRTEEN: THE MAN IN THE IRON MASK

1 Lair, volume II, 454.

2 Adrien Huguet, *Le Marquis de Cavoye: Un grand maréchal des logis de la maison du Roi* (Paris: Édouard Champion, 1920), 27.

3 Ibid., 135.

4 Emile Laloy, *Enigmes du Grand Siècle: Le Masque de fer, Jacques de La Cloche, l'abbé Prignani, Roux de Marsilly* (Paris: Librairie H. Le Soudier, 1912), 209–210.

5 Ravaisson, volume VI, 375.

6 Laloy, 214–219.

7 Noone, 229.

8 Petitfils, *Masque*, 144.

9 Caire, 43.

10 Petitfils (*Masque*, 167) points out that the sculptor, Pierre-Jean David, is known as David d'Angers because of his place of birth.

11 Petitfils, *Masque*, 166–167.

12 Furneaux, 43.

13 Delort (1829), volume I, 286–288.

14 Ellis, 248–249.

15 Ellis, 255–256; Delort (1825), 217; Roux-Fazillac, 67.

16 Ravaisson, volume IX, 168–169.

17 Ibid., 171.

18 Barnes, 293.

19 Courtilz de Sandras, volume III, 72.

20 See, for example, Delort (1829), volume I, 182.

21 Robert Ambelain, *La Chapelle des damnés: La véritable Affaires des poisons, 1650–1703* (Paris: Éditions Robert Laffont, 1983), 113.

22 Barnes, 288. There is also the question of Eustache's clothing, which Louvois said should last for three or four years (see above, p. 135). This suggests that Eustache was not considered to be a person of quality. Certainly, his social status was not equal to that of Foucquet or Lauzun.

23 Duvivier, 216–217.

24 Petitfils, *Masque*, 144.

25 Marie-Thérèse of Austria, although Spanish, was descended from the Habsburgs, as was Louis's own mother, Anne of Austria. The two queens were aunt and niece and became mother- and daughter-in-law upon Louis's marriage to Marie-Thérèse.

26 England had not yet adopted the Gregorian calendar, and so was ten days behind the rest of Europe.

27 Cyril Hughes Hartmann, *Charles II and Madame* (London: William Heinemann Ltd., 1934), 233.

28 Ibid., 264.

29 Ibid., 227.

30 Ibid., 230.

31 Ibid., 228.

32 Ibid., 230.

33 Ibid., 243, 246.

34 Ibid., 246.

35 Henriette gave birth to her second daughter, Anne-Marie, who would become duchesse de Savoy, on August 27, 1669.

36 Hartmann, 267.

37 Ibid., 275–276.

38 Ibid., 281.

39 Jacqueline Duchêne, *Henriette d'Angleterre, duchesse d'Orléans* (Paris: Librairie Arthème Fayard, 1995), 342.

40 Petitfils, *Masque*, 176.

INDEX